A GUIDE TO

Itinerant Early Childhood Special Education Services

A GUIDE TO
Itinerant Early Childhood Special Education Services

by

Laurie A. Dinnebeil

and

William F. McInerney

University of Toledo
Ohio

·P·A·U·L·H·
BROOKES
PUBLISHING Co. ®

Baltimore • London • Sydney

Paul H. Brookes Publishing Co.
Post Office Box 10624
Baltimore, Maryland 21285-0624
USA

www.brookespublishing.com

Typeset by Integrated Publishing Solutions, Grand Rapids, Michigan.
Manufactured in the United States of America by
Sheridan Books, Inc., Chelsea, Michigan.

Some individuals described in this book are composites or real people whose situations are masked
and are based on the authors' experiences. In these instances, names and identifying details have
been changed to protect confidentiality.

Library of Congress Cataloging-in-Publication Data

Dinnebeil, Laurie A.
    A guide to itinerant early childhood special education services / by Laurie A. Dinnebeil and
William F. McInerney.
        p.   cm.
    Includes bibliographical references and index.
    ISBN 13: 978-1-55766-965-0 (pbk. : alk. paper)
    ISBN 10: 1-55766-965-1 (pbk. : alk. paper)
    1. Children with disabilities—Education (Early childhood)   2. Chidlren with disabilities—Services
for.   3. Community-based child welfare.   4. Early childhood education.   I. McInerney, William F.
II. Title.
    LC4019.3.D56 2011
    371.9'0472—dc22
                                                                                          2010044428

British Library Cataloguing in Publication data are available from the British Library.

2021   2020   2019

10   9   8   7   6   5   4   3

Contents

About the Authors

Laurie A. Dinnebeil, Ph.D., Professor and Judith Daso Herb Chair, ECE, Judith Herb College of Education, University of Toledo, MS 954, 4500E Gillham Hall, 2801 West Bancroft Street, Toledo, Ohio, 43606

Dr. Laurie Dinnebeil is a professor of inclusive early childhood education. She was a preschool special education teacher for 5 years before entering higher education. She has taught a range of undergraduate and graduate courses related to early childhood education and early childhood special education (ECSE) and has published extensively in the area of itinerant ECSE service delivery. Dr. Dinnebeil is a proficient grant writer, having secured more than $6 million in national and state funding since the late 1980s. She is very active in the field of ECSE at the local, state, and national levels. Dr. Dinnebeil is a past president of the Council for Exceptional Children's Division for Early Childhood and the Ohio Higher Education Consortium for Early Childhood Education. She is Associate Editor for *Topics in Early Childhood Special Education* and serves on editorial boards for numerous academic journals related to early childhood education and special education. Dr. Dinnebeil is a 2002 Mid-Career Fellow for ZERO TO THREE. She also has college administrative experience as a department chair and associate dean for graduate studies and research.

William F. McInerney, Ph.D., Professor of Special Education, Judith Herb College of Education, University of Toledo, MS 954, 4500E Gillham Hall, 2801 West Bancroft Street, Toledo, Ohio, 43606

Dr. McInerney teaches graduate-level courses in the early childhood special education (ECSE) area. Throughout his career, Dr. McInerney has secured U.S. Department of Education–Office of Special Education Programs (USDOE-OSEP) funding to support graduate-level training of ECSE teachers and early intervention personnel. He has managed several grants that have focused on itinerant early childhood special education (IECSE) services and has coordinated, with his associates and the Ohio Department of Education, a statewide professional development program for IECSE teachers and their supervisors. He and his colleagues at the University of Toledo have presented their work at professional conferences and have consulted with school districts and state education agencies concerning the status and future of IECSE services.

Foreword

The early childhood world has evolved significantly since I first entered it as a preschool teacher in the mid-1970s. At that time, the vast majority of children with disabilities were served in self-contained classrooms with little or no access to peers who were typically developing. Back then, my role as a classroom teacher was to work directly with children to promote their development and learning and to partner with their families to address their priorities and concerns. Today, approximately one half of preschoolers with disabilities receive special education services in some form of inclusive early childhood program or home setting. This reality has created a new professional role in early childhood—the itinerant early childhood special education (IECSE) provider. The role expectations for an itinerant teacher differ dramatically from those of a classroom teacher, yet many professionals who assume this role may not be adequately prepared to work with other adults as a consultant, coach, or inclusion specialist.

Laurie A. Dinnebeil and William F. McInerney have produced an incredible volume that promises to be the single most reliable source on a topic that to date has received little attention—itinerant early childhood special education services. Although itinerant services (and related models such as consultation and coaching) are widely used in the United States to support high-quality inclusion of children with disabilities and their families, the policies and practices that define this approach are not well understood in the early childhood field. Dinnebeil and McInerney unpack the itinerant service delivery model, thoughtfully peeling back the layers to reveal its essential components in terms that readers from a wide array of backgrounds can understand and appreciate.

The authors address fundamentally important questions: Who are IECSE providers? What is the nature of direct versus indirect service delivery? What are the various roles that these professionals play? What does the process of implementing itinerant services look like? Perhaps the most valuable contribution that this volume makes is defining what it means to be an IECSE provider. Dinnebeil and McInerney debunk the myth that an itinerant professional is an expert who comes into an early childhood setting once a week for 60–90 minutes to provide "episodic and intensive intervention." Instead, they paint a picture of an itinerant provider as someone whose goal it is to partner with another adult (a teacher, specialist, or family member) to support the use of evidence-based, child-focused interventions (e.g., embedded interventions, response prompting, modeling) that they plan and evaluate together. The authors rightly assert that any approach to providing services to young children and families must begin with a broader vision of the key components of an effective service delivery system—access, participation, and supports related to high-quality inclusion; tiered models of instruction and intervention; and implementation science. Drawing on their wealth of knowledge and experience on this topic, Dinnebeil and McInerney provide a step-by-step model of itinerant early childhood service delivery, complete with all of the resources and forms for managing the logistics, caseloads, communication, and documentation that are needed to be effective. *A Guide to Itinerant Early Childhood Special Education Services* will become the go-to resource that professionals will want to keep handy as an essential text to working collaboratively with others in the context of inclusion to help each and every young child reach his or her full potential.

Virginia Buysse, Ph.D.
Senior Scientist
FPG Child Development Institute
University of North Carolina at Chapel Hill

Preface

Itinerant early childhood special education (IECSE) is a service delivery model that supports the inclusion of young children with disabilities whose primary placement is a community-based program such as a private preschool, child care center, or Head Start classroom. Itinerant teachers, also called *inclusion specialists, early childhood consultants,* or other terms, visit children's community-based classrooms on a regular basis to provide individualized education program (IEP)–based services. The prevalence of itinerant services for young children with disabilities served in community-based programs is growing nationwide. Even though this service delivery model is used to support early childhood inclusion, the role of the itinerant teacher is poorly defined not only in policy but also in practice and research. IECSE teachers often perform their jobs without the benefit of a job description, and their supervisors rely on supervision practices that are based on the role of a classroom-based teacher. Without guidance from state policy makers and administrators, IECSE teachers are left to rely on their instincts and previous experience as classroom teachers to guide their day-to-day responsibilities. As a result, most itinerant teachers function in the role of direct service provider to children, providing individual or small-group instruction that addresses IEP goals and objectives. On average, they see a child once a week for an hour, pull the child aside, and "work on" IEP objectives. Essentially, they function as tutors, a role that severely limits their ability to effectively support the child's inclusion in the community-based program.

An alternative view to the itinerant teacher as direct service provider or tutor is the role of the itinerant teacher as consultant and coach. In this model, the primary function of the itinerant teacher is to work directly with a child's primary caregivers (classroom teachers, parents, paraprofessionals) in order to support inclusive practices. Itinerant teachers partner with their community-based colleagues to find ways to embed IEP-based instruction into the child's daily routine, provide information to their adult partners, teach adults how to use research-based instructional strategies, and provide emotional support to adults who doubt their abilities to effectively work with children who have disabilities. Many view the role of itinerant teacher as consultant or coach as "best practice" in early childhood special education. This recommendation is based on results of research focused on the effectiveness of school-based consultation and peer coaching practices. It is also based on the premise that learning opportunities should be distributed across the day and integrated into daily routines and activities that naturally interest children.

Early childhood special educators who function as itinerants need to have access to a knowledge base that will help guide their practice. Itinerant teachers generally feel ill prepared to work collaboratively with other adults. Due to a lack of knowledge and confidence in their abilities, they often resist accepting the role of "expert" in their work with adults or children, even though parents and general education early childhood teachers regard them as the experts. This resistance often pushes them to retreat into the role of a tutor, where they can work safely and comfortably with children.

The field of early childhood special education desperately needs guidance about the role of itinerant teachers. Without a research-based approach to providing itinerant services to young children with special needs, itinerant teachers will continue to resist the role of consultant and coach and will continue to limit their professional responsibilities to those that relate directly to children.

The purpose of this book is to help early childhood special educators acquire the knowledge they need to function in effective itinerant roles. This book examines the critical roles of IECSE teachers including: 1) assessor, 2) consultant, 3) coach, 4) direct service provider, 5) service coordinator, and 6) team member. In addition, this book details a framework composed of the following features for the provision of itinerant services: 1) gathering baseline information, 2) planning for itinerant services, 3) providing itinerant services through triadic intervention, and 4) reflecting on the quality of itinerant services.

In addition, this book provides information helpful to itinerant teachers in managing the logistical components of their job (e.g., travel time, scheduling, completing paperwork). Chapters include many real-life examples that students and instructors may use to provide the necessary dialogue and reflection critical to meaningful learning. Finally, appendixes in the book contain varied forms and protocols that IECSE teachers may use to provide effective itinerant services.

Acknowledgments

The authors acknowledge the support that Dr. Lyn Hale has provided in coordinating U.S. Department of Education–Office of Special Education Programs (USDOE-OSEP) grants that have advanced the practice of consultation in early childhood special education (ECSE). The authors also recognize Ms. Margie Spino for her invaluable assistance with research related to the development of key content for this book. In addition, the authors acknowledge and appreciate the work of itinerant ECSE teachers and their colleagues who have inspired and challenged us, particularly our ECSE colleagues across Ohio. They are developing and refining the practice of consultation every day. We respect their skills and commitment, and value their good will in helping us move forward.

To Doug, Elissa, Jeff, Mark, Megan, and Addison,
who mean the world to me.
To Betty and Bill Pollock,
loving parents who always put
their children first.

—LD

To my loving wife, Marcia,
and our wonderful daughters, Brigid and Shea.
And to the newest members of the family, Owen and Andrew.

—WM

CHAPTER 1

Introduction to Itinerant Early Childhood Special Education Services

Early childhood inclusion embodies the values, policies, and practices that support the right of every infant and young child and his or her family, regardless of ability, to participate in a broad range of activities and contexts as full members of families, communities, and society (Division for Early Childhood [DEC]/National Association for the Education of Young Children [NAEYC], 2009. See also Appendix C.).

The purpose of this book is to discuss itinerant early childhood special education (IECSE) services, the different roles that IECSE teachers assume, the details of putting an IECSE service delivery model into place, and what the future holds for this aspect of early childhood special education. This book is grounded in a practical discussion of how the IECSE service delivery model functions at present and describes options for more efficient delivery of IECSE services.

Who Are Itinerant Early Childhood Special Educators?

Itinerant early childhood special education teachers work with young children ages 3–5 years. They travel to a number of different sites where they teach, consult, participate in meetings, coordinate children's educational goals with other service providers, and partner with parents. The IECSE service delivery model necessitates having a qualified, certified early childhood special education (ECSE) teacher who is able to balance large caseloads with the demands of travel to different sites. The IECSE teacher may be asked to consult with teachers, related service providers, and other members of the individualized education program (IEP) team; plan professional development for program and school staff; and participate in IEP meetings and other meetings about children with disabilities.

What Are Itinerant Early Childhood Special Education Services?

Itinerant early childhood special education services can be provided directly, with IECSE teachers teaching children in various environments; or on a consultative basis, with IECSE teachers working with early childhood education (ECE) teachers or ECSE teachers as consultants, coaches, mentors, and trainers. There are several options for delivery of IECSE services. The most common option is delivery of services to a child who is enrolled full time or part time in a community preschool program and receives no other services from the local education agency (LEA). An alternative option is the provision of services in the home of the child, when the child is not enrolled in any program outside of the home. Another option is provision of IECSE services for children who are enrolled in community child care programs part time and also receive IEP-focused services in an ECSE classroom on a part-time basis. More information about this topic is provided in Chapter 12.

Where Are Itinerant Early Childhood Special Education Services Provided?

Although interest in IECSE services continues to grow (see Figure 1.1), it is difficult to determine the number of children receiving these services under Part B of the Individuals with Disabilities Education Improvement Act (IDEA) of 2004 (PL 108-446). The U.S. Department of Education Office of Special Education Programs (OSEP) does not require state departments of education to report the number of children receiving itinerant services. They do, however, require reporting of the number of children served in different educational environments. In 2006–2007, the following educational environment categories were established:

- A child with a disability receives services in the general early childhood program at least 80% of the time.

- A child with a disability receives services in the general early childhood program 40%–79% of the time.

- A child with a disability receives services in the general early childhood program less than 40% of the time.

- A child with a disability receives services in his or her home.

   One problem in interpretation of current enrollment data is the result of the recent (2006) redefinition of an *early childhood program* as "a program that includes at least 50 percent nondisabled children" (Table 3-RE5, Part B, Individuals with Disabilities Education Act Implementation of free appropriate public education [FAPE] requirements, p. 2). This means that a child can be counted as being in a "general early childhood program at least 80% of the time" even if the child is in a special education classroom with

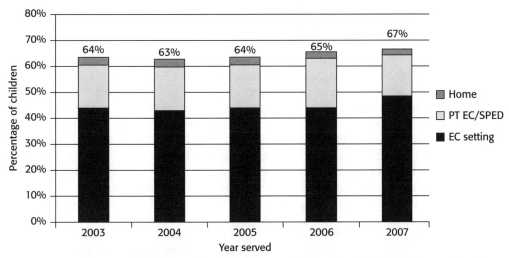

Figure 1.1. Percentage of children (3–5 yrs.) receiving IDEA Part B 619 services (2003–2007). (*Source:* https://www .ideadata.org/default.asp; *Key:* PT EC/SPED, part-time early childhood special education; EC, early childhood.)

an ECSE teacher that is composed of six children with disabilities and six children without disabilities. As a result, an estimation of the number of children who are receiving IECSE services nationwide is not available at present.

What Is the Current Spectrum of Itinerant Early Childhood Special Education Services?

IDEA 2004 (PL 108-446) requirements stipulate that children be educated in the least restrictive environment possible and that there shall be a continuum of placement options under this provision. This continuum of placement options—from education in a separate school to full inclusion in the general education classroom—is necessary to support the FAPE provision of IDEA in providing services to children with disabilities.

Placement and service options for young children with IEPs usually include the following:

- Placement in a separate or segregated prekindergarten (pre-K) school or early learning center

- Home instruction featuring home visiting consistent with the IECSE services model

- Placement in a self-contained pre-K classroom in a neighborhood school

- Placement in an inclusive pre-K classroom in a neighborhood school that may feature variable ratios of children with disabilities to children without disabilities

- Placement in an LEA-operated pre-K classroom in which proportional enrollment of children with special needs is maintained

- Placement in community pre-K programs in which the primary focus is children who are developing typically (this is the model in which IECSE consultation services are most viable)

These options are consistent with the traditional Cascade Model (Kavale & Forness, 2000), which is the frame of reference for many IEP teams in determining how restrictive a child's educational placement should be. The Cascade Model is a graduated reference for evaluation of the relative restrictiveness of placements. The Cascade Model is based on the extent of physical separation from peers that is necessary to meet the minimum requirements of the FAPE clause of IDEA, as identified in the IEP. As an example, the Cascade Model suggests that, without reference to the IEP, placement in a self-contained special education classroom, in a separate setting, is more restrictive than placement in a self-contained special education classroom in a neighborhood school.

Although home-based service delivery has been the staple of early intervention services for infants and toddlers (ages 0–3) since 1986, it has only been since 2000 that IECSE services have been embraced for 3- to 5-year-olds with special needs. Several factors have contributed to the rising profile of IECSE services. The continuing interest of professionals and parents in providing natural environments for students coupled with an increasing awareness of the importance of early childhood intervention have been primary factors. In addition, there also has been a growing interest in serving young children with special needs in community child care and preschool programs (Craig, Haggart, Gold, & Hull, 2000; DEC/NAEYC, 2009; DeVore & Bowers, 2006; Sandall, Hemmeter, Smith, & McLean, 2005; Walsh, Rous, & Lutzer, 2000). Finally, awareness of the inherent value of early inclusion experiences (Allen & Schwartz, 1996; Odom & Diamond, 1998) also has fueled interest in IECSE services.

Who Are Itinerant Early Childhood Special Educators?

The pool of practicing IECSE teachers is quite diverse. Many IECSE teachers hold bachelor, master, or advanced degrees in early childhood education, special education, or early childhood special education as well as other human services degrees (e.g., psychology, nursing, social work). Practicing IECSE teachers may be novice educators or mature professionals. Some IECSE teachers have had prior experience as classroom teachers in early childhood or early childhood special education programs, whereas others may have had experience as teachers in general education or special education classrooms. IECSE teachers may enter the field as traditional graduates of undergraduate teacher preparation programs; reenter the profession after brief or extended leaves of absence; enter the profession in response to layoffs or collective bargaining requirements; or be seeking a career change after years of classroom teaching in preschool or elementary, middle, or high school programs. These career path options have led to heterogeneity within the ranks of the IECSE teacher population. This heterogeneity has significant implications for the profession and the practice of IECSE intervention.

The Structure of This Book

The remainder of the chapters in this book address the following subjects:

- Chapter 2 addresses the differences between the direct services model of IECSE and the consultation model of IECSE. Because our position is that the consultation model of IECSE is more desirable, a rationale will be presented for moving from a direct services model to a consultation model.

- Chapter 3 discusses the various roles that an IECSE teacher may have—direct services provider, consultant, coach, monitor and/or assessor, service coordinator, team member, and lifelong learner.

- Chapters 4–8 examine in more detail the IECSE teacher's various roles as enumerated earlier in this chapter.

- Chapters 9 and 10 present several models through which IECSE services may be provided and the responsibilities of the IECSE teacher within these frameworks with respect to gathering information, planning for intervention, coaching, consultation, and evaluation of partner and child progress.

- Chapter 11 presents a case study in which the consultation model of IECSE service delivery has been successful.

- Chapter 12 reviews important logistics in providing IECSE services.

This sequence of content was developed to address policies and practices related to IECSE service delivery, examine models for more efficient and effective IECSE service delivery, review theoretical aspects of IECSE service delivery, as well as to address pragmatic aspects in delivery of IEP-focused instruction in community-based early childhood education programs.

CHAPTER 2

The Rationale for Consultation in IECSE Services

The focus of this chapter is a discussion about why a consultation model in IECSE services is preferable to a direct and episodic intervention model. In addition, the chapter discusses the process of learning and how this research-based knowledge must drive decisions related to recommended practice in IECSE services.

This chapter addresses the following questions related to the efficacy of direct instruction and assumptions or presumptions underlying the child-focused instruction model:

1. What do we know about the process of learning, and how does this affect our decisions regarding what form of instruction should occur within IECSE services?

2. Does learning occur more quickly as a result of brief and intensive instruction (e.g., 60 minutes per week), or is learning more likely to occur when there are opportunities for teaching and learning spread out across the day or week?

3. Is intensive instruction more effective in the initial or acquisition stage of learning?

4. Is subsequent movement to fluency, maintenance, and generalization more effectively supported through direct and intensive instruction or through opportunities for practice that occur systematically throughout the week?

5. Is the process of learning the same for all children, regardless of type or extent of disability?

6. What is the effect of the learning environment on child learning?

7. What effect do peers who are typically developing have on the learning of children with special needs?

Implications of Learning Theory in Choice of Model for IECSE Service Delivery

There are several possible explanations for how children learn and how that learning can be enhanced. We must consider *environmental factors* that occur within the early childhood learning settings—specifically in child care and pre-K settings—such as parent, teacher, and peer expectations and the arrangement of rooms, including access to items. Also, we must consider *developmental factors* such as impairment in motor skills, cognitive skills, or sensory functions. Finally, we must consider the interaction between developmental factors and environmental factors. These factors present a rich base for reflection on the range of variables that may affect the learning of children.

Environmental Factors

Our experiences in Ohio as well as our conversations with colleagues across the United States indicate that many young children receiving IECSE services are children with mild delays or high incidence conditions, rather than children with severe impairments. A number of these children would be identified as children with speech or language delays, with or without accompanying cognitive impairments. These speech or language delays or developmental discrepancies are also often within the mild range. As a result of the nature of these developmental delays, these children would be expected to have speech and expressive and/or receptive language objectives as priority items in their IEPs. Some of these objectives might relate to semantic functions and syntactic skills, whereas other learning objectives might address the pragmatics of communication. Other IEP objectives might relate to the quality of speech (e.g., articulation errors). Over the course of a school year and a number of weekly visits and direct instruction by the IECSE teacher, a child might evidence improvement in one or all of these areas of language development. Although the initial inclination might be to attribute these gains to the effect of IECSE services, other, competing variables also might explain or contribute to these positive developments. For example, what effect would parent and teacher expectations for communication have on the child? What if the ECE teacher had systematically introduced and labeled items in his or her classroom for all children and encouraged the naming of these items? What if several peers in a multiage pre-K classroom had decided to help a younger or less able peer in naming more items? In doing so, they might develop a strategy to withhold an item unless the child provided an approximation of the word that described the item. What if the teacher had established a reading buddy program with third-grade students who visited the classroom and read to children twice a week? What if the teacher had systematically paired a child with deficiencies in pragmatic skills with helpful peers who modeled high-quality communication skills? These environmental variables might have contributed to the child's positive developments.

Developmental Factors

We have explored some environmental factors that may shape children's learning. Developmental factors also may be helpful in explaining a child's progress. Discussion of how motor skills, sensory impairments, and cognitive skills can affect children's learning is provided in the following sections. As we discuss the effect of these factors on learning, we will also discuss how authentic, embedded, and longitudinal instruction in a consultative setting can be of more benefit than intensive, direct instruction provided solely by an IECSE teacher.

Motor Skills

Motor skills can influence child development. For example, for the child who may have an IEP objective of *developing a mature pincer grasp*, it is difficult to see the benefit of intensive intervention occurring once a week (i.e., via direct IECSE services) as opposed to distributed and embedded opportunities to develop this skill in authentic and motivating activities (i.e., through the use of consultative IECSE services) (Campbell & Sawyer, 2004; 2007; Case-Smith & Rogers, 2005; DeVore & Russell, 2007; Milbourne & Campbell, 2007; Rainforth & York-Barr, 1997). A *matrix planning model* (Hemmeter & Rous, 1997; McWilliam & Casey, 2007), in which priority learning skills are indexed with routines or instructional opportunities, is a very useful tool for helping parents and ECE partner teachers to see opportunities for the learning of skills, including motor skills, in routine activities. If a parent or ECSE partner teacher was aware of when and where use of a modified or mature pincer grasp could be expected within an activity, he or she could be more vigilant in making sure these opportunities were planned. In the home, for example, a parent or sibling could place a number of Froot Loops on a small plate and ask the child to pick up seven pieces (with the parent or sibling providing counting help, if necessary) and place them in a cereal bowl before the remainder of the cereal is poured into the bowl. The identification of the color or selection of colors in securing the requested seven pieces also could be embedded into this motivating task. And, of course, the child could be encouraged to use the pincer grasp in picking up the cereal and placing the pieces in the bowl.

Using another example from the classroom, an ECE teacher could require a child to help secure "Helper of the Day" assignments displayed on a cord using clothespins or similar fasteners that require the pincer grasp to affix or release the cards. Also, during an art activity or a nature hike, the child could be required to use tweezers to secure, place, affix, and bag items. Once again, providing longitudinal opportunities for practice is more likely to enhance fine motor skills than intensive manipulations that take place for only 1 hour per week of instruction.

Biological Maturation

The effect of biological maturation, specifically improvement in coordination and differentiation of movement, cannot be overlooked. This may be particularly relevant in the case of a younger child who has mild, spastic hemiplegic or diplegic cerebral palsy and who has typical intelligence or minimal cognitive impairment. In addition to neurological and neuromuscular maturation, this child may be learning to inhibit dysfunctional movements with alternative forms of movement. This interaction of biology and maturational experience—particularly within a learning environment that provides frequent opportunities for functional, authentic, and motivated practice—is the most probable platform for child development of fine motor skills. The same observations could be made with respect to gross motor movements such as mobility. Although bracing and adaptive mobility devices provide the support necessary for intentional movement, it is likely that movement in motivating circumstances (e.g., transition to learning centers) with implicit requirements for movement (e.g., adoption of a passport requirement in which children must visit three centers during center time, verified by ECE teacher) would contribute to potential mastery of movement.

Cognitive Skills

The developmental domain that some educators and parents would describe as perhaps most responsive to intensive intervention would be *cognitive skills*. For example, *seriation,* a premath concept, requires arrangement of items in descending or ascending order based on the extent that these items (three or more are necessary) differ with respect to a key physical (e.g., length) or perceptual (e.g., degree of hue or color) feature of the item. This is an essential early cognitive skill that can be taught and practiced in intensive teaching sessions, but the concept is only evidenced through display of seriation skills across multiple items. In the absence of the IECSE teacher, there are many opportunities for instruction and practice. Comparing sizes of cups or diameters or areas of plates; stacking blocks, Duplos, bristle blocks, or Legos in ascending order; reading books that feature seriation; arrangement and storage of art materials; and arrangement of children's footwear in the entry area by relative length or height are all opportunities to learn seriation skills and to practice this skill throughout the day, moving toward fluency and generalization. Although there are many opportunities to teach, practice, and assess child progress in seriation, it is essential that parents or ECE partners recognize, plan for, and take advantage of these opportunities. This is more likely to occur as a result of consultation and coaching versus trust and optimism.

These examples illustrate the dilemma within IECSE instruction. Although an IECSE teacher may be perfectly qualified to teach young children with special needs, to the extent that the focus of his or her intervention is on the child and not the ECE teacher or parent, the probability of success of the intervention is limited. Also, if the child does demonstrate the learning objectives specified in his or her IEP, it is possible that these gains were related to environmental or maturational factors or a combination thereof rather than caused by direct instruction by an IECSE teacher. Furthermore, developing an intentional consultation relationship with an ECE partner or a parent, with the objective of transferring critical skills and knowledge to this partner, is more likely to lead to learning than one-to-one or small-group instruction delivered by the IECSE teacher during his or her weekly visit. Considerations for the progression of learning or present state of the child's learning are addressed in the following section.

Stages of Learning and Implications for IECSE Service Delivery

It may be helpful to consider how children learn with respect to the stages of learning and the potential value of systematic transfer of skills and knowledge to the ECE partner or parent versus direct instruction provided by the IECSE. It is widely acknowledged that learning advances through four stages: *acquisition, fluency, maintenance,* and *generalization* (Fox & Lentini, 2006; Haring & Eaton, 1978). It also is generally accepted that skills are most functional when they are manifested in generalized forms (Stokes & Baer, 1977). In fact, the ability to generalize a skill across materials within a number of environments (e.g., home, school, and community) and in the presence of different people is often understood to be the benchmark for demonstration of having learned a concept. In other words, it is only when a child can select the closest, biggest, longest, or first in order of a group of objects that it is said that the child has mastered that particular concept. For example—with regard to the concept of *first*—whether the block that is at the beginning of the lineup of five blocks is the biggest, is red, or is smaller than the next block is irrelevant to the block being first in the series. This understanding of the concept *first* can only be inferred through errorless responses of the child across a number of exemplars.

It is instructive to examine the link between the stages of learning and the efficacy of IECSE intervention. If there is value in the child-focused, direct instruction approach within the IECSE service delivery model, it may be limited to the *acquisition* phase of learning. This phase of learning is the period when a child is beginning to show approximations of a skill or behavior or is able to execute the initial components of a skill. The acquisition phase is characterized by frequent errors on the part of the learner and is the phase during which the need for instruction is most apparent. In fact, this is the stage of learning during which errorless learning strategies (Glaser, 1990; Terrace, 1963, 1972) are recommended to limit child error and improve the efficiency of learning.

As an example, consider puzzle assembly, a typical early childhood cognitive and fine motor skill. In the acquisition phase of puzzle assembly, a child usually is provided with a four-piece puzzle with cut-out inserts for each piece of the puzzle. A good example would be the common four-piece puzzle that consists of illustrations of a bunch of grapes, a pear, a banana, and an orange. To limit child error, a teacher or parent might leave three pieces of the puzzle in the inserts and remove only one piece (e.g., the orange). If that did not result in the child inserting the single piece that was removed from the puzzle, the teacher or parent might provide guidance in accordance with the hierarchy of prompting (Noonan & McCormick, 2006) and the principle of partial participation (Baumgart et al., 1982). This might take the form of minimal physical prompting (providing support at the child's elbow) in conjunction with time delay procedures or moving the piece to be inserted closer to the location where the piece is to be inserted. Another strategy might be to place a graphic cue in the insert (e.g., a small orange circle) or to color the insert orange. This effectively prompts the child to move the item to the appropriate insert and to match the sample provided. As the child becomes more accustomed to moving this piece to the insert, another piece may be removed (e.g., the banana). Removing the second piece (i.e., the banana) that shares few of the characteristics of the initial puzzle piece (i.e., the orange) also is a form of errorless learning. It is less likely that the child would attempt to insert the banana into the insert for the orange than the apple, for example. Of course, the child's response to this task will provide the information the teacher will need to adjust his or her teaching strategies.

After the child is able to insert the four pieces with no or minimal assistance, he or she enters the *fluency* phase of learning in which performance is characterized by minimal latency when presented with the same puzzle. The child completes the task fairly quickly and with limited or no errors (e.g., the child does not attempt to place the pear in the orange insert). *Fluency* can be observed in most children with respect to less time required to complete the task as well as significant decrease in errors. *Maintenance* occurs when the child is able to demonstrate fluency without adult cueing or with minimal adult or peer assistance. *Generalization* occurs when the child can complete a number of different four-piece puzzles and also is able to begin to assemble insert puzzles with more than four pieces as well as puzzles without inserts.

Direct instruction of the child may be necessary during the acquisition phase of learning. The IECSE teacher could accomplish direct instruction during his or her weekly visit; however, without guided instruction during his or her absence, the child may revert to trial-and-error learning, which, despite its positive press in folklore, is inefficient and not a recommended practice (Davis, 1966). If the IECSE teacher chose to alter the focus of his or her instruction to model a skill within the hierarchy of prompting, the child may, through the efforts of a well-informed parent or ECE partner, continue to approximate the target skill with greater efficiency. It is also possible that the IECSE teacher could assist her ECE partner in understanding how selected peers also could assist in adoption of a skill by helping the child (e.g., with assembling the puzzle).

The need for parent or ECE partner awareness of the process of learning in the fluency, maintenance, and generalization phases is more obvious. There is a need for systematic manipulation of materials as well as planned exposure of the child to an increasing number of opportunities to demonstrate or practice this skill across the curriculum and daily routines. Adoption of a consultation model would address this need for direct instruction in the acquisition phase and would address child learning during the fluency, maintenance, and generalization phases of learning.

Research Base for Adoption of Consultation Versus Direct Services Delivery

Adoption of a consultation model as the primary mode of intervention in IECSE services must be based on the efficiency of this practice versus the traditional pattern of practice (i.e., direct instruction). If periodic or episodic intervention—usually 60–90 minutes per week in traditional IECSE service delivery—is as efficient as distributed instruction and practice, then there is no need to adopt a consultation model as the primary mode of intervention. If, however, distributed or spaced instruction or practice is proved to be a more efficient model of service delivery, then adoption of a consultation approach in IECSE services is warranted. In either case, the research base related to the effect of both practices on child learning must be examined.

Some research proposes that instruction is most effective when opportunities to acquire and practice skills occur across the day rather than at single points during the day (Hemmeter, 2000; Sandall & Schwartz, 2002; Wolery, Anthony, Caldwell, Snyder, & Morgante, 2002; Wolery, Ault, & Doyle, 1992). This is not a recent concern, as evidenced by the interest of Vander Linde, Morrongiello, and Rovee-Collier in the "fundamental question of whether information that a very young infant repeatedly encounters will accumulate over the course of successive encounters or whether each successive encounter with that information will be encoded as a distinct and separate event, unrelated to what came before" (1985, p. 148).

Before a review of pertinent research evidence can be presented, it is necessary to define, in general, the basic tenets of *massed instruction* versus *distributed instruction*.

Massed Instruction

In the condition of *massed instruction*, children are provided with intensive instruction and multiple opportunities to practice within a single learning session. This condition is most similar to the child-focused, one-to-one instruction that often occurs during the weekly visit of an IECSE teacher. For example, the IECSE teacher could provide 20 minutes of instruction that targets a child's IEP objective of *vocabulary development* in a single session in one day. Another example of massed instruction would be when a child is instructed with the same materials (e.g., use of a shape box or different shaped items that can be presented by the IECSE teacher and secured by the child) multiple times in a single session. This is the practice that is mimicked in traditional child-focused, one-to-one instruction as delivered in the traditional IECSE model.

Distributed Instruction

In the condition of *distributed instruction*, children are provided with many planned learning opportunities across the day and throughout the week. These opportunities occur when the targeted skill is most likely to be required within the learning environment or in response to direct instruction or manding of the ECE teacher. For example, for the IEP objective of *vocabulary development*, the child's teacher or primary caregiver plans for and provides opportunities for the child to learn new vocabulary. The ECE teacher or parent also plans for practice using this new vocabulary at different times across the day or week when opportunities to use these words occur, sometimes spontaneously, in context. Another example of distributed instruction would be when a child is instructed with different materials multiple times during the day and across the week. For example, for the IEP objective of *shape identification,* instruction could occur through identifying basic shapes in 10-minute direct instruction sessions (one-to-one or small group) at different times during the day or across the week. In addition, natural opportunities for instruction and practice could be scheduled by creative adaptations of tasks (e.g., the child might be required to match a cardboard shape to the shape of a preferred activity on the center time planning board) or materials (e.g., sponges for art activity are different shapes). Now that the basic characteristics or conditions of these strategies have been described, an analysis of their relative efficacy can be conducted.

Research Studies Related to Distributed Versus Massed Practice in Instruction of Children

Since the 1800s, researchers have demonstrated that distributed practice supports learning significantly better than massed practice, particularly for language-based skills (Ebbinghaus, 1885/1964; Jost, 1897; Thorndike, 1912). More recently, Cepeda, Pashler, Vul, Wixted, and Rohrer (2006) and Donovan and Radosevich (1999), as a result of in-depth meta-analyses of relevant research literature, suggested that the effects of distributed practice are consistent across the human life span. Infants as well as older adults learn better when opportunities to learn are distributed across time rather than massed. Although the general benefits of distributed instruction have been supported by research findings for more than a century, it is appropriate to focus additional attention on research evidence that compares the relative benefits of distributed versus massed instruction for IECSE services for young children with special needs.

Rea and Modigliani (1985) taught spelling words and math facts to a group of third graders. Students were identified as Level 1 (top half of class) or Level 2 (bottom half of class) students. The results of the study indicated that students performed better on spelling and math tests when instruction was distributed rather than massed. Distributed instruction was more efficient for both Level 1 and Level 2 students, suggesting that the ability level of the students was not related to their response to distributed versus massed instruction.

Seabrook, Brown, and Solity (2005) conducted a study in which 34 children (mean age 5 years, 6 months) were taught phonics over a period of 2 weeks. The students were taught under two different conditions. Condition I, clustered (or massed) instruction, consisted of one 6-minute session per day within a general classroom setting. Condition II, distributed instruction, occurred in three 2-minute sessions per day within a general classroom setting. The results of this study indicated that children who received distributed instruction earned test scores 6 times greater than those children in the clustered (or massed) condition.

Childers and Tomasello (2002) also were interested in the early vocabulary acquisition of toddlers and the influence of distributed exposure to words versus massed exposure. The focus of their study was how many times and over how many days would a 2-year-old need to hear a new word in order to learn the word. In two experiments, 2-year-olds were taught silly nouns and verbs (words they had never heard or seen) over the course of a month in instruction sessions lasting 5–10 minutes. The toddlers learned best when exposure to the words was distributed. The more days that the children heard the word, the better able they were to learn the word. Children learned words better if they heard the words once a day for 4 days rather than eight times in a single day.

An important issue related to distributed instruction is the time that elapses between instruction sessions. Rovee-Collier (1995) studied the behavior of 3-month-old infants who were taught to kick at and move a crib mobile during two 15-minute sessions that were separated by a variable number of days. The second session occurred 1, 2, 3, or 4 days after the first session, with a test of retention scheduled for 8 days after the first session. The results indicated significant retention of the mobile activation skill *if* the second session was 1, 2, or 3 days after the first session. However, the infants who participated in a second training session that was 4 days later than the initial session performed no better on the retention test than did infants who received only a single training session. As Rovee-Collier stated,

> The critical issue in session-spacing effects is whether or not a second session or study trial will be integrated with the memory of the preceding session or study trial. If it is, then individuals will exhibit a retention advantage; if it is not, then individuals will exhibit retention no better than had they received only a single training session. If sessions are too widely spaced to be integrated, then they are represented in memory as completely independent events that are neither associated nor otherwise linked. (1995, p. 150)

This is a powerful observation regarding the process of human learning. This basic study of infant learning suggests that one instruction session per week, the traditional model of massed instruction in IECSE service delivery, is inherently inefficient. Instruction in this model is likely to result in limited retention of previously taught content unless there is intentional and planned repetition of instruction in the intervening 3 days after the initial presentation of content. This finding emphasizes the importance of distributed instruction in supporting the learning of young children.

Other studies also confirm the advantage of distributed instruction. Wolery et al. (2002) taught a small group of young children (ages 5–7 years) to recognize words through the use of embedded and distributed instruction that occurred during circle time and transition activities. The children were able to acquire the target skills, and the children generalized these skills across adults and materials. Chiara, Schuster, Bell, and Wolery (1995) sought to examine the effectiveness of small-group, massed-trial instruction versus individual, distributed-trial instruction with a group of preschoolers. Eight children ages 3–6 years learned to label pictures via massed instruction that consisted of 10 trials within a single session in 1 day. Each teaching session lasted no more than 12 minutes, with 5 seconds in between instructional activities (or trials). In the distributed instruction condition, the 10 instructional activities (or trials) were distributed throughout the day (8:30 a.m.–3:00 p.m.) during natural breaks in the schedule, with 15–30 minutes between teaching sessions. The authors found that regardless of the mode of instruction, distributed instruction yielded more efficient learning (fewer trials to criterion and lower error percentage) than the small-group massed condition. Maintenance and generalization of skills were reported following either form of instruction.

Venn, Wolery, and Greco (1996) studied the effects of daily instruction versus every-other-day instruction. Preschool children in the study were taught manual signs, letter naming, or numeral naming. All of the children in the study received *both* types of instruction (every day and every-other-day). Children were assigned in groups of three, with each group comprised of two children who were typically developing and one child with disabilities. The typically developing children received 9 instructional trials in each session, whereas the children with disabilities received 12 instructional trials per session. Instruction was delivered in an alternating instruction format. Five of the six preschool-age children (four were typically developing, one child had autism, and one child had pervasive developmental disorder [PDD]) reached criterion on all skills regardless of the schedule of instruction. The every-other-day schedule, however, was more efficient for *all* children, resulting in fewer sessions, trials, and minutes of instruction necessary to reach criterion. No difference in generalization was observed after either method of instruction.

Sigafoos and colleagues (2006) tested the effects of embedded instruction versus discrete-trial training on self-injury, correct responding, and mood of a 12-year-old child with autism. Embedded instruction featured one learning trial every 1.5 minutes that was incorporated into one of three activities—walking, swinging, or music. The discrete-trials model of instruction featured four learning trials per minute (one trial every 15 seconds). Ten imitation trials were followed by 10 receptive labeling trials. All sessions lasted 5 minutes and occurred 2–5 times a day, 1–2 days per week. The authors concluded, "Embedded instruction was the more effective instructional format in terms of being associated with less self-injury, more intervals with correct responding, and higher mood ratings" (p. 201).

In another study of children with autism, Miranda-Linne and Melin examined the process of acquisition, generalization, and spontaneous use of color adjectives. They compared the relative efficiency of incidental teaching and traditional discrete-trial training procedures in the learning of these children. The results suggested that "discrete trial training led to faster acquisition, while embedded instruction was associated with greater maintenance and generalization of target behaviors" (1992, p. 197).

This analysis of historical and contemporary research findings suggests that distributed instruction benefited children and adults regardless of whether the tasks were physical or cognitive. Also, the spacing or distribution of instruction within the day (e.g., three 2-minute sessions per day) or across days (e.g., one time per day for 4 days) helped children learn. Although these findings may be intuitive, it is necessary to cite this research base in establishing the evidence that distributed instruction is the recommended practice in IECSE services. Furthermore, the best method to ensure distributed instruction within the IECSE model of service delivery is the adoption of consultation and coaching strategies as the key mode of intervention. It is also important to note, in this context, that IECSE teachers have limited time with children. As such, it is impossible for the IECSE teacher to implement a distributed practice model. Early childhood teachers and parents, however, are present all day, every day. They are positioned to provide opportunities for distributed practice across the day and during the week. Although they enjoy the benefit of continuous contact, they cannot be effective in addressing the priority IEP goals of their student(s) if they do not have the knowledge and skills to do so. It is, therefore, incumbent that IECSE teachers should spend their time helping their ECE partners see their vital role in supporting the development of the child. This is best accomplished through discussing and planning for learning opportunities that will be distributed across the day and will occur during the week between the visits of the IECSE teacher.

The consensus among professional practitioners and the weight of research evidence has resulted in the Council for Exceptional Children, Division for Early Childhood, acknowledging consultation within ECSE inclusive services as a recommended practice (McWilliam, 2005). As McWilliam (1996a) noted, prior to adoption of this recommendation, it is not the intensity or amount of direct instruction that occurs during the consultant's visit that should be the focus of attention, because the child's learning occurs between these consultation sessions.

Implications for Adoption of the Direct Services Model

The culture of early childhood education emphasizes a holistic focus on the child. This focus may assume the form of systematic arrangement, manipulation, or engineering of the learning environment; management of learning centers and learning materials; encouragement of peer engagement; and development of a child-centered curriculum (Johnson & Johnson, 1992). Children with special needs, however, may present a challenge with respect to their response to a discovery-oriented, child-initiated curriculum (Carta, Schwartz, Atwater, & McConnell, 1991; Wolery, 1997). Children with special needs, when left to their own devices, may elect to engage in activities that are not necessarily beneficial to their development. In fact, some children with special needs may consistently elect to withdraw from engagement with their peers who are typically developing or to persist in engaging in the same activities or with the same materials with which they are comfortable and that are well within their range of developmental skills. These predictable patterns of interaction, or avoidance of interaction, often precipitate more direct intervention on the part of the teacher that is consistent with the special education approach to instruction.

Unfortunately, this may begin a cycle of expectation and fulfillment with respect to the relationship among the IECSE teacher, his or her ECE partner, the child, and the parent(s) of the child. On the part of the ECE teacher, this expectation may be that the IECSE teacher will provide this requisite, IEP-focused direct instruction during his or her weekly visit. This expectation, in effect, absolves the ECE teacher of responsibility for addressing the child's IEP objectives throughout the remainder of the week. This expectation also shapes parent perceptions of the role of the IECSE as a visiting special education professional who will focus his or her complete attention on the child during the weekly visit to the child care or pre-K program. Finally, the IECSE teacher, who already may have an inclination to adopt a pull-out or small-group direct instruction model, is now rewarded by the ECE partner teacher and the parent for assuming this role. For many IECSE professionals, the trap has been set. Without redirection from an informed supervisor or advocacy from the IECSE community, the IECSE teacher may adopt this now expected role of visiting expert. This role may or may not be more personally and professionally comfortable for the IECSE teacher. Regardless of his or her personal preference and professional inclination, there is likely to be considerable pressure from key constituents to conform to this expectation and to assume this role.

Unfortunately, although episodic and intensive instruction may be attractive to the adult stakeholders, the efficacy of this model has not been established. More importantly, as discussed previously in this chapter, there are compelling reasons why the presumed efficacy of the direct services model must be questioned. Let us now examine the basic elements of the direct services delivery model and the consultation model in light of this research evidence and the characteristics of children receiving IECSE services.

Characteristics of Children Receiving IECSE Services

The Individuals with Disabilities Education Act of 1990 (PL 101-476) requires that all children with an IEP be educated in the least restrictive environment (LRE). This continuum of services, particularly in Part B 619 services, includes a spectrum of learning environments that typically ranges from extremely limited interaction with typical peers (e.g., home instruction or ECSE classroom in segregated school), to some interaction with typical peers (e.g., inclusive ECSE classroom), to extensive opportunities for interaction with peers who are typically developing (e.g., community pre-K program or Head Start). There are no prescriptive recommendations for placement options in IDEA based on extent or type of disability. Under IDEA, no children are precluded from daily and longitudinal contact with peers who are typically developing. This mandate notwithstanding, it is likely that the vast majority of children who are determined to be appropriately placed in non–LEA-managed, community-based child care or pre-K programs are children with high-incidence disability conditions. These conditions may include mild-to-moderate cognitive delays, mild sensory impairments (e.g., vision or hearing), mild-to-moderate motor impairments (e.g., spastic hemiplegic or diplegic cerebral palsy), and milder forms of autism. This range of conditions also would include a significant number of young children with communication disorders.

Adopting Unified and Longitudinal Intervention in Natural Environments

The rationale for adoption of a longitudinal model of intervention is compelling. As a result, the focus of attention for the IECSE teacher should be engagement of the parent or ECE partner teacher in a triadic model of consultation (Buysse & Wesley, 2005). In a triadic model (see Figure 2.1), which has been the recommended model of intervention in Part C programs for many years (Barnard, 1997; Cripe & Venn, 1997; McCollum & Yates, 1994; Woods, 2004), the IECSE teacher plans his or her visits with the intent to engage in reactive and proactive consultation and coaching strategies designed to transfer

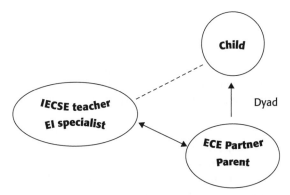

Figure 2.1. Illustration of the triadic model of consultation, focusing on the dyadic interaction and triadic exchange. In this model, the IECSE teacher plans visits with the intent to engage in reactive and proactive strategies in order to transfer specific knowledge and skills to his or her partner, who then transfers them to the child. (From PIWI Projects, Children's Research Center, University of Illinois at Urbana-Champaign; adapted by permission.)

specific knowledge and skills to his or her partner. The focus is not on direct instruction of the child. Although the child is always the focal point in the triadic model, there is recognition that the most effective means to influence child development is through change in the frequency and quality of the partner's interaction with the child. The triadic model recognizes that the ECE partner or parent has many more opportunities to address the priority learning objectives of the child across the week than the IECSE teacher has in a 60- to 75-minute weekly visit, even if the visit features intensive and direct instruction of the child. If the value of the consultation model is now apparent, then adoption of intentional and planned interaction with a partner is the recommended model of intervention. The ultimate objective of the consultation model is to ensure that the target child has multiple opportunities to acquire, master, and generalize those priority skills and behaviors identified in the child's IEP. This can occur as the child seeks to meet the expectations of the learning environment, through "spaced" or distributed direct instruction, as a result of incidental teaching, and through planned peer engagement.

This model for addressing priority IEP objectives involves assisting the parent or partner teacher in seeing opportunities for instruction or intervention and providing them with the information and skills that they will need to address these learning opportunities. This is best accomplished through a consultation model that features mapping of priority IEP objectives with typical activities and routines in the home, the child care setting, or the pre-K classroom. The matrix planning model (Hemmeter & Rous, 1997; McWilliam & Casey, 2008; Raver, 2004; Wilson, Mott, & Bateman, 2004) is helpful in providing the partner with specific examples of when and where during the day IEP objectives can be linked to typical activities.

The matrix planning format (see Figure 2.2) includes a listing of priority IEP objectives in the left-hand column. These IEP objectives also may be linked with local or state curriculum standards for ECE, effectively indexing the child's IEP objectives with the ECE general education curriculum, as well as a recommendation for an appropriate teaching strategy to address this objective. In Figure 2.3, the column headers are typical routines or activities in the classroom or home environment. Opportunities for addressing priority IEP objectives within these activities are indicated by entry of an X or a brief description of the parallel activity that will address this IEP objective. A more advanced matrix (see Figure 2.4) could be developed for more than one child in an instance in which several children with IEPs might be enrolled in the same classroom, such as a Head Start program. It also could include a recommended strategy for instruction to address this priority IEP objective within this routine or activity. After this matrix mapping has been completed, the IECSE teacher can then, through modeling and provision of other materials, help the partner develop key teaching skills to address these learning objectives.

The final stage of this process is monitoring child progress. This can be the province of the IECSE teacher or a responsibility shared with the partner. These key activities in the consultation model are addressed, in detail, in Chapters 5, 10, and 12.

After this proactive planning has occurred, priority IEP objectives should be addressed in a unified and longitudinal manner that is consistent with the principles of learning that guide the consultation model. The development of a unified and longitudinal approach to instruction will ensure that priority learning objectives are addressed in activities that occur throughout the day, across a range of learning materials, and in authentic situations. An example of a unified and longitudinal approach to instruction in which the parent or ECE partner teacher is responsible for instruction might be a

ACTIVITY-BASED MATRIX
IEP Objective x Activity

Child: Brian L.

ECE Teacher: Ms. Slattery

IECSE: Ms. Browner

Location: Play to Learn Pre-K

School Year: 2010–2011

Goals/ objectives	Table tasks	Circle	Snack	Centers	Closing circle
Identify letters	ABC letter-matching book and file folder activities; ask to name letters	Identify first letter in name using name cards when called to go to the restroom		Reading center: ladybug matching game, ABC file folder games	Identify first letter in name using name cards when called to go home
Follow directions	Follow picture schedule to complete morning jobs	Follow directions when asked to sit for circle	Follow picture directions to make milkshakes	Follow picture schedule to complete center rotations	Follow directions when asked to sit for circle
Answer yes/no questions	Ask, "Did you complete your job, yes or no?"		When asked if done, respond with yes or no		
Participate in a verbal exchange		Say hello at circle	Request snack; respond with thank you		Say good-bye at circle

Figure 2.2. Sample activity matrix for a child.

Activity Planning Matrix

Instructions: In the first column, enter the child learning outcomes and the related state department of education general education early learning content standards (ELCSs) that you identified in your activity plan. Across the top row, enter five opportunities for instruction that could occur daily or in conjunction with planned activities for the week. You may use one form for EACH focus child, or you may include other focus children on the same form. For EACH outcome for EACH child describe, in observable terms, the behaviors or skills that the child is expected to perform within these activities.

Activity: ELCS and child learning outcomes	Introduction to art project	Transition to tables	Task 1 Cutting grass	Task 2 Coloring duck/gluing feathers	Task 3 Fingerpainting mud
ELCS: Reading/Reading Applications #4: Participate in shared reading of repetitive or predictable text. **Child learning outcome:** Michael will press the switch to repeat the message "There is 1 duck stuck in the muck" during the activity with 1 pointing prompt.	After reviewing the story, Michael will answer the question "What happened to the duck?" by pressing the switch.			Michael will answer the question "What did the duck get stuck in?" by pressing the switch.	Michael will press the switch after completing his One Duck Stuck project.
ELCS: Math— Use Measurement Techniques and Tools #3: Sequence and order events in the context of daily activities and play. **Child learning outcome:** Michael will use visual cues to follow the direction "work first, then play" during the table time and free choice routines with 1 adult verbal prompt.		Michael will use the transition card to move to the appropriate table in the classroom.	Michael will follow the picture schedule to complete Step 1 of the art project (cut).	Michael will follow the picture schedule to complete Step 2 of the art project (color).	Michael will follow the picture schedule to complete Step 3 of the art project (paint).

ELCS: Social Studies—Rights and Responsibilities #3: Demonstrate increasing abilities to make independent choices and follow through on plans. Child learning outcome: Luis will follow the direction "pick up" and clean up toys/objects during the activity	Luis will follow the direction "pick up" and put art project on the chalkboard at the end of circle time.		Luis will follow the direction "pick up" and place scissors in bin when finished cutting.	Luis will follow the direction "pick up" and place glue in bin when finished gluing.	Before transitioning to finger paint, Luis will follow the direction "pick up" and clean up toys.
ELCS: Science—Abilities to Do Technological Design #4: Demonstrate the safe use of tools such as scissors, hammers, and writing utensils with adult guidance. Child learning outcome: Michael will hold scissors correctly to cut straight lines and hold writing instrument with an appropriate grasp with 1 verbal/physical prompt. Luis will use loop scissors to cut a straight line and hold writing instrument with an appropriate grasp with 2 verbal/physical prompts.	Michael and Luis will use scissors to demonstrate cutting grass.		Michael will use FISCAR scissors to cut a straight line while making grass for the art project. Luis will use loop scissors to cut a straight line while making grass for the art project.	Michael will hold the crayon correctly while coloring the duck. Luis will hold the crayon correctly while coloring the duck.	Michael will hold a paintbrush correctly to put paint on paper. Luis will hold paintbrush correctly to put paint on paper.

Figure 2.3. Sample activity matrix including child learning outcomes and the related state department of education general education early learning content standards (ELCSs).

ACTIVITY-BASED MATRIX

IEP Objectives x Child Grouping

Instructions: Use this form to plan when you will focus on each of your children's priority individualized education program (IEP) objectives in a group situation. Across the top of the form, list the everyday activities and routines that occur in the classroom. Then, down the left-hand column, list the goals and objectives and the children who have these goals/objectives in common. For each of the objectives, identify at least two activities during which you could provide IEP-based instruction.

ECE teacher: Ms. Dawes

IECSE teacher: Ms. Belanger

ECE program: Olivet Early Learning Center

School year: 2010–2011

Children	Goals/ objectives	Arrival/breakfast	Free play	Snack/lunch	Outdoor/gross motor play	Craft	Departure
Damian Neshaun	Communicating wants/needs	Picture cues for food Repeating model for drink, eat (e.g., sign, word).	Preferred toys: repeating models, spontaneous	more eat please (e.g., word/ sign/picture for desired food)	Preferred toy (e.g., bike, ball) Preferred area (e.g., bean bag, picnic area, grass)	Craft materials: (e.g., glue, scissors) Assistance: (e.g., help, more)	
Danielle Steven	Using two- to three-word phrases (response form)	Answering question, "What do you need to do next?" (e.g., "Eat food") with or w/out model	Questions about play: "What are you building?"	Reach for/grasp cooking utensils	Reach/grasp to hold onto swing/ side of slide	Answering questions about what is being made	Answering question, "What do you need to do next?"
Damian Neshaun Danielle	Participate in turn-taking		Building with blocks Playing a board game	Washing hands	Swinging Sharing bikes	Waiting for materials	
Danielle Steven	Matching letters and shapes		Pattern blocks Magnetic letters		Large wooden shape board outside	Matching foam shapes	

Figure 2.4. Sample activity matrix for a group of children.

series of learning opportunities related to recognition of shapes, a prerequisite reading (visual discrimination) and math skill.

The IECSE teacher would consult with the parent or ECE partner to identify activities that occur throughout the day, during which opportunities for instruction might be embedded (Grisham-Brown, Hemmeter, & Pretti-Frontczak, 2005; Horn, Lieber, Li, Sandall, & Schwartz, 2000; McWilliam & Casey, 2008). This is an essential aspect of the consultation process and the initial step in developing a holistic intervention plan. Teachers and parents often do not see the range of opportunities for learning and instruction that occur in everyday routines and activities. Before they can take advantage of these opportunities, they need to recognize them. For example, shape discrimination, the underlying skill in recognizing different shapes, can become part of many activities. The children's personal cubbies can include the name and/or photo of the child mounted on a different shape (e.g., variations of triangles, rectangles, squares, circles). The child could be prompted to identify the shape on which his or her name was mounted. The shapes for each child, or for the target child, could be changed frequently to afford additional opportunities for teaching as well as to increase motivation via novelty. Other opportunities for learning and teaching could occur by asking the children to indicate which friends are present or absent during morning circle. If the names and/or photos of the children also were mounted on different-shaped backing (also, different colors for an additional teaching option), the teacher could ask the children to count the number of children absent (or present) and to identify the shape under the student's name.

Other opportunities for direct or indirect instruction could occur in the puzzle or block corner, during a planned collage activity in art, during snack time if different shapes or sizes of paper plates were available or if children's placemats were shaped differently, at story time, during a nature walk, in classroom signage that indicates center areas (e.g., hanging icons on backgrounds of differing shapes), through matching of children's names (and shapes of name cards) for grouping during activity, by providing different shapes of sponges for painting or cleanup, and so forth. There are many natural opportunities to address this objective; however, intentional manipulation of learning materials is necessary to extend the number of opportunities for learning and instruction. Intentional adaptation of activities and materials is a skill that must be taught to some parents and partners.

After the IECSE teacher and his or her partner have examined the range of learning opportunities and discussed suggestions for expansion of opportunities, then strategies for instruction should be considered. The IECSE teacher will have to provide specific examples of how shape recognition can be taught through direct and incidental teaching strategies. It will be during this stage that information describing the hierarchy of prompting (Karlan, 1991), for example, would be shared. The partner or parent could be provided with implementation checklists, articles, PowerPoint slides, or web site addresses (e.g., SPIES Project of Utah State University) that describe the rationale for the hierarchy of prompting, also known as the system of least prompts (Godby, Gast, & Wolery, 1987), as well examples of these strategies. The IECSE teacher also might model—with a child or his or her partner—how to use these strategies. The teacher also should discuss what the partner should look for in the behavior or response of the child that would suggest a change in prompting strategy. The IECSE teacher also should explain the differences between direct and incidental teaching as well as provide examples of several of these strategies. The parent or partner teacher should be reassured that creating and managing a high-quality learning environment in which activities and materials are engaging would complement direct instruction.

Embedding Related Services in Typical Routines in Natural Environments

Some children receiving IECSE services also may need to receive related services as a component of their IEP program. Speech pathology, physical therapy, and occupational therapy are the most common of the related services provided to young children with special needs. Children with disability-specific conditions such as visual impairment or severe cerebral palsy also may require related services of consultants in vision impairment or assistive technology (Corn, Hatlen, Huebner, Ryan, & Siller, 1995). Each of these disciplines has examined the role of direct services and consultation in addressing priority IEP objectives. Adoption of a consultation model in physical and occupational services has been recommended since the 1980s (Campbell, 1987; Dunn, 1990; Rainforth, 1997; Rainforth & York-Barr, 1997). Recent publications have described the process of consultation in much greater detail (Case-Smith & Rogers, 2005; Hanft, Rush, & Shelden, 2004; McEwen, 2000). This continuing dialogue has sought to balance tension among these related services practitioners. Some of this tension is related to concern about the potential dilution of professional authority and responsibility for provision of services under medical prescription as well as a growing understanding of the benefits of therapeutic activities or exercise that are provided, longitudinally, in authentic, motivating, and age-appropriate activities.

An example of this apparent dilemma would be the case in which a child with a condition such as Down syndrome had an occupational therapy objective related to improved pincer grasp versus persistent use of palmar grasp. Development of a functional pincer grasp might precede the development of a modified tripod grasp that is considered a prerequisite to the development of print skills and linked with improved fluency in fingers dexterity, which is necessary in accessing a keyboard. In this situation, the related services professional faces the same dilemma as the IECSE teacher. The occupational therapist often provides direct instruction in a one-to-one or pull-out model. The rationale for one-to-one direct services provided by any related services professional often is attributed to the need to use specialized equipment (e.g., Bobath ball, modified light board, software for visual training) or orthotic and assistive devices (e.g., wrist splints, adaptive gloves). The need for direct, one-to-one intervention also may be based on the need for precisely executed therapeutic exercise regimens (e.g., range of motion, visual target tracking, articulation exercises). Although there are legitimate reasons why direct instruction or therapeutic intervention may be necessary, there are still benefits to follow-up or longitudinal intervention in the absence of the therapist.

No related services professional would argue that multiple opportunities to practice communication, visual discrimination and decoding skills, or gross and fine motor skills in age-appropriate activities would be detrimental to a child's development or would undermine the child's acquisition of key skills. Related services professionals might argue that it is essential that any learning and practice opportunities be provided in accord with the minimal therapeutic support necessary to improve the probability of success of the child. This is a reasonable assumption and sets the expectation for transfer of basic knowledge and skills. This transfer, depending on the nature of the knowledge and skills, can be addressed through a triadic consultation relationship of the related services professional and the ECE teacher. This transfer also can occur within the IECSE teacher and ECE partner teacher relationship as long as the related serviced professional is open to collaboration with the IECSE teacher.

The process for addressing related services objectives within typical routines and activities involves the same planning process as that which occurs in addressing general developmental goals. The matrix planning model is the primary curriculum planning tool. The related services professional also should engage in an IEP prioritization process—such as the Maturation, Environment, Peer and Intensive (MEPI) model (the rationale for the model as well as specific applications as a planning tool are described in Chapters 9 and 10)—similar to the process in which the IECSE teacher and his or her ECE partner participate. Within a triadic model of consultation, the related services professional would engage in the prioritization process with the ECE teacher or his or her LEA associate, the IECSE teacher.

A range of motor and communication objectives can be addressed effectively within typical activities. Examples include opportunities to practice fluency with specific phonemes and to respond to social bids of peers with appropriate syntactic constructions; improvement of quality of gait or efficiency of movement through participation in scavenger or adventure hikes or completion of classroom jobs; and use of selected forms of grasp in securing food, art, and play items, with or without tools. It is not difficult to imagine how use of a matrix planning model coupled with adoption of incidental teaching strategies could result in the ECE teacher identifying multiple opportunities across the day to address key related services objectives.

CHAPTER 3

Essential Roles of IECSE Teachers

This chapter provides a framework for discussing the roles of IECSE teachers. The work of two groups of researchers will form the basis of this framework. In addition, this chapter describes differences between IECSE teachers and their classroom-based colleagues. Finally, we will discuss one way to assess the performance of IECSE teachers.

Building a Service Delivery System

Striffler and Fire (1999) suggested that an effective service delivery system must be built on a clear understanding of the vision an entity has for early intervention (EI) and ECSE services. This vision serves as the foundation for all other work, including the way a service delivery system is designed and the roles and responsibilities associated with jobs of individuals who work within this system. Figure 3.1 depicts Striffler and Fire's model of personnel development that we have used to guide our personnel development work with IECSE teachers. Identifying a vision for ECSE service delivery is the first element under Striffler and Fire's model and is essential to operationalize in order to build a framework of professional development in a state.

Inclusion

The Council for Exceptional Children's Division for Early Childhood's (DEC) position statement on inclusion provides the vision on which we believe an IECSE service delivery system should be built. The DEC's position on inclusion is built on the promises of 1) access to high-quality early learning experiences, 2) full participation in all learning activities, and 3) "an infrastructure of inclusion supports" (2008, p. 3). Critical to this infrastructure of supports is access to information and technical assistance that general early childhood educators and parents need to ensure that all children have access to and can fully participate in high-quality learning experiences. IECSE teachers can be important sources of support for other adults. Serving as consultants or coaches, they can share information with others and support early childhood inclusion in a variety of ways.

Least Restrictive Environment, Free
Appropriate Public Education, and Natural Environments

Also pertinent to the discussion on inclusion are the concepts of LRE and FAPE that are mandated by IDEA 2004 (PL 108-446). Identifying the LRE for school-age children is relatively easy given the compulsory nature of K–12 education. However, because

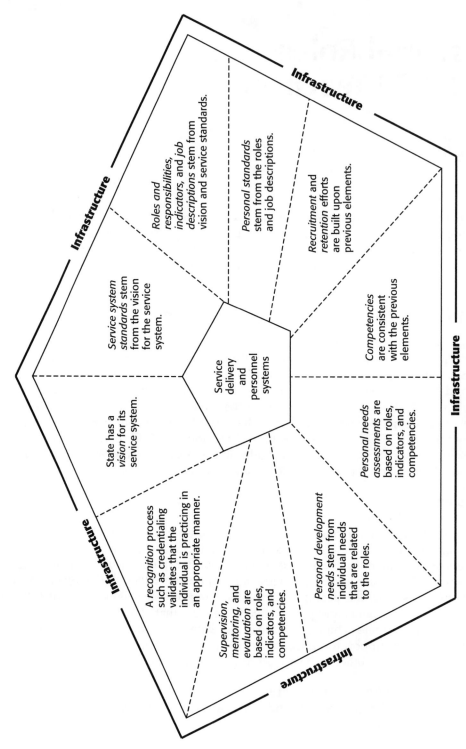

Figure 3.1. Model of personnel development showing integrated systems: Service delivery and personnel. (From Striffler, N., & Fire, N. [1999]. Embedding personnel development into early intervention service delivery: Elements in the process. *Infants and Young Children, 11*, 52; reprinted by permission.)

Infrastructure

Infrastructure

Infrastructure

Infrastructure

Infrastructure

Service delivery and personnel systems

State has a *vision* for its service system.

Service system standards stem from the vision for the service system.

Roles and responsibilities, indicators, and *job descriptions* stem from vision and service standards.

Personal standards stem from the roles and job descriptions.

Recruitment and *retention* efforts are built upon previous elements.

Competencies are consistent with the previous elements.

Personal needs assessments are based on roles, indicators, and competencies.

Personal development needs stem from individual needs that are related to the roles.

Supervision, mentoring, and *evaluation* are based on roles, indicators, and competencies.

A *recognition* process such as credentialing validates that the individual is practicing in an appropriate manner.

preschool education is voluntary, it is much more difficult to identify the LRE for a preschool-age child with disabilities. Given this difficulty, it is helpful to understand the concept of *natural environments* as discussed in Part C of IDEA. A *natural environment* is one in which early intervention services are to be provided; this refers to home and community settings where typically developing infants and toddlers are likely to be served and includes settings such as playgroups, child care, story times, and, of course, children's homes. Extending the concepts of *natural environment* and *LRE* to preschool services leads us to identify community-based programs such as child care centers, Head Start classrooms, private preschools, and families' homes as inclusive settings. This legislation identifies the *place* where children should receive services. However, it does not stipulate the *nature* of those services. To best understand how to build a system of high-quality preschool services, it is also imperative to examine the nature and quality of services that children receive in inclusive settings as well as the qualifications of individuals who will provide them.

Recognition and Response

Another body of literature promotes a vision for inclusive early childhood practices but extends a framework to the roles of early childhood professionals within inclusive settings. The recognition and response model (Buysse & Peisner-Feinberg, 2010) is developed after the response to intervention (RTI) model (Fuchs & Fuchs, 2006) that is helping to define the importance of tiered instruction and early intervention services vital to prevent school failure. This intervention framework is comprised of three components: 1) the use of increasingly complex interventions, 2) a problem-solving approach to assist educators in identifying and evaluating intervention strategies, and 3) a coordinated system of data collection and progress monitoring in order to make informed decisions as part of the problem-solving approach.

The term *tiered intervention* refers to a hierarchical approach to the implementation of increasingly complex interventions. Tier 1 is that of a high-quality early learning environment that provides rich experiences to all children. Tier 2 reflects group interventions designed for small groups of children who share learning difficulties. Tier 3 is individualized intervention. This level is designed for children who have not achieved success using Tier 1 or Tier 2 interventions. Decisions about which tier of intervention to use are based on screening, assessment, and progress monitoring strategies. The recognition and response model is based on the assumption that interventions used to support young children's learning are evidence-based and implemented based on data from progress monitoring efforts (Buysse & Peisner-Feinberg, 2010).

Central to the success of the recognition and response model (Buysse & Peisner-Feinberg, 2010) is the extensive use of behavioral consultation and collaborative problem solving. Within this approach, adults (e.g., parents; ECSE professionals such as itinerant teachers, ECE teachers, related service providers) work together to design, implement, and evaluate the success of interventions reflected in Tiers 1, 2, or 3. A recurring theme across current literature on educational reform in early childhood special education stresses the importance of collaborative problem solving and consultation, a central focus of this book and the work of IECSE teachers within a consultative model.

Setting Service Delivery Standards Based on a Vision

Striffler and Fire (1999) identified the second element in their model as the development of service delivery standards that embody the shared vision of the group and serve as the foundation for further action. These standards provide guidelines that support the effective evaluation of the system. State operating standards for ECSE services compose one set of standards that are commonly found across the United States. Because we are familiar with Ohio's work in this area, we use Ohio's operating standards as an example (Ohio Department of Education, 2008). Section 3301-51-11 describes service delivery standards for preschool-age children with special needs. This section delineates case-load ratios for teachers, including IECSE teachers. It briefly describes permitted roles and functions of IECSE teachers and reflects the state's vision for early childhood services by permitting itinerant services to be provided through a consultative model and for intervention to be delivered by a team of professionals that include the IECSE teacher, family members, or other caregivers who work in public or private preschools (see 3301-51-11[G][3] and [5]). It is important to note that these operating standards, adopted in July 2008, differ significantly from the previous operating standards, which did not articulate how itinerant services should be provided or the functions of an IECSE teacher, especially as it relates to consultation. Ohio, like many other states, is working to operationalize its vision of inclusive early childhood services through legislation and promulgation of regulations that support this vision.

Roles, Responsibilities, Performance Indicators, and Job Descriptions

Striffler and Fire (1999) identified the third element of their model as the way in which the entity describes the job functions of personnel who work in the system. Once an employee's job function is identified, it is then possible to determine personnel standards as well as proceed with recruitment and/or retention efforts. Roles are defined by the scope of job-related responsibilities assumed by the individual. Striffler and Fire emphasized that the role of an individual can differ dramatically depending on the setting in which he or she provides services. For example, an IECSE teacher assumes very different roles than a classroom-based ECSE teacher, even though they are both credentialed as early childhood special education teachers.

Once a state has identified roles and responsibilities, it can further differentiate performance indicators. Developing performance indicators for a job helps to set personnel standards and provides mechanisms for effective supervision and self-reflection. Each indicator should be formulated using measurable, observable terms and should reflect behaviors that occur within the context of the early childhood job setting (Striffler & Fire, 1999).

IECSE Teacher as Intensive Technical Assistance Provider

Also pertinent to this discussion is the conceptual work done by Fixsen, Blasé, Timbers, and Wolf (2007) concerning implementation research. These researchers have written extensively about what is needed to ensure implementation of an evidence-based practice and how critically important it is to verify that an intervention has occurred as planned. Given the field's commitment to early childhood inclusion, understanding what happens (and what should happen) during itinerant visits is necessary to determining under which parameters early childhood inclusion is successful. We assume that IECSE teachers work with other adults to enhance learning environments and ensure that young children with disabilities have access to high-quality, child-focused interventions in the absence of the itinerant teacher.

The relative success of an intervention is dependent, in large part, on the degree to which it is implemented with integrity. Although it is easy to isolate the effects of yeast in making bread or how holding a golf club a certain way results in a longer drive, identifying the effects of human intervention on another human's behavior is much more challenging. Fixsen and colleagues suggest the following:

> Other than most chemical interventions and surgical interventions, any treatment endeavor in the human services is labor intensive. It is the skillful interaction of a Practitioner with a child, parent or other adult that produces benefits. The more difficult the problem, the more skillful and complete the performance of the Practitioner must be in order to achieve a beneficial outcome. The [work between the] Practitioner–child or Practitioner–adult is where and how treatment is actualized in the human services. (2007, p. 97)

If we accept Fixsen and colleagues' (2007) premise as stated above, then it is essential that we understand what people *do* as part of their jobs in EI and ECSE. And, although it is necessary to understand what they do, it is not enough. We must also understand *how* they do it; that is, the degree to which there is consistency between what they are *supposed* to do and what they *actually* do. This is the essence of implementation research and forms the basis for a type of support Fixsen, Blasé, Horner, and Sugai (2009) term *intensive technical assistance* (ITA, p. 1). Intensive technical assistance is a form of technical assistance that is needed to help individuals adopt new ways of functioning. In the case of early childhood inclusion, we assume that early childhood teachers and other caregivers need to adopt new ways of interacting with young children who have disabilities to maximize developmental and academic outcomes. In essence, we realize that IECSE teachers provide ITA during their visits to community-based programs. Table 3.1 outlines primary components of ITA and is consistent with what we believe to be the essence of a consultative approach to IECSE service delivery.

Defining the Work of the IECSE Teacher

It is not enough for IECSE teachers to understand their job-related roles and responsibilities; there must be a common understanding across all individuals who are involved in the service delivery system. Although it is relatively easy to identify and agree on essential roles and responsibilities for individuals who hold traditional positions such as teachers or administrators, it is much more difficult for positions with titles such as *home visitor* or *itinerant teacher*. The term *itinerant teacher* implies that the individual who assumes this position functions in a teacher role—that is, primarily instructing students during visits to their homes or other classrooms. Odom, Horn, and colleagues (1999), however, found two major models of IECSE service delivery. In the *itinerant-direct* model, the itinerant teacher assumed the role of an instructor to students. However, in the *itinerant-consultative* model, IECSE professionals served as consultants to other adults—either caregivers or teachers. Odom and his colleagues described this model more favorably than the itinerant-direct model because it helped to ensure that children benefited from IEP-based instruction outside of visits from the itinerant teacher. Given the important distinctions between these two approaches to IECSE service delivery, we were interested in examining the perspectives of various stakeholder groups familiar with IECSE service delivery.

In an attempt to identify essential roles and responsibilities of IECSE teachers, we conducted a study using the Delphi method with four stakeholder panels comprised of individuals across the United States. These panels (ranging in size from 22 to 29 members)

Table 3.1. Core features of intensive technical assistance

1. Clarity
    a. Purposeful activity to understand, but not be "consumed by," the current context (e.g., reviews of system strengths, stressors, policies, regulations, data)
    b. Mutually established clear needs, roles, and responsibilities among the technical assistance (TA) entity, the TA recipients, and other partners
    c. Agreement about how to create the new structures needed to support educators employing new methods (e.g., points of contact, communication routines, feedback methods, workgroups)

2. Frequency
    a. Regular (daily, weekly, monthly) on-site and in-person communication and shared activities to initiate and manage change
    b. Regular (daily, weekly, monthly) use of planning, execution, evaluation, and next step cycles to quickly correct errors and solve problems

3. Intensity
    a. Prompting and creating opportunities for collective reflection to inform and guide "next steps" (e.g., planning retreats; use of learning communities)
    b. Creating opportunities to infuse into the system relevant skills (e.g., training and coaching events) and knowledge (e.g., use of technology to provide didactic information)
    c. Regular on-site coaching and assessments of skill development and overall progress based on active participation and direct observations supplemented with long-distance planning and work sessions (e.g., video and telephone meetings)

4. Duration
    a. Doing whatever it takes to create desired changes and resolve issues in ways that help develop and expand capacity
    b. Systematic, focused, and sustained change efforts carried out over a period of several years (2–5 years may be typical)

5. Integrity
    a. Focus on integrating current activities, roles, and functions to create more effective and efficient education systems
    b. Comprehensive work with whole systems instead of piecemeal activities that may contribute to further fragmentation
    c. Collecting and using reliable and accessible data for decision-making at local and system levels

6. Accountability
    a. Responsibility for actively providing information and necessary supports for assuring that intended outcomes occur in a timely and effective manner
    b. Use of negative feedback and setbacks as opportunities to create new methods, bring in new partners, and develop new knowledge, skills, and abilities to adapt to challenges and continue to make progress toward agreed-upon goals
    c. Benefits to students, families, teachers, and education systems define the success of an intensive TA effort

From Fixsen, D.L., Blasé, K.A., Horner, R., & Sugai. G. (2009, February). *Intensive technical assistance. Scaling Up Brief #2.* Chapel Hill: The University of North Carolina, FPG Child Development Institute, State Implementation and Scaling Up of Evidence Based Practices (SISEP); reprinted by permission.

included IECSE teachers, ECE partner teachers, parents of preschool-age children served by IECSE teachers, and supervisors of IECSE teachers (Dinnebeil, McInerney, & Hale, 2006b). In addition to discovering professional roles and responsibilities individuals consider important, our research also allowed us to examine the degree to which members of each stakeholder group achieved consensus on the relative importance of a responsibility (Linstone & Turoff, 2002). We asked individuals in these groups to respond to the same set of questions:

1. What are the primary responsibilities of IECSE teachers?

2. What are the secondary responsibilities of IECSE teachers?

3. What are the key roles of IECSE teachers?

Table 3.2. Definitions of itinerant roles used in Delphi survey with all groups

Role label	Role definition
Assessor/monitor	Engages in formal and informal assessment activities ranging from observations of child in natural settings to administering tests for the purpose of determining eligibility. Also includes activities such as writing progress reports, keeping records of child's progress, completing other paperwork related to services described on the individualized education program (IEP), and collecting/managing data related to children's progress in meeting IEP objectives.
Consultant/coach to other adults	Works with parents, caregivers, teachers, and other adults involved in child's life. Provides written information, activity plans, and materials/equipment related to child's special needs to other adults. Assists other adults in planning appropriate activities and modifying materials, equipment, or activities for child. Models or demonstrates intervention strategies that other adults might use to address IEP goals and objectives. Provides feedback to other adults about their implementation of intervention strategies. Plans and conducts inservice sessions and other trainings targeted to general education teachers and/or caregivers.
Direct service provider	Works directly with child to address IEP objectives individually, in small groups, or in large groups. Prepares materials and activities to use directly with child. Prepares lesson/activity plans that address child's IEP goals and objectives. Helps other children in classroom interact appropriately with children with IEPs. Interacts with and teaches all children in classroom.
Lifelong learner	Accesses materials to improve knowledge about child's specific disability and related needs. Engages in a range of professional development activities designed to remain current in the field.
Service coordinator	Coordinates the provision of services as outlined in the child's IEP. Links parents and other members of inter/transdisciplinary team to other community resources to meet child's needs. Coordinates transition activities as child moves from one program to the next.
Team member	Serves as a member of the child's IEP team. Works with the team to develop the IEP. Participates with colleagues in district planning and engages in public relation activities to promote the services the school district has to offer.

Note. IEP = Individualized education program.

The roles for IECSE teachers that we identified based on the results of the Delphi process are listed in Table 3.2. In addition to identifying key roles of IECSE teachers, we also asked respondents to identify responsibilities associated with those roles (Dinnebeil et al., 2006b). Using content analysis procedures (Johnson & LaMontagne, 1993), we linked each responsibility with one of the roles described previously. Finally, we asked respondents to rate the degree to which each responsibility was "important for effective itinerant service delivery" (Dinnebeil et al., 2006b, p. 157) and the degree to which these responsibilities should be addressed in preservice training. We also examined the degree to which there was consistency in the responsibilities identified by each group. As one might expect, IECSE teachers generated the largest number (44) of different responsibilities. Early childhood teachers identified 26 responsibilities, parents identified 29 responsibilities, and supervisors of IECSE teachers identified 33 responsibilities. Members of the IECSE teacher panel reached consensus about the importance of responsibilities associated with the role of consultant and/or coach and differed most often on the importance of responsibilities associated with the roles of a direct services provider and a service coordinator. Members of the parent panel consistently rated as essential responsibilities associated with the role of direct services provider but differed on the degree to which they believed the responsibilities associated with the role of consultant and/or coach were important. Members of the supervisor panel and the ECE teacher panel also had difficulty reaching consensus on the importance of responsibilities associated with the role of a consultant and/or coach. One thing was clear from the results of this study—there was not a great deal of consistency in the perceptions of those most familiar with IECSE service about the importance of roles and responsibilities of an IECSE professional.

Major Roles of IECSE Teachers

As discussed above, the results of the Delphi study (Dinnebeil et al., 2006b) identified major roles that IECSE teachers assume as part of their work. Next, readers will find a description of those roles.

Direct Service Provider

At times, IECSE teachers might need to work with a child directly, primarily to help him or her acquire or learn new skills or behaviors (as opposed to practice, increase fluency, or generalize use of a skill to other settings). They also may engage in direct services to develop a relationship with the child and get to know the child's learning characteristics. Within the role of direct services provider, the IECSE teacher might provide individualized instruction in the classroom or home. She might also work with the child in small-group activities and, sometimes, in large groups. Consistent with the views of ECSE leaders, we believe that a "pull-out" (including a "pull-aside") approach in which the teacher removes the child from the learning environment to provide specialized instruction is not desirable (McWilliam, 1996b). Providing direct instruction outside of the context of the learning environment makes generalization very difficult. In addition, providing instruction outside of the classroom removes the child from the learning environment. Naturalistic instruction (Rule, Losardo, Dinnebeil, Kaiser, & Rowland, 1998) that is embedded within the children's daily routines and activities (Horn, Lieber, Li, Sandall, & Schwartz, 2000) should serve as the foundation for child-focused interventions; thus, we do not devote a chapter to discussing the role of direct services provider in more detail, though many chapters will make reference to the direct services model versus the consultative model.

Consultant and/or Coach

The roles of consultant and coach are important ones to IECSE teachers because it is through these roles that they can best support high-quality early childhood inclusion. Although both of these roles differ (see Dinnebeil, Buysse, Rush, & Eggbeer, 2007), they both characterize indirect, consultative (McCollum, Gooler, Appl, & Yates, 2001) service delivery. IECSE teachers who function as consultants or coaches work primarily with other adults as opposed to working directly with children (Buysse & Wesley, 2005). As consultants, they may help other adults to modify the learning environment or the curriculum to meet children's needs. They work collaboratively with partners to align specialized instruction that children need with the general early childhood curriculum and academic content standards prescribed by many states (DEC, 2007). Along with their partners, they analyze the learning environment to ensure that children are engaged in learning (McWilliam & Casey, 2007) and have access to the general curriculum (Nolet & McLaughlin, 2000). They help partner teachers plan activities, embedding specialized instruction within the context of daily classroom routines and activities. They share information about the child's special learning needs or resources that might be available to support the child in the community-based setting. They problem-solve with their adult partners to address challenges or roadblocks to successful inclusion. The IECSE teacher's role as consultant and coach are discussed in more detail in Chapters 4 and 5, respectively.

As coaches, IECSE teachers help other adults learn new skills or enhance their use of existing skills (Hanft et al., 2004). Coaching is a widely used form of professional development that has demonstrated effectiveness in a variety of contexts (Kohler, Crilley, Shearer, & Good, 1997; Kohler, McCullough, & Buchan, 1995; Showers & Joyce, 1996; Vail, Tschantz, & Bevill, 1997). Rush, Sheldon, and Hanft describe coaching as "an interactive process of observation and reflection in which the coach promotes a parent's or other care provider's ability to support a child's participation in everyday experiences and interactions with family members and peers across settings" (2003, p. 33). Observation, performance, feedback, and reflection are important components in the coaching process. IECSE teachers who serve as coaches work with learners to jointly identify goals or desired outcomes for the coaching relationship. They provide explicit modeling or demonstration to the learner and offer specific, constructive feedback that enables the learner to learn a new skill or behavior. The role of the coach is more fully described in Chapter 5.

Assessor and/or Monitor

As the individual who is primarily responsible for implementing services outlined on the child's IEP, the itinerant teacher plays an important role in assessing and monitoring the child's progress. Chapter 6 of this text focuses on the role of the IECSE teacher as assessor. Assessment is a key element of a curriculum framework that supports positive developmental outcomes for young children (DEC, 2007). Assessment serves many purposes including 1) screening to identify children who might have or be at risk for a special learning need, 2) diagnosis to determine the etiology of the delay or disability, 3) determining eligibility for specialized services, 4) monitoring progress and making curriculum decisions, and 5) program evaluation (both formative and summative) (Wolery, 2004). IECSE teachers work with the IEP team including family members, educational partners, and related services colleagues to design, implement, and evaluate a system of assessment to guide the provision of high-quality, child-focused services. Within a consultative model of IECSE service delivery, all team members work collaboratively to collect and interpret data central to the assessment progress. Within this model, IECSE teachers play a role in the assessment process that is different from their classroom-based colleagues. Although a classroom-based ECSE teacher is the individual who most often actually implements assessment efforts and collects data, the IECSE teacher must rely on the individuals who see or work with the child on a regular basis. Working with family members or general education partners, IECSE teachers devise efficient and feasible data collection methods that yield useful information. That is not to say that IECSE teachers do not engage directly in assessment efforts. They must work with the child directly on occasion to monitor progress and collect data through formal and informal assessment efforts. The IECSE teacher is probably also the person on the team who is responsible for managing data and using it to write progress reports. However, in general, the role of the IECSE teacher as assessor or monitor is more indirect and behind-the-scenes. This role is described more fully in Chapter 6.

Service Coordinator

Even though the role of a service coordinator is most often associated with early intervention providers, participants in the Delphi study described above (Dinnebeil et al., 2006b) identified responsibilities associated with the role of a service coordinator as important to the work of an IECSE teacher. Indeed, we have found that the IECSE teacher is the person who is often called on to arrange transportation schedules, coordinate related services, and identify community resources that may be useful in supporting the child's progress toward meeting his or her IEP goals. To fulfill the role of the service coordinator, IECSE teachers must have an extensive working knowledge of community resources that might be available to support the child—resources such as volunteer organizations, toy-lending libraries, or parent-to-parent support groups. In addition, the IECSE teacher is often the individual who coordinates the child's transition from EI programs to preschool or from preschool programs to kindergarten. IECSE teachers often coordinate parent visits to receiving classrooms as well as coordinate the paperwork associated with transition activities. Relationships between adults and adults and children are important for successful transitions (Rosenkoetter et al., 2009). IECSE teachers must have strong positive relationships with other teachers and must also foster these relationships among partner teachers (e.g., between the general education preschool teacher and the kindergarten teacher). Developing strong partnerships with others is at the heart of the IECSE model and is crucial to successful consultation and coaching. All of these activities are related to the role of service coordinator and will be discussed in Chapter 7.

Team Member

Participants in the Delphi study identified "team member" as a key role of an IECSE teacher. Please see Chapter 8 for a more in-depth view of the IECSE teacher's role as a team member. This role is particularly important because the membership of an IEP team of a child receiving IECSE services can be diverse. The IECSE teacher, because she visits the child in the home or community-based program, usually has a stronger relationship with these other adults and can easily be viewed as the team leader. As a team member, IECSE teachers have responsibilities to other team members. Dependability, follow-through, and reliability are important qualities of a good team member. In addition, competent team members must be able to communicate effectively with others, understanding the dynamics of team meetings and team development (Friend & Cook, 2000).

In addition to serving on IEP teams, IECSE teachers often are asked to serve on districtwide teams such as early childhood assessment teams and community-based councils (e.g., local Part C interagency coordinating councils) (Dinnebeil et al., 2006b). Although the same qualifications as discussed apply to these roles, IECSE teachers who serve on these broad-based teams and committees should possess a greater degree of sophistication and savvy about public relations than their classroom-based colleagues. In some ways, they are their LEA's "diplomats" to the early childhood community and should feel and behave comfortably in that role. Again, the IECSE teacher as an IEP team member is discussed more fully in Chapter 8.

Performance Indicators

Striffler and Fire (1999) explained that, after roles and responsibilities of personnel have been established, it is important to develop *performance indicators*. Performance indicators represent operational statements that include performance criteria linked to each job role. Performance indicators are stated in behavioral, measurable terms and reflect setting-specific competencies. Performance indicators can be used to develop job descriptions and can allow supervisors and professionals a mechanism for providing constructive and critical feedback regarding the IECSE teacher's job performance. Personnel standards can be developed from these performance indicators to create a cohesive system of personnel development.

Performance Indicators for Early Childhood Education Specialists

As part of our partnership with the Ohio Department of Education's Office of Early Learning and School Readiness, we worked with field-based colleagues to develop the Performance Indicators for Early Childhood Education Specialists (PIECES; Dinnebeil, McInerney, et al., 2007). The PIECES is a document that outlines performance indicators for IECSE teachers and provides a set of rubrics to identify the user's level of competency associated with each performance indicator. The purpose of the PIECES is to provide a method of self-assessment for IECSE teachers. Supervisors might also be interested in using this document to support the performance of the IECSE teachers they supervise. In addition, this document provides performance-based examples at three levels: *basic, proficient*, and *distinguished*. IECSE teachers who are new to their positions can be expected to operate at the *basic* level of performance; however, those with more experience and expertise can be expected to operate at either the *proficient* or *distinguished* levels. We hope this document is useful to those wishing to improve their performance as IECSE teachers as well as to those who supervise the work of IECSE teachers. (Please see Appendix C for a photocopiable version of the PIECES.)

After the PIECES was developed, more than 300 potential users in Ohio (e.g., IECSE teachers, supervisors, state level personnel) reviewed it and responded to an electronic questionnaire regarding its utility and potential to support the work of IECSE teachers (Dinnebeil, Denov, Hicks, & McInerney, 2007). Based on their feedback, we revised some of the wording and terminology used in the document. Overall, users viewed the PIECES positively, stating that it would be useful in guiding the work of IECSE teachers and helping to support meaningful supervision. One drawback questionnaire respondents identified was the length of the PIECES. It was viewed as too long and comprehensive. However, given the complexity of an IECSE teacher's job, we believe that it should stay intact and have left it as such.

Overview of the PIECES

As we have indicated, an IECSE teacher is a "value-added" professional. All ECSE professionals must have a clear understanding of principles of early childhood special education and specialized instruction. They must all possess comprehensive knowledge about typical and atypical child development as well as early childhood and early childhood special education curriculum and assessment practices. All ECSE professionals must understand how to work effectively with family members and other professionals and must know how to collaborate with others. However, in addition to having the foundational competencies associated with any ECSE professional, IECSE teachers must possess a range of other competencies. Specifically, we believe that IECSE teachers must have a working knowledge of operational and program standards for a range of community-based early childhood programs (e.g., Head Start, child care, Title I programs, kindergarten). They also must be skilled at engaging in consultation and coaching strategies. IECSE teachers, more so than their classroom-based colleagues, also must be proficient and creative problem solvers and collaborators. They must be skilled at working with other adults with a range of demographic characteristics, including adults and children from diverse cultural, ethnic, and racial backgrounds. Finally, given their job roles as described above, IECSE teachers must be effective team leaders.

In addition, readers should note that the knowledge and skills described in the PIECES (Dinnebeil, McInerney, et al., 2007) are not the *only* competencies needed by early childhood special educators. The Council for Exceptional Children's (CEC) Common Core and Early Childhood Specialty Standards provide a comprehensive overview of the knowledge and skills needed by beginning early childhood special educators. These standards are included on the CEC's web site (http://www.cec.sped.org/Content/NavigationMenu/ProfessionalDevelopment/ProfessionalStandards/default.htm).

Finally, the field of early childhood special education has identified a code of ethics that guides the practice of early childhood special educators, including IECSE teachers (DEC, 2009). This code of ethical conduct identifies key principles that should guide professional conduct. It should also serve as a guideline to be used to solve professional dilemmas and problems facing personnel who serve young children with disabilities and their families. The DEC's Code of Ethics is the foundation of all of the work of IECSE professionals and is included in Appendix C as a resource for readers.

Organization of the PIECES

The performance indicators outlined in the PIECES (Dinnebeil, McInerney, et al., 2007) are divided into three parts. Embedded within each part are a series of rubrics designed to help IECSE teachers and/or their supervisors identify their current or desired skill level, described previously. Each part of the PIECES is described next:

Part A focuses on requisite knowledge and skills related to ECSE service delivery and includes the following:

1. Knowledge of the organizational context of the child's environment

2. The ability to design and implement child-focused interventions

   a. Knowledge of typical and atypical child development

   b. The ability to appropriately use special education intervention strategies

   c. An understanding of how aspects of the environment affects children's development and learning

   d. The ability to embed interventions into routines and daily activities

e. The ability to monitor the effect of the intervention on children's progress toward meeting IEP goals

f. The ability to assess the effectiveness of interventions.

Part B focuses on communication skills and specialized knowledge related to coaching and information sharing in order to develop family, professional, and community relationships that support learning in the LRE. It includes the following:

1. The ability to build a collaborative team

    a. The ability to identify and actively include key members of the child's IEP team

    b. The ability to guide the team to use conflict resolution and problem-solving strategies

2. The ability to establish and implement a plan for regular communication among team members

    a. The use of systematic procedures to communicate with team members

    b. The ability to document communication events

3. The ability to demonstrate appropriate use of specific interpersonal communication skills to establish ongoing relationships with families and providers

    a. The ability to adhere to schedules and follow through on requests

    b. The ability to use appropriate communication strategies

4. The ability to help others develop skills and use strategies via a coaching model that includes the following components:

    a. Jointly identifying opportunities for coaching and intended outcomes

    b. Observing the partner teacher's skills

    c. Demonstrating or modeling the targeted skill

    d. Observing the partner teacher using the skill or strategy

    e. Providing feedback about the partner teacher's performance

    f. Continuing through the cycle of observation, demonstration, and feedback until the intended outcome is achieved

    g. Providing information to support the child's success in the community-based program

Part C: The IECSE teacher uses specialized knowledge to coordinate and facilitate integrated service delivery to support learning in the LRE in the following ways:

1. Coordinates and monitors service delivery

    a. Coordinates and monitors delivery of services specified on the child's IEP

    b. Effectively plans for visits

    c. Coordinates and completes paperwork as required by federal, state and local guidelines

    d.   Meets mandated timelines for procedural compliance

    e.   Designs and implements professional development (PD) activities

The PIECES can be completed by IECSE teachers as a way to monitor their yearly professional growth and development. Supervisors also can use the PIECES to provide feedback to IECSE teachers and determine the need for further professional development opportunities. We suggest completing the PIECES at the beginning of the school year to establish a baseline of skills and then at the end of the school year as a way of documenting one's professional growth in each of the areas the PIECES covers.

Summary

To develop service delivery systems that have a positive impact on the developmental and academic outcomes for young children with disabilities, we must identify components of such a system and determine the relative efficacy of each component. Our work is built on the work of Striffler and Fire (1999) and reflects the current educational reform movement associated with recognition and response (Buysse & Peisner-Feinberg, 2010; Peisner-Feinberg et al., in press) as well as the recent emphasis on implementation research by Fixsen and colleagues (2007). If we are to value early childhood inclusion and work to increase high-quality inclusive learning environments for children, then we must understand the components of a service delivery *system* that supports it. That is, it is critically important to define the "active ingredient" in the service delivery system or the elements in the system that serve to support (or challenge) positive outcomes.

It is clear through this chapter that IECSE teachers play many roles that incorporate diverse responsibilities. In addition to serving children directly, IECSE teachers also serve as consultants and coaches, assessors, team members, and service coordinators. In the next chapters, readers will find detailed discussions of each of the roles IECSE teachers assume when they take on the job of serving young children with disabilities in community-based settings and other natural environments.

CHAPTER 4

The IECSE Teacher as Consultant

One of the most important roles of an IECSE teacher is that of a consultant. A consultant provides strong support for young children with special needs. Buysse and Wesley defined *consultation* as

> [A]n indirect, triadic service delivery model in which a consultant (e.g., early childhood special educator, therapist) and a consultee (e.g., early childhood professional, parent) work together to address an area of concern or a common goal for change. Through a series of meetings and conversations, the consultant helps the consultee through systematic problem solving, social influence, and professional support. In turn, the consultee helps the client(s) with full support and assistance from the consultant. (2005, p. 10)

Important Terms to Consider

Several terms in the definition provided above merit discussion. First are the terms *indirect* and *triadic*. *Indirect* refers to the fact that the consultant (in our case, the IECSE teacher) works primarily with other adults to provide specialized services to young children with special needs as opposed to working primarily with the child. McCollum and Yates (1994) are credited with first using the term *triadic intervention* to refer to a service delivery model that originally focused on the quality of parent–child interactions for young children with disabilities. Its central logic, however, can be applied to itinerant consultation, in that two adults (e.g., a parent or general ECE teacher and the IECSE teacher) work together to improve outcomes for young children. This is also the central focus of a consultative approach to early childhood intervention. The work these adults may do varies depending on the needs of the child.

It is also important to recognize that early childhood consultation is process-based. As Buysse and Wesley (2005) pointed out previously, consultation occurs *over time* as consultants and the consultees work through issues and problems. In that regard, consultation is a type of service delivery model (Odom et al., 1999). Consultants and consultees work together *over time* to address issues and solve problems so that young children with disabilities receive the specialized intervention they need to be successful. *Over time* in this context can be interpreted in various ways, but the key point is that the consultation occurs on a longitudinal basis.

Another key term Buysse and Wesley (2005) used is *systematic*. Consultation is a service delivery approach that is explicit and deliberate. It does not just happen, nor is it incidental in nature. "Checking in" with another person about how a child is doing is not consultation. Key to the provision of successful consultation is the fact that both parties (the consultant or IECSE teacher and the consultee or general EC teacher or parent) recognize the importance of consultation. Dinnebeil, Buysse, Rush, and Eggbeer (2008) asserted that consultation reflects a problem-solving approach common to other collaborative models such as coaching, teaming, and reflective supervision. The process of providing consultation is discussed later in this chapter.

In addition to a problem-solving approach to consultation, Buysse and Wesley (2005) also identified *social influence* and *professional support* as important characteristics of early childhood consultation. Wilson, Erchul, and Raven (2008) provided an excellent discussion of the concepts of social power and social influence within a school-based consultation model. They define social power as the "potential of an individual (i.e., agent) to produce a change in another individual's (i.e., target's) beliefs, attitudes, or behaviors" (pp. 101–102) and social influence as the "demonstrated change in the beliefs, attitudes, or behaviors of a target" (p. 102). Wilson and colleagues as well as Buysse and Wesley acknowledged the importance of understanding the degree to which one person's actions can influence or change the beliefs, attitudes, or actions of another person. Citing Raven's 1992 work on social power bases, Wilson and colleagues discussed the importance of expertise. Table 4.1 illustrates the positive and negative effects of various types of social power.

Professional support refers to the words and actions of a consultant that help consultees reach mutually agreed-on outcomes. Professional support helps consultees feel comfortable, confident, and competent in their abilities to achieve important outcomes through discussions, conversations, and dialogue. For example, Irene, a consultant, knows that Sandy, her consultee, is nervous and anxious about positioning her daughter, Riley, in her chair and makes a special point to provide information and encouragement to Sandy whenever she comes to Sandy's home. IECSE teachers who serve as consultants help consultees achieve this comfort level by doing the following:

- Ensuring that the consultee believes she or he has the knowledge, skills, and motivation necessary to get the job done

- Ensuring that the consultee believes she or he has the capacity *to gain* the knowledge, skills, or motivation necessary to get the job done

- Helping the consultee to realize that the consultant believes in the consultee

- Providing the help or support the consultee needs to get the job done

- Indicating where the consultee can find help or support

Within the context of a consultative model, the consultant (e.g., IECSE teacher) may assist the consultee (e.g., general early childhood teacher) in many different ways. For example, the IECSE teacher may help the general education teacher modify the physical environment to better meet the learning needs of the child. She may help the general education teacher revise the daily schedule if needed or find ways to embed interventions into the child's daily routines. She may identify ways to collect data to monitor the child's progress on IEP objectives. Here are some other ways that consultants might provide professional support to consultees in helping young children with special needs (Hanft & Place, 1996):

- *Assist partner in acquiring a new skill.* For example, a consultant can present information about the importance of using a system of prompts to help the child practice a new skill.

- *Introduce a new resource.* A consultant working with a general ECE teacher may discuss using a Picture Exchange Communication System (PECS) to help a child with autism spectrum disorder (ASD) learn to communicate with others in the classroom.

- *Adapt materials.* A consultant working with a parent may help the parent modify a toy by adding a microswitch so that the child can more easily play with the toy.

- *Modify environment.* A consultant can help his or her general ECE partner teacher to rearrange learning centers to decrease distraction and increase meaningful engagement with materials.

- *Reframe perspective of partner.* A consultant may help a parent understand the underlying causes of challenging behaviors so the parent better understands how to help the child.

- *Modify routines or schedules.* A consultant may help a parent modify the child's nighttime schedule to promote positive behavior.

Table 4.1. Positive and negative effects of various types of social power

	Positive	Negative
Expert	The consultee goes along with the consultant's advice because she believes the consultant is an expert in her field.	The consultee rejects the consultant's advice because she believes that the consultant is acting in her own best interests.
Referent	The consultee acts on the consultant's advice because she wants to be perceived as similar to the consultant.	The consultee rejects the consultant's advice because she doesn't want to be perceived as similar to the consultant.
	Personal	Impersonal
Reward	The consultee goes along with the consultant's advice because she wants the consultant to approve of her.	The consultee goes along with the consultant's advice because she believes that doing so will result in a tangible reward.
Coercion	The consultee goes along with the consultant's advice because she believes the consultant will disapprove of her if she doesn't.	The consultee goes along with the consultant's advice because she believes the consultant has the power to punish her.
	Indirect	Direct
Informational	The consultee goes along with the consultant's advice because she hears from another source that the advice is sound.	The consultee goes along with the consultant's advice because it makes sense to her.
Legitimate position	The consultee accepts the consultant's advice because she believes that the consultant holds a position of authority.	
Legitimacy of reciprocity	The consultee believes that the consultant has done something positive for the consultee and feels the need to reciprocate.	
Legitimacy of equity	The consultee does something that the consultant recommends because she believes the consultant has worked hard on her behalf.	
Legitimacy of dependence	The consultee complies with the consultant's request because she believes the consultant is dependent on the consultee.	

From Raven, B.H. (1992). *The bases of power: Origins and recent developments.* New York: Wiley; reprinted by permission.

Roots of Early Childhood Consultation

The foundation of the proposed model of consultation is the behavioral consultation model as articulated by Sheridan, Kratochwill, and Bergan (1996) and Erchul and Sheridan (2008). Sheridan and colleagues identified three primary characteristics of a conjoint behavioral consultation approach. First, as previously mentioned, it is an indirect service delivery model (1996). The consultant provides indirect services to the child with special needs by working directly with the consultee (i.e., other adults such as parents and teachers who see the child on a daily basis). Second, the model is based on an ecological systems approach to viewing human development (Bronfenbrenner, 1979). That is, there is an understanding that humans develop within the context of various ecological systems including their immediate and extended families, their communities (including schools and classrooms), and society. Third and finally, the behavioral consultation model assumes a problem-solving approach as discussed in detail in the sections that follow.

The Process of Consultation

Within early childhood special education, a successful consultative relationship is built on the assumption that both the consultant and the consultee share the same overarching goal for the relationship—to help a young child with disabilities reach his or her goals as identified on his or her IEP. Similar to other types of collaborative relationships (Dinnebeil, Buysse, et al., 2007), consultation is built around a problem-solving approach and consists of the following steps, adapted from Buysse and Wesley (2005).

Gaining Entry

As the first step of the process, consultants and consultees learn about each other and the context within which they will be working. If the consultee is an early childhood teacher, the consultant will want to become familiar with the child, the family, and the program, including its general history and its history in serving young children with disabilities. In addition to the consultant becoming familiar with the program, it is also important for the consultee to get to know the consultant, including his or her background and qualifications. It is during this stage that consultants and consultees may face one or more of the following issues that must be resolved in order for the relationship to progress:

1. The consultant and consultee may be aware of unequal levels of formal education. For example, the IECSE teacher may have a graduate degree, whereas the general ECE teacher has a high school diploma. Conversely, the IECSE teacher may have a bachelor's degree, whereas the general ECE teacher has an advanced graduate degree such as an educational specialist or doctoral degree. Depending on how it is handled, different educational levels may present challenges to developing a positive and effective relationship.

2. Consultees also may be concerned about their lack of knowledge or skills related to special education or early childhood intervention. They will need confidence to believe that they have or will gain the requisite knowledge and skills to help the child be successful in the learning environment.

3. Consultees may be uncomfortable having another person in their classroom and may feel as if the consultant is intruding. Again, a clear understanding of the pur-

pose of the consultative relationship is integral to allaying fears that the consultant is judging or evaluating the qualifications of the consultee.

4. The consultee may question the trustworthiness of the IECSE teacher. If there is no previous relationship between the two individuals, the consultee may not trust the consultant's motives or ability to keep information confidential. Again, it is important to establish ground rules early in the relationship so both partners feel comfortable working together. Wesley and Buysse (2006) provided an excellent overview of ethical concerns related to consultative relationships.

5. The consultee may be concerned that child outcomes may become his or her sole responsibility. For example, a general ECE teacher may believe that the IECSE teacher and other specialists might abandon him or her after a certain period of time or when he or she reaches a certain level of proficiency. It is possible that some consultees begin to believe that they bear the entire responsibility for the child's success. It is critically important that consultees understand that they are working with another person who will be available to guide and support them and deliver services as appropriate.

Building the Relationship

As discussed before, consultation is a relationship-based approach to service delivery, and its success depends on the degree to which two people can work together effectively. Building a positive and productive relationship is an important first step in the consultation process. It allows partners to understand each other's motives, priorities, and perspectives. Consultants and consultees must get to know each other and be able to work productively together to help children reach their goals and objectives. Building a relationship takes time and requires consultants and consultees to spend time together. Finding focused time to spend together may be difficult, especially for consultants who work with general ECE teachers. Early childhood teachers have many responsibilities in the classroom and can face innumerable distractions that disrupt discussions and conversations necessary to building a relationship. It is important, then, that the teachers as well as their respective administrators find ways of providing focused, uninterrupted time to develop their relationship and use it to support the child. In Chapter 10, we discuss the need for a shared understanding of the consultative relationship by program directions, LEA administrators, and parents. Suffice it to say that relationships between IECSE consultants and their partner teachers can be enhanced by savvy administrators who can arrange for an extra pair of hands in the classroom or a quiet place to meet and talk.

Critical to the efficacy of this professional support are the interpersonal skills necessary for successful consultation. Buysse and Wesley (2005, pp. 31–32) identified a number of tools for effective communication in consultation, which are included in Table 4.2.

Interpersonal skills can make or break a partnership. Individuals who can listen attentively to others, communicate effectively, and display a willingness or openness to learn from others are more likely to be engaged in positive professional relationships with others (Erchul & Martens, 2002). Effective consultants do the following:

*   Use body language that indicates that they are interested in engaging with someone else (e.g., leaning forward, maintaining eye contact).

Table 4.2. Tools for effective communication in consultation

	Function	Example
Attending and active listening		
Body language	Physical posture characterized by a relaxed, open manner and good eye contact demonstrate interest and concern.	Leaning slightly toward the speaker while sitting, hands relaxed in the lap
Reflecting content	Paraphrasing the content of a message is one way to let the speaker know you understand what has been said.	"You've tried limiting the number of toys and materials in each center."
Reflecting feelings	Using your own words to identify the feelings expressed in a message is one way to let the speaker know you understand his or her sentiments and sense the world as he or she perceives it.	"You're pretty excited about Jon coming to your classroom!"
Encouraging words	Acknowledging the speaker through simple verbalizations encourages the speaker to continue.	"Yes." "Uh-huh." "Please go on."
Seeking and verifying information		
Questioning	Probing through the use of different types of questions yields information that helps to define an issue or concern.	"How many teachers are assigned to this room?" (closed question) "In what ways do you acknowledge cultural differences in your program?" (open-ended question)
Silence	Waiting patiently and quietly while another person thinks or prepares to answer a question lets the speaker know you want to hear from him or her.	N/A
Clarifying	After encouraging the speaker to elaborate or expand on a topic, reflect the message and ask if you understand what has been said.	"Tell me more about departure time . . . Do I understand what happens correctly?"
Building	Adding to the speaker's ideas or statement lets the other person know you value his or her input.	"Yes, and . . ." "That's a great starting point for . . ."
Summarizing	Integrating the relevant facts into a succinct statement is one way of obtaining closure when speakers appear to have said everything they have to say.	"Let's see. We've identified two goals today . . ."
Seeking consensus	Verifying information and agreement throughout the process prevents misunderstanding.	"Would you say that increasing literacy opportunities in the classroom is our biggest priority now?"
Encouraging, influencing, and supporting		
Self-disclosing	Sharing one's personal or professional experiences or perspectives helps establish rapport and minimize perceptions of power.	"I struggled with the same issue when I taught preschool."
Demonstrating	Showing or modeling a desired behavior can boost success during implementation.	"Watch how I hold his hand over the spoon."
Coaching	Making periodic suggestions can support or improve skill development.	"Try pointing to the picture and then showing Ennis the sign."
Informing	Sharing information and knowledge enhances understanding.	"Her behaviors are characteristic of children with Asperger syndrome."

	Function	Example
Drawing inferences	Forming and sharing hypotheses is an important part of solving problems and uncovering possible meanings of behaviors.	"Chih Ing may need a little more encouragement and assistance to use the new communication cards."
Evaluating	Forming and sharing conclusions helps practitioners determine when they have been successful in implementing their strategies.	"The strategy you used in the transition to nap time worked well today."

From Buysse, V., & Wesley, P.W. (2005). *Consultation in early childhood settings* (p. 31). Baltimore: Paul H. Brooks Publishing Co.; reprinted by permission.

- Demonstrate that they have listened to others by reflecting back content or feelings (e.g., "It sounds as though you're pretty concerned about how you're going to meet Katie's needs while still meeting the needs of all of the other children in the class").

- Use words and terms that others can easily understand and refrain from using jargon or slang unless it is commonly understood and appropriate for a professional conversation.

- Ask questions when they do not understand something and work to make sure that others understand them.

- Share information about themselves (i.e., self-disclose) when it helps to build a rapport and a productive professional relationship (e.g., "The first time I had to use a feeding tube, I was really nervous too!") (Buysse & Wesley, 2006).

A Word About Relationships

The relationship between a consultant and a consultee is professional in nature and is directed toward helping each other to meet the specialized needs of the child. A consultative relationship is not a personal relationship or a friendship. Time spent working together focuses on moving forward to help the child reach his or her goals. When two people hit it off, it is easy for them to move the relationship to another level such as a friendship. Developing friendships with a consultant or a consultee can lead to confusion, concern, or worse. In addition, consultants and consultees who become friends can have difficulty attending to the goals of the consultative relationship. It becomes very easy to talk about things that are irrelevant to the child or situation, and time is wasted. It can become difficult to deal with touchy situations—situations in which feedback is not appreciated or accepted. For these reasons, we strongly encourage consultants to ensure that the relationships they have with others are of a professional and not personal nature.

Gathering Information

The third step in the consultation process is gathering information. For a consultative relationship to move forward effectively, both the consultant and consultee must have background information about the child's strengths and needs, the quality of the child's learning environment, the consultant's and consultee's expertise and values as they relate to the child with special needs, and other factors that may influence the consultative relationship and the child's success. Consultants gather information in a variety of ways—through conversations and interviews with other adults as well as through observation of the child in his or her learning environment and the teacher (or parent) along with other children in the learning environment.

Many excellent texts are available that focus on standard types of formal and informal child assessment measures. IECSE teachers and their partners will have access to a range of child-focused assessment information. To successfully support young children with disabilities in general early childhood settings, however, different foci for assessment must occur: 1) how the child performs within the context of a learning environment, 2) the quality of the learning environment itself, and 3) the ability of the consultee (i.e., general early childhood teacher, parent, other adult) to use targeted intervention strategies appropriately. Each of these is discussed in more detail below:

Child Performance in the Learning Environment

To successfully support children's growth and development in the learning environment, it is necessary to collect data on the degree to which the child engages with the environment as well as the quality of those engagements. McWilliam and Casey (2007) offered a systematic approach to studying child engagement that includes strategies for assessing the degree and quality of the child's engagement in the classroom. Meaningful child engagement is strongly correlated to academic success. Young children who are positively engaged in their environment reach higher levels of developmental and academic outcomes (Shonkoff & Phillips, 2000).

In addition to McWilliam and Casey's (2007) work, Wolery, Brashers, and Neitzel (2002) offered another way of assessing the child's success in the learning environment through a focus on ecological congruence assessment (ECA). Using this approach, IECSE teachers and their partner teachers would collect data on child performance in typical routines and activities, noting the quality of the child's engagement in the activity in terms of how similar or deviant his or her behaviors are in relation to other children also engaged in the activity. In addition to assessing the quality of the child's behavior in an activity, the partner teacher would rate the degree to which the deviant behavior is acceptable to the teacher. For example, if during story time, the target child stands up and engages in behaviors that distract the other children, the teacher might rate that behavior as highly deviant (if none of the other children engage in that behavior) and also would rate that behavior as highly unacceptable. Both the consultant and the consultee would then identify a list of skills or behaviors that the child would need to appropriately function in that activity and identify interventions that would be appropriate to support the development of those skills. A comprehensive analysis across the preschool day would allow the consultant and the teacher to prioritize their efforts. Using an approach such as ECA helps consultants to address immediate problems that are important to the ECE teacher and may help create "buy-in" that will result in the consultant's improved social influence through increased *legitimacy of reciprocity and legitimacy of equity* (Wilson et al., 2008).

Finally, IECSE teachers can use functional behavior assessments to identify and understand difficulties children are having in classroom routines and activities and positive behavioral supports to alleviate the difficult behaviors these children present (Sugai et al., 2000). These assessment approaches have become standard approaches in special education services, and a detailed discussion of each is beyond the scope of this book.

Quality of the Learning Environment

Researchers have validated what many early childhood practitioners already know; the quality of the early learning environment has a significant effect (positive and negative) on the academic and developmental achievement of young children, including young children with disabilities (Belsky, 2006; Hynes & Habasevich-Brooks, 2008; NICHD Early Child Care Research Network, 2006). Given the importance of the quality of the learning environment, an important consideration for supporting inclusion is to ensure that the child's learning environment is such that it supports and sustains development. IECSE teachers must be knowledgeable about characteristics of high-quality learning environments and must be able to identify strengths and weaknesses of early learning environments. Fortunately, a number of tools exist that help to structure observations and pinpoint strengths and areas of concern. Perhaps most commonly used is the Early Childhood Environment Rating Scale–Revised (ECERS–R; Harms, Clifford, & Cryer, 2005), which measures the quality of the early learning environment along seven subscales including 1) space and furnishings, 2) personal care routines, 3) language-reasoning, 4) activities, 5) interaction, 6) program structure, and 7) parents and staff. The ECERS–R is one type of quality assessment measure that is widely used for statewide quality improvement initiatives (National Child Care Information Center, 2009). Buysse and Wesley (2005) recommended that consultants and consultees use the ECERS–R together to pinpoint areas of strength and concern that can form the basis of consultation goals. In addition to the ECERS–R, Harms and her colleagues have developed other environment rating scales that focus on different settings, including family child care (Family Child Care Environment Rating Scale–Revised [FCCERS–R]; Harms, Cryer, & Clifford, 2007) and infant and/or toddler programs (Infant Toddler Environment Rating Scale–Revised [ITERS–R]; Harms, Cryer, & Clifford, 2003). Each of these rating scales has provisions for rating the degree to which young children with special needs are served appropriately.

Another instrument designed to assess the learning environment is the Classroom Assessment Scoring System™ (*CLASS™*; Pianta, La Paro, & Hamre, 2008). The CLASS™ assesses the quality of the environment as it relates to 1) the emotional climate (i.e., the degree to which teachers are sensitive to and supportive of children's social-emotional development); 2) the instructional climate (i.e., the degree to which the teacher fosters learning through concept development, modeling, and feedback); and 3) the classroom organization, including behavior management, student productivity, and instructional and/or learning formats. The CLASS™ has been widely used in research and professional development efforts.

Harms and colleagues' environment rating scales (Harms et al., 2005; Harms et al., 2003, 2007) as well as Pianta and colleagues (2008) classroom assessment are generalized environmental rating scales. If the IECSE consultant wants to investigate dimensions of the environment specific to a certain disability condition or learning need, he or she has other options such as the Early Language and Literacy Classroom Observation Tool, Pre-K (ELLCO Pre-K; Smith, Brady, & Anastasopoulos, 2008) or the Child/Home Early Language and Literacy Observation (CHELLO; Neuman, Dwyer, & Koh, 2007). The ELLCO focuses on the degree to which the early childhood classroom (Pre-K) supports literacy and language development, whereas the CHELLO focuses on how family child care settings support literacy and language development. Both of these tools can be very useful for IECSE consultants and their partners who work with children who have language disorders or delays. Finally, Odom and his colleagues developed the Autism Program Environment Rating Scale, which focuses on how the learning environment supports individuals with ASD (Odom & Cox, 2009).

Ability to Use Intervention Strategies Appropriately

The success of any child-focused intervention, instructional strategy, or evidence-based practice depends largely on how well it is delivered or implemented by the teacher or other adult. There is a significant focus on evidence-based practice (Buysse & Wesley, 2006), with numerous questions focusing on how one builds the "research to practice bridge" (Winton, 2006). How do educational leaders ensure that teachers are using evidence-based practices in their classrooms *as they were intended to be used*? Consultation becomes an important vehicle for helping to address issues about appropriately using evidence-based practices in classrooms.

In terms of gathering information to make decisions about the direction of the consultation relationship, IECSE teachers must also understand how well the general early childhood teacher or parent can use an intervention strategy or instructional approach. As such, it is legitimate to include here strategies for assessing the expertise of adults in implementing instructional strategies. The fidelity with which an intervention is delivered as planned is a topic of great concern to researchers (Fixsen et al., 2007; Pence, Justice, & Wiggins, 2008).

An implementation checklist is one promising strategy to use in assisting general education teachers and others to use intervention strategies as intended. In partnership with other professional organizations, Ohio Center for Autism and Low Incidence (OCALI) has developed a series of Internet training modules that include video-based training as well as a set of implementation checklists that can be used to document the degree to which a teacher or other adult uses a specific strategy as intended (http://ocali.org). The checklist can be used to structure an observation and provide meaningful feedback to a learner about his or her use of a specific intervention strategy. An example of one of the checklists is included in Figure 4.1 (Smith & Collett-Klingenberg, 2009).

Setting Goals

Once the consultant and consultee have gathered the information they need to identify key issues and formulate a plan, they need to set goals that will guide their future actions (Buysse & Wesley, 2005). Some of these goals will reflect priority goals for the child. We offer a process of identifying priority goals in Chapter 9 of this book. However, within a consultative approach to IECSE service delivery, these goals do not all have to relate directly to the child. Indeed, Buysse and Wesley stressed the fact that some goals might be extraneous to the child, the needs of the general early childhood teacher, or the parent. Goals vary from child to child, setting to setting, and time to time. As IECSE teachers and their partners identify goals, it is important to remember that incremental changes can lead to dramatic effects. Small improvements can lead to greater feelings of confidence and accomplishment that will serve to sustain the partners and reinforce positive efforts. In addition to "starting small," it also makes sense for the consultant and consultee to be realistic when identifying goals. Buysse and Wesley advised that consultants and consultees prioritize goals and try to make sure that their work is manageable and feasible. Wolery et al. (2002) offered one way of prioritizing goals through their process of ECA. We also offer a way of prioritizing child-focused goals through an analysis of the type of intervention needed to achieve the goal (see Chapter 9 for a discussion of this process).

In general, we identify a range of potential outcomes of a consultative relationship between an IECSE teacher and another adult (e.g., general early childhood teacher, parent) as follows:

- *Increase the learning opportunities available to a child that are embedded within the context of daily routines and activities.* For example, as a result of consultation, Mariah's

Module: Visual Supports
Implementation Checklist for Visual Boundaries

Instructions: The Implementation Checklist includes steps for the development and implementation of visual schedules. Please identify the step that was being implemented during the observation, as well as the date, time, and children present. Then check "yes," "no," or "NA" next to each item to indicate whether it was addressed. The final column can be use for taking notes during observations.

Teacher/practitioner: _____   Observer: _____

Date: _____   Time: _____

Step observed: _____

Others present: _____

Step 1. Defining the Need	Yes	No	NA	Notes
1. Teachers/practitioners identify visual supports required by learners to acquire or maintain skills.				
Step 2. Defining the Boundary				
1. Teachers/practitioners define or establish where the visual boundary is or should be, if it does not yet exist.				
2. Teachers/practitioners use natural physical boundaries, objects, and furniture to clearly designate the boundary.				
Step 3. Teaching the Boundary				
1. Teachers/practitioners introduce the learner to established boundaries.				
2. Teachers/practitioners use modeling to teach the learner to stay within the boundary.				
3. Teachers/practitioners model and use reinforcement when learners stay within the boundary.				
4. Teachers/practitioners model and use corrective feedback when learners do not stay within the boundary.				
5. Teachers/practitioners are consistent with boundary settings.				
Step 4. Evaluating Success				
1. Teachers/practitioners collect data on learners' use of boundaries.				
2. Teachers/practitioners collect data on learners' related target behaviors.				
3. Teachers/practitioners make data-based decisions regarding the effectiveness of established boundaries.				
4. Teacher/practitioners monitor on-going effectiveness of boundaries and their impact on learner behavior.				

Figure 4.1. Sample implementation checklist for visual boundaries. (From Smith, S., & Collet-Klingenberg, L. [2009]. Implementation checklist for visual boundaries. Madison, WI: The National Professional Development Center on Autism Spectrum Disorders, Waisman Center, University of Wisconsin; reprinted by permission.)

teacher offered more opportunities for Mariah to practice using three- to four-word sentences to indicate her wants and needs.

- *Increase the consultee's comfort level in regard to working with a child who has special needs.* For example, after working with an IECSE professional who functions as a consultant, a general ECE teacher may feel more confident and positive about her ability to address the child's needs.

- *Increase the consultee's knowledge in regard to working with a child who has special needs.* The IECSE consultant may share information about certain disability conditions or information about other resources that increases the general education teacher's knowledge base. This information can help the general education teacher better understand aspects of the child's disability and how the child's disability affects behavior or success in the classroom.

- *Enhance the consultee's ability to provide individualized instruction to the child with special needs.* For example, the IECSE teacher may coach the child's parent to help them learn to use time delay (Wolery, Ault, et al., 1992) as an intervention strategy. Helping other adults learn ways to meet children's needs broadens the adult's repertoire of teaching strategies and makes it possible for the child to receive individualized instruction in the absence of the IECSE teacher.

- *Improve the quality of the child's learning environment.* IECSE teachers who work as consultants can help other adults modify the child's learning environment to maximize child outcomes or to make it feasible to include the child in daily routines or activities. As an example, an IECSE teacher may help a parent modify daily routines or activities to better accommodate his or her child's needs. The IECSE teacher may help a general education teacher change the physical environment by creating boundaries between learning centers that help a distractible child stay more engaged in an activity.

Documenting progress made toward goal achievement will help determine the success of the consultation relationship. As consultants and consultees discuss the goals that they would like to address, it is important to provide operational definitions of those goals with clear, measurable outcome statements as well as timelines and responsibilities of those involved in achieving the goal. Just as IEP goals are written in a way as to allow evaluation for success, so should consultants and consultees write goals for their work. For example, consider the goal "The IECSE teacher (Ann) and general EC teacher (Sarah) will improve the quality of Ben's learning environment." How will the IECSE teacher and general EC teacher (as well as other members of the IEP team) know when they have reached that goal? Instead of a global statement such as the one above, consider the following statement: "The IECSE teacher and general EC teacher will create a dramatic play center, a literacy center, and a fine motor center in the classroom." Of course, this goal could be further detailed with materials to be included in the centers as well as other properties of the centers. The second statement provides much more direction to Ann and Sarah as well as others who will review the work of these two partners. Review the following goal statements next in Table 4.3 to determine how helpful each is in supporting the needs of young children.

When selecting goals, it is important to record the goals as well as the strategies used to reach them along with other pertinent information (e.g., timelines, individuals' responsibilities, outcomes). Readers can find sample log forms in Appendix B of this

Table 4.3.   Sample goal statements for consultants and consultees

General goal statement	Specific goal statement
Increase opportunities for Ritu to practice communication skills.	Provide Ritu with at least two opportunities to initiate interactions with her peers during snack time.
Help Riley stay engaged with toys and materials.	During center time, help Riley play with a specific toy or material for at least 3 minutes.
Increase Jenni's knowledge in regard to working with a child who has special needs.	Jenni will feel comfortable identifying characteristics of children with Down syndrome and describing how those characteristics affect the children's learning.
Enhance Pat's ability to provide individualized instruction to the child with special needs.	Pat will correctly use a system of backward chaining to help Jeremy put on his coat twice a day—once when it is time for recess and once when it is time to go home.
Improve the quality of Parker's learning environment.	Tanisha and Erin will increase the number of materials (e.g., blocks of different sizes, shapes, and colors; signs, cars, and toy people in the block area) to create a rich learning environment for Parker and the other children in the classroom.

book. Although many teachers and education professionals complain about "more forms," they are very useful in keeping track of activities and can serve as reminders for follow-through and implementation.

Selecting Strategies

The type of strategy chosen by the consultant and consultee is dependent on a number of factors. First, if it is a child-focused strategy, does it have an evidence base to support its use? Is it ethical to use? Do all parties "buy in" to the use of the strategy? Second, is its implementation matched to the goal set by the consultant and consultee? Third, is implementation of the strategy feasible? Is it realistic to expect that the strategy can be implemented effectively and appropriately? For example, if it is a child-focused strategy, can the parent or general early childhood teacher implement it appropriately and still fulfill other responsibilities? If it is a strategy focused on increasing the parent's or teacher's knowledge or skill base, is it targeted to his or her ability level? Fourth, can use of the strategy and its effects be monitored and documented appropriately? Monitoring the use of a strategy and its effect is vital to appropriately evaluating the success of the strategy. Consultants and their partners must decide on ways that they will document the effects of the strategies chosen. Data collection efforts can focus on self-report data (e.g., Do the consultees think the strategies work? How do they know?), observational data related to consultee or child goals (e.g., Was the consultee able to use the response-prompting strategy correctly? How many times did the child initiate interactions with peers after using a response-prompting strategy?), or permanent products or artifacts (e.g., copies of children's handwriting documenting fine motor skills). Finally, what types of additional resources or supports are needed to use the strategy effectively and efficiently (Buysse & Wesley, 2005)?

In choosing strategies, it is important for both consultees and consultants to remember to prioritize their work. Using planning matrices such as the ones developed by Grisham-Brown and her colleagues (Grisham-Brown, Pretti-Frontczak, Hemmeter, & Ridgley, 2002) are very useful in planning intervention use. Chapter 9 includes an example of a planning matrix. Note how it can be used to identify and plan for specialized interventions in children's routines and activities.

Implementing the Plan

Implementing the plan developed by the consultant and consultee requires foresight, follow-through, and commitment. If the plan includes implementing child-focused intervention strategies, general early childhood teachers or parents will need help in preparing and organizing activities and schedules, using a matrix such as the one in Chapter 9 or another version. In addition to planning to use a strategy, parents or general early childhood teachers may need to learn how to implement a strategy or to refine their skills in using a child-focused intervention strategy. A coaching model such as the one described in Chapter 5 is critical to the success of the implementation plan. Consultants and consultees must set aside time to learn or practice using the strategy. In addition, consultants or others who help consultees learn a strategy must make sure to provide high-quality performance feedback on a regular basis (Gilbertson, Witt, Singletary, & VanDerHeyden, 2007; Mautone, Luiselli, & Handler, 2006; Noell et al., 2005; Rathel, Drasgow, & Christle, 2008).

Implementation checklists such as ones developed by the National Professional Development Center on Autism Spectrum Disorder and OCALI are very useful in helping teachers and other adults implement a child-focused intervention as planned (Smith & Collett-Klingenberg, 2009). These checklists provide support for implementing an intervention or instructional strategy systematically, accurately, and effectively. They also support the use of high-quality performance feedback, or feedback that is specific, targeted, meaningful, and supportive to the learner. The checklist provided in Figure 4.1 is an example focused on using visual boundaries to organize environments for students with ASD. Consultants also can develop checklists addressing other types of strategies, though it is critical that the checklist reflects correct steps and procedures needed for implementation. Those interested in developing checklists for different naturalistic intervention strategies may find texts such as Wolery, Ault, and Doyle (1992) helpful in developing procedural checklists for different types of response-prompting intervention strategies. Refer back to the example of an implementation checklist is included in Figure 4.1.

Evaluating the Plan

To assess the success of a plan, consultants and consultees must document that the plan was implemented as intended (e.g., Were the child-focused intervention strategies implemented in accordance with the evidence base? Were they implemented to the extent to which the consultant and consultee initially planned?) and that the anticipated outcomes were achieved. Consultants and consultees cannot judge the success or the failure of a plan without knowing that the interventions were delivered as intended. In addition to verifying that the interventions were delivered as planned, consultants and consultees must also have data on the outcome of the interventions, including those interventions that were child-focused, environment-focused, and consultee-focused. How did children respond? How did the environment change and what effect did it have on children's developmental outcomes? Did the consultee acquire the knowledge or skills that were planned? How satisfied was the consultee with the changes that emerged from implementation of the plan?

Key to evaluating the success of a plan is data collection efforts that are strategically targeted on child-, environmental-, and consultee-focused outcomes. Evaluators use a logic model to evaluate the effects of an educational program (McLaughlin & Jordan,

Input ⇒	Output ⇒	Short-term outcomes ⇒	Intermediate outcomes ⇒	Long-term outcomes ⇒
Coaching to help the teacher learn to use positive reinforcement strategies	The teacher will become proficient at using positive reinforcement strategies to support Justin's success in the classroom.	Justin will stop running away from the teacher.	Justin will engage in meaningful learning activities in the classroom.	Justin's language and cognitive skills will be enhanced.

Figure 4.2. A visual representation of a logic model that a consultant and consultee might follow in determining the success of their efforts.

1999). A key component of a logic model is the identification of desired outcomes—both short-term (e.g., stopping Justin from running away from the teacher) and long-term (e.g., helping Justin engage in sustained meaningful play) as well as direct (e.g., the teacher does not have to worry about Justin's safety) and indirect (e.g., Justin's language and cognitive skills improve as he engages in meaningful active learning opportunities). Wesley and Buysse (2006) advocated the use of a logic model to assist early childhood consultants in documenting the efficacy of the consultation relationship. For example, evaluating the effects of a consultative relationship might focus on its success in improving the learning environment with the understanding that improving the learning environment will help children reach their goals and objectives. In another case, a consultant and consultee might focus on enhancing the consultee's ability to work with the child; and in that case, one of the outcomes of the consultative relationship would be improvements in the consultee's targeted instructional skills. In either case, the logic is that by focusing efforts on changing the environment or teacher behavior, child outcomes will be enhanced. Figure 4.2. provides a visual representation of a logic model that a consultant and consultee might follow in determining the success of their efforts.

When operating from a logic model perspective, it is critical that consultants understand the evidence base of variables such as the quality of the learning environment or use of teacher's skills. Buysse and Wesley (2005) reminded us that consultants must have an extensive understanding of evidence-based or recommended practices in early childhood special education in order to make recommendations or suggest a course of action. Chapter 6 focuses on the IECSE teacher's role in the assessment process. Readers can find more detailed descriptions of assessment and evaluation efforts that will assist them in helping to determine the success of a consultative relationship.

Summary Conference

The purpose of the summary conference is to review the outcomes of the evaluation and plan next steps (Buysse & Wesley, 2005). This last step of the consultation process provides an opportunity for reflection and critical analysis of the success of the consultant's and consultee's efforts. It is during this time that consultants and consultees discuss challenges they faced and the degree to which those challenges impeded the success of the plan. For example, in discussing Justin's challenging behavior (e.g., running away, lack of meaningful engagement), Erin and Charlie might ask, "What would we do differently next time?" Critically reflecting on this question and others is appropriate at this stage.

In addition to reflecting on the success of the consultation efforts to date, Buysse and Wesley (2005) also suggested that the Summary Conference provides an opportunity to plan for next steps and review options for continuing or modifying the plan. For example, after arriving at a solution to help Justin remain safely in the classroom, Erin and Charlie might sit down to think about ways that they can increase Justin's active engagement in classroom activities. In the case of young children who receive IECSE services, a consultative relationship would not end until the end of the academic year. As such, it is possible that summary conferences could occur at multiple times during the relationship, providing an opportunity to take stock of current efforts and make modifications or changes to the plan.

Characteristics of Effective Consultants

IECSE consultants require knowledge, skills, and dispositions that are, in many cases, unique from their classroom-based peers. In addition to possessing the competencies for initial level practitioners as specified by the Council for Exceptional Children (2009), IECSE professionals require an additional set of skills—primarily related to working with other adults who work in a range of early childhood settings. Chapter 3 outlines the knowledge and skills we believe to be critical for those functioning as IECSE professionals. Earlier in this chapter we presented a table from Buysse and Wesley (2005) outlining skills of effective communicators. Chandler and Maude (2007) identified a set of competencies related to preparing personnel to support young children in inclusive or natural learning environments. In addition to these, effective consultants are often those who display an interpersonal style of communication that promotes collegiality and collaboration (Dinnebeil, Buysse, et al., 2007). Dinnebeil, Buysse, and colleagues summarized research concerning personal characteristics of effective consultants as individuals who

- Adapt their approach to meet unique aspects of a situation

- Work in a flexible manner

- Rethink, revise, or modify their thoughts or a course of action to reach a goal

- Consider multiple perspectives and set aside their own beliefs or expectations if they interfere with a productive working relationship

- Demonstrate the ability to make informed, objective decisions based on realistic expectations and sound logic

- Help others feel comfortable in a range of situations

- Are viewed as sincere in their beliefs and actions

- Demonstrate respect for others through their words and actions

- Are sensitive to cultural, racial, ethnic, or other individual differences

- Can honestly reflect on their professional strengths and shortcomings

- Are comfortable in their role as a consultant or an expert in their field

- Demonstrate expertise without being a "know it all"

Challenges to Effective Consultation

Challenges to effective consultation can be grouped into four distinct categories: 1) attitudes or values toward consultation, 2) expertise and skill as a teacher and a consultant, 3) logistical concerns, and 4) expectations and administrative support. Each of these will be discussed separately next.

Attitudes, Values, and Interpersonal Style

As discussed above, effective consultants have the self-confidence they need to be successful in their work. They believe in their abilities to make a difference on behalf of children, their families, and their teachers but do not have an inflated sense of self-worth. For example, Charlie believes that he has the knowledge and skills related to working effectively with young children who have disabilities, but he does not believe that he is the only person who can help children or that he has the right answer every time. To the degree that consultants do not possess the personal characteristics discussed above, they will be challenged to serve as consultants. It is critically important that administrators in a position to hire IECSE professionals carefully consider the interpersonal qualifications of candidates because these characteristics are difficult to learn or cultivate. We have emphasized the importance of hiring IECSE professionals who possess a certain degree of maturity and experience in providing services to young children with disabilities. Hiring a "newly minted" ECSE teacher for an itinerant position could be a challenge to effective consultation because he or she could lack the professional maturity needed to be successful in his or her job.

In addition to examining the attitudes, personal characteristics, and values of the consultant, it is also important to consider the same dimensions in a consultee. For example, a consultative relationship will be challenged if the consultee lacks self-confidence in his or her ability to work with young children with special needs or if he or she does not value inclusive ECE. Consultees who are not open to new ideas, are judgmental of others, or find it hard to work collaboratively with others may find it difficult to work with a consultant. Consultants must be in tune with the thoughts, feelings, and perspectives of those with whom they work and may be challenged to help consultees feel more comfortable, confident, and competent in their abilities to provide high-quality inclusive services.

Expertise and Skills

To the degree that IECSE professionals lack the expertise as consultants, the success of the consultative relationship will be challenged. However, perhaps before considering expertise related to consultation, we should consider a consultant's competence as a provider of high-quality, specialized services to young children with special needs. We have worked with many IECSE teachers who are hired on a temporary or provisional credential because of a shortage of highly qualified candidates. Not only do these individuals lack experience working with other adults but also they lack experience working directly with young children with special needs as well as formal preparation in early childhood special education. They lack the knowledge and professional credibility needed to work effectively with others. Consultees might be appropriately apprehensive of a consultant with little direct experience "under his or her belt."

What about the expertise and skills of a consultee? Certainly, the efficacy of a consultative relationship may be challenged when the consultee lacks knowledge and skills related to working with young children who have special needs, but there should be no expectation for that knowledge and skill set. An IECSE professional who serves as a consultant should be prepared to work with individuals with a range of expertise and skills. The knowledge and skills of a consultee should not unduly affect the success of a consultative relationship.

Logistics

Logistical concerns can very effectively sidetrack a consultative relationship, and unfortunately, these concerns are very real when considering IECSE service delivery in early childhood settings such as child care centers or community-based preschools. These early childhood settings often face staffing challenges. Adult/child ratios are higher then in LEA-sponsored preschool classrooms and group sizes are larger. Teachers work long hours and often do not have access to professional planning time that could be used for consultation. Although some early childhood centers might have other adults who can free up the teacher to spend time with the consultant, many do not, and this can challenge the success of a consultative relationship. It is very difficult for an early childhood teacher to work effectively with a consultant if he or she is also responsible for his or her regular duties at the same time. To mitigate this situation, the IEP team should think clearly and strategically when agreeing to provide services in a specific classroom. Upfront discussions need to occur to make sure that teachers have the time they need to work effectively together on behalf of a child.

In addition to ensuring that early childhood teachers can appropriately participate in a consultative relationship, consultants and consultees are often challenged by conflicting schedules and lack of privacy. IECSE teachers have busy schedules and may not be able to meet the early childhood teacher at a time when she may be free to meet (e.g., during children's nap time, early in the day before children arrive). It is often valuable for an IECSE teacher to visit during a time of day that is challenging for a child (e.g., a child with difficulty attending during large group time). However, it may not always be possible and this can create challenges to the efficacy of a consultative relationship. The IECSE teacher and ECE teacher may lack a quiet place to work together, and this can compromise confidentiality and the ability to attend to the topic at hand. Again, some of these logistical problems can be addressed or avoided altogether by careful and strategic planning during the development of the IEP. In cases in which planning does not occur at the IEP meeting, the IECSE teacher, her general ECE partner, and their supervisors should work together at the onset of the relationship to rectify the situation.

IECSE professionals who work with parents in a consultative relationship can face similar challenges. Parents or family members are busy, and it may be difficult to find a time when the parent can focus exclusively on the consultant. It also may be difficult for the consultant to visit during the time of day that would provide the parent with the direct support she or he needs. For example, the consultant and parent may both decide that working on self-help skills is an important goal and that intervention should be embedded during daily dressing routines. If that is early in the morning or in the evening, it may be difficult (if not impossible) for the IECSE professional to visit at that time, which could compromise the consultant's ability to demonstrate, model, or provide important performance feedback. In situations such as these, parents might be able to videorecord a dressing session (parents love to videotape their kids!) and share it with the IECSE teacher during a visit. Using a doll to simulate an intervention strategy is also an option. Finally, it may be difficult to find a quiet place at a family's home to meet, especially when young children are around. Televisions can be noisy and can distract parents or family members from paying attention to the consultant. Telephone calls and text messages can have the same effect. It may be helpful to tactfully discuss ways to minimize these distractions at the beginning of the consultative relationship.

Expectations and Administrative Support

Major challenges to an effective consultative relationship are unclear or unrealistic goals or expectations. Consultees who believe that the consultant's role is to solve the problem or meet all of a child's needs will be frustrated when this does not occur. Consultants who believe that executing the intervention plan should be the paramount concern of the consultee will be disappointed when the consultee is sidetracked or unable to meet these expectations. As always, communication is key to making sure that both partners have clear and realistic expectations of their partner and are understanding when things do not always happen according to plan.

In addition to unrealistic expectations, a lack of support from either the consultant's administrator or the early childhood teacher's administrator can challenge a successful consultative relationship. Administrators should have clear ideas about the purpose of the consultative relationship and how they can best support its success. Early childhood administrators can increase the likelihood of a successful consultative relationship by providing logistical support that includes an extra pair of hands in a busy early childhood classroom or offering the consultant and consultee a quiet place to work together. Appendix A of this book offers practical ideas for letters of introduction and other types of written communication that help all parties involved understand and support the working relationship.

Resources to Enhance Consultation Services

Even the most knowledgeable and skilled IECSE consultant needs access to resources to support child progress in early childhood programs and homes. Fortunately, the digital age has resulted in immediate access to a range of downloadable resources including written information as well as video and audio clips. Skilled IECSE consultants know about many of these resources and are always on the lookout for others. In addition, savvy consultants have the ability to match these resources to the consultee's needs, interests, and abilities. For example, a consultant might know that a consultee does not have time to read an entire book about Down syndrome but would like to see a short abstract. Alternatively, a consultant might know that a consultee is a visual learner and might share short video clips that highlight use of a particular intervention strategy. The National Early Childhood Technical Assistance Center (NECTAC), at http://www.nectac.org, provides a wide range of web-based resources and useful links to resources that IECSE teachers who work as consultants can use to support children's success.

Summary

The role of consultant is one of the most important ones for an IECSE professional. Built on the foundation of a triadic service delivery model, IECSE professionals who function as consultants work primarily with other adults to bring about positive outcomes for children. Early childhood consultation is built on a behavioral consultation model (Sheridan, Kratochwill, et al., 1996) and follows a problem-solving approach as outlined by Buysse and Wesley (2005). Skilled IECSE consultants work with consultees such as parents of young children with special needs or their teachers to 1) gain entry, 2) build a relationship, 3) gather information through assessment, 4) set goals, 5) select strategies, 6) implement the plan, 7) evaluate the plan, and 8) hold a summary conference. Social influence and professional support play a critical role in successful early childhood consultation. IECSE consultants must be skilled communicators and have an interpersonal style that promotes partnership and collaboration. A number of factors support and hinder successful consultation including 1) personal and professional beliefs and values, 2) expertise, 3) logistical issues, and 4) administrative support. Finally, the digital age has resulted in a range of excellent resources that IECSE consultants can use to support the consultative relationship.

CHAPTER 5

The IECSE Teacher as Coach

The effective IECSE teacher must move beyond providing child-focused and episodic instruction to adopting a model of indirect instruction. In this model, the IECSE teacher intentionally and systematically moves toward a consultation relationship and, eventually, develops a coaching relationship with an engaged ECE partner. In order to more fully understand the relative benefits of consultation and coaching versus direct instruction of children, it is necessary to define the process and objectives of coaching within an IECSE service delivery model.

Coaching: Definition and Process

Whereas consultation opens the door to opportunity, coaching is the process that moves the ECE partner teacher from passive participant to active agent. Coaching, with the scaffold of consultation, seeks to engage the consultee in a mutually respectful, personal, and longitudinal process of empowerment and self-discovery. The use of the term *coaching* to describe the fully engaging process of consultation within the delivery of IECSE services is not an accident. Those descriptors often associated with athletic coaching, or the more recent emergence of career coaching, fit within the IECSE context. The effective coach will have certain experience, knowledge, and skills that can be transmitted to a partner, protégé, or player. The transfer of this knowledge and skills is often accompanied by genuine encouragement of the partner as well as authentic satisfaction with the accomplishments of the partner.

Although consultation may conclude with sharing of information or modeling of skills, coaching is more active and longer term. In coaching, the relationship extends beyond static, point-in-time consultation sessions to a protracted relationship. In consultation, the perception of the consultant that targeted skills were demonstrated by the consultee or that useful and topical information was shared with the partner might serve as the primary indicators of successful consultation. In the coaching model, the continuing professional and personal progress of the partner becomes the benchmark for the effectiveness of the coaching process. Observation of enhanced skills and application of current knowledge in the practice of the partner teacher is the hallmark of effective coaching. In some sense, this is similar to the RTI model in that the intensity, frequency, and focus of consultation services is titrated by the response of the ECE partner teacher as evidenced by change in practice and development of the target child. Ultimately, the effectiveness of consultation (or coaching) can only be verified by change in the practice of the partner teacher.

Coaching is a process that is used in business, education, athletics, medicine, and many other aspects of life. Coaching is an effective interpersonal process that results in improved commitment to goals by the key parties involved in the process. Commitment is facilitated through clarification of goals and priorities and improvement in the knowledge and skills of the participants in the coaching partnership. As Kinlaw stated,

> People are more likely to use their discretionary energy and time to pursue organization goals when 1) they have greater clarity about these goals and their importance, 2) they can exercise influence over these goals, 3) they are more competent to achieve these goals, and 4) they receive more appreciation for working . . . to achieve these goals. (1999, p. 4–5)

Within the domain of IECSE services, the focus of the process is to help the ECE partner in defining the task, analyzing current opportunities and challenges in addressing key IEP objectives, evaluating the appropriate use of recommended intervention strategies, and determining how to implement the intervention plan agreed on by both parties. Stroh and Johnson succinctly described the role of the consultant in the business world as providing "a specialized skill or expertise that the client . . . is unable to provide on [his or her] own" (2006, p. 3). This expectation is consistent with the formal basis for the relationship between an IECSE teacher and his or her ECE partner teacher.

It is important to understand that coaching is, in many respects, a sales job. The effective coach engages in a process of collaboration that leads to an agreement between the partners. This agreement resolves ambiguity about the goals of the relationship as well as communicates a promise to support the consultee (e.g., ECE partner teacher) in acquiring the knowledge and skills he or she will need in assuming this new role as primary facilitator of child progress. This is a critical element of the coaching relationship. The partner teacher must have confidence that the IECSE teacher will provide the information and skill training necessary to develop competence in addressing these priority IEP goals.

Kinlaw suggested that coaching describes a process rather than a function. This is an insightful observation. He further describes the relationship as "conversations of personal discovery . . . that focus on performance-related topics and are . . . shaped by discovering what the other person does know and does not understand" (1999, p.23).

Models of Coaching

Several varieties of coaching models need to be examined in describing the model of coaching in IECSE services.

Peer Coaching

Peer coaching is a model in which there is equity between partners. In peer coaching, both parties hold equivalent credentials. These credentials may be in the same field (e.g., special education certification) or may be similarly respected within the professional community (e.g., special education certification and ECE certification). An example would be a partnership between teachers who hold special education licensure or ECE licensure. Although these partners may not have identical professional experience, they may share enough parallel professional practice that there is a perception of equivalence. An example of inequity in a coaching relationship might be a child development associate (CDA) credentialed Head Start teacher who is completing an associate's degree and a special education licensed teacher who holds a master's degree. From an egalitarian perspective, one might wish to view this relationship as a peer coaching relationship; however, it is unlikely that either of the partners would perceive this partnership as a peer relationship. As an IECSE coaching relationship progresses, an environment can be established that could foster a transition into a peer relationship.

Reciprocal Coaching

The basic premise of reciprocal coaching is straightforward. It is a *quid pro quo* relationship: In response to your offer to coach another individual, you agree to be coached in return. This may be a one-time relationship or it may expand into a chain of reciprocal coaching options. In many respects, the transdisciplinary model of staff interaction and professional development is a blend of a reciprocal coaching relationship and an expert coaching relationship. An example is the interaction between the occupational therapist (OT) and the early childhood special education teacher. The OT would explain the dynamics of motor development related to key tasks in daily living and might model the appropriate application of hand splints or microswitches that improve child function. The teacher could provide information on the cognitive dimensions of an art activity, explain incidental teaching opportunities related to targeted fine motor skills, and also describe a range of typical activities in the classroom where opportunity for practice or refinement of fine motor skills and use of orthoses or environmental control devices might be appropriate. In this situation, both professionals have mastered content and developed practices that may be outside of their professional scope. These skills and knowledge enrich the instruction of the target child as well as his or her peers.

Expert Coaching

This model of coaching is, perhaps, the most familiar. It also presents significant challenges to the expert. Some IECSE teachers express great discomfort with being designated, formally or informally, as an expert. In some cases, particularly in the case of the novice professional or the IECSE teacher employed under a temporary credential, this discomfort is understandable. The perception of expertise on the part of one partner does, in fact, create or acknowledge an imbalance of power. It is important to note that the very nature of the IECSE teacher relationship with an ECE partner teacher is based on differences in expertise and professional responsibilities. This imbalance is manifested in differences in licensure and/or certification, the focus of formal education (e.g., ECE, special education, early childhood special education) of the partners, and sometimes distinctly different professional experiences. The requirements of IDEA and the No Child Left Behind (NCLB) Act of 2001 (PL 107-110) dictate this difference in expertise in that the IECSE teacher must have formal training and licensure and/or certification in some area of special education to meet federal and state requirements as a Highly Qualified Teacher.

This imbalance does not necessarily undermine the consultation relationship. In fact, a survey of ECE partner teachers (Dinnebeil, McInerney, et al., 2006b) indicated that ECE teachers expected their IECSE partner to have greater expertise in identifying and addressing the needs of young children with developmental differences. The perception of expertise is an essential element of the IECSE model. Although we may agree that the expectation of expertise is rational and desirable, it is how this expertise is revealed that will determine its utility in the coaching relationship. No ECE partner will be energized and reassured by an IECSE teacher who begins (and maintains) a relationship based solely and exclusively on an imbalance of power.

The Dynamics of Coaching

The coaching process involves the intentional development of a professional and personal relationship between a professional with specific expertise in an area of interest or need and a partner. In the instance of IECSE services, this partnership is mandated by the least restrictive environment (LRE) placement decision. This mandate, however explicit, may change the nature of the coaching relationship. In the case of IECSE services, the partner in this coaching relationship may be unwilling or skeptical. Although this potential uneasiness may be present in any coaching relationship, it may be more pronounced in IECSE services in which the ECE partner may not have requested assistance and may be uncomfortable with having another teacher in his or her classroom. As a result of these realities, the nature of the coaching process becomes a delicate balance.

Although the basis for this relationship between the IECSE teacher and his or her partner is primarily a business relationship, it is unlike other experiences that the ECE partner may have had in previous consultations that may have been of the expert variety. Although expertise is inherent in coaching, as discussed previously, the duration of this relationship may be outside of the experience of the ECE partner. Also, in addition to the stages or phases of coaching that are examined in detail in this chapter, the stage or phase of coaching for the 12–16 ECE partner teachers with whom the IECSE teacher may be partnered will differ. These differences can be related to how successfully and seamlessly the IECSE teacher helps his or her partner navigate through the stages of coaching. The characteristics of the child being served also can affect the progression of coaching. Consider the possibly immediate impact of coaching on facilitating pre-academic skill development of a child versus the probability of coaching resulting in an immediate reduction in peer-threatening behavior, which may be more resistant to change. The motivation of the ECE partner as well as his or her trust of the IECSE teacher also will affect the progression of coaching. Trust and motivation of the ECE partner may be related to any number of factors, including positive or negative experiences of the ECE partner in previous consultation or coaching relationships. Finally, the recent nature of the initiation of this coaching relationship will affect the stage of coaching. As children age into Part B 619 services, sometime around their 3rd birthday, or move within or into the school district, IECSE teachers will need to initiate or transition from a coaching relationship. It is safe to say that many IECSE professionals, post–mid-school-year in particular, will be engaged in coaching relationships with a number of ECE partner teachers.

Stages of Coaching

The process of consultation or coaching is usually viewed as a series of distinct stages or phases (Buysse & Wesley, 2004; DeVore, 2007). The model that is proposed here includes five stages: 1) *cultivating awareness,* 2) *introduction* (establishing the relationship), 3) *rapport building,* 4) establishing *comfort,* and 5) recognizing *partnership.* The relationships between these stages or phases are shown in Figure 5.1.

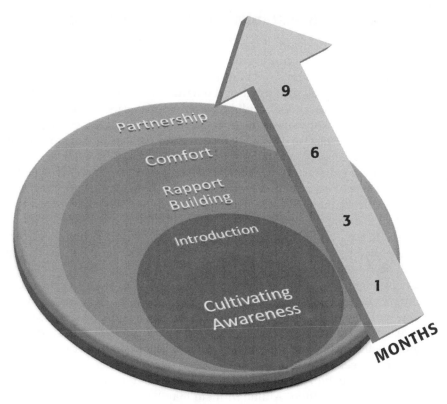

Figure 5.1. Progression of consultation partnership: A linear and temporal model.

Stage 1: Cultivating Awareness

In this initial stage of the coaching relationship, both the IECSE teacher and the ECE partner must understand the nature of their impending relationship. This is accomplished through clear and consistent communications with key stakeholders in the consultation and/or coaching process. ECE program administrators must be aware of the intent and process of the coaching relationship so that they are prepared to discuss this with ECE classroom staff. Also, the distinction between direct instruction in a one-to-one or small-group paradigm and coaching an ECE partner teacher must be discussed with parents before the IEP meeting, particularly when there is an increased probability that a community placement option might be discussed in the IEP meeting or when it is apparent that the parents strongly support community placement as the appropriate LRE option for their child. The LEA Part B 619 supervisor also must articulate the role and responsibilities of the IECSE teacher to potential IECSE teachers in the recruiting and interview process as well as maintain consistent communication with current IECSE personnel. Finally, the distinction between this model and the traditional pull-out and classroom respite model must be addressed whenever any confusion becomes apparent. Consistency in the practice of consultation and coaching as the primary mode of service delivery in IECSE services will establish a public awareness of this model among key constituents. Accomplishing this will accelerate progression to Stage 2. Failure to persistently and publicly promulgate awareness of coaching as the primary model for IECSE services will delay and undermine progression to partnership.

Stage 2: Introduction—Establishing the Relationship

Following the placement decision of the IEP team, the IECSE teacher is matched with his or her ECE partner teacher. In the recommended model of IECSE service delivery, the key stakeholders (i.e., parents of child, supervisor of community-based program, ECE partner teacher) are fully informed of the nature of a consultation model (versus the traditional direct services model) and the objectives of this model. This proactive notification informs key constituents of the form of impending IECSE activities (coaching versus one-to-one IECSE teacher-to-child instruction) as well as the function of the services (longitudinal engagement of child in IEP-focused learning activities versus episodic engagement limited to interaction with the IECSE teacher during weekly visits).

The critical stage of consultation leading to a coaching relationship begins at this time. In the introduction stage, the IECSE assists the ECE partner teacher in understanding the wealth of learning opportunities that, although inherent in the curriculum, may not be apparent to the ECE partner teacher. In effect, the IECSE teacher reassures his or her ECE partner that he or she has already established the learning scaffold that the target child will need to be successful. The IECSE teacher also reassures the ECE partner teacher that although he or she may not have formal training and/or experiences with young children with special education needs, the IECSE—through consistent visits and consultation—will ensure that he or she has the knowledge and skills necessary to support the development of the child. In effect, the IECSE teacher explains, through formal letters of introduction, that he or she has the expertise and experience to assist his or her partner teacher in meeting the needs of the child in question.

During the introduction stage, the IECSE teacher, from the perspective of the ECE partner teacher, is on probation. Although there may be a grace period during which the ECE partner will refrain from personal or professional judgment, this honeymoon period is not indefinite. The competence of the IECSE teacher in providing guidance and insight to his or her partner teacher will be decisive in winning the trust and respect of his or her ECE partner teacher. Trust and respect are engendered through stable presence at scheduled weekly or biweekly consultations, evidence of preparation for these consultation sessions, and subsequent follow-up on key issues that are raised in these sessions. From the perspective of the ECE partner teacher, an uninvited guest has been assigned to his or her classroom for an extended period ostensibly to provide him or her with assistance. The form of that assistance, consultation and coaching, may not be what the ECE partner teacher had in mind. It is necessary for the IECSE, during the introduction stage, to define the model of IECSE intervention through consistent and predictable interactions with the ECE teacher and child. It is important to note that not all partnerships will progress through the introduction stage with the same degree of success or on the same timetable. As has been discussed, the IECSE teacher with a caseload of 12–16 children may be in different stages of the coaching relationship with different ECE partner teachers at different times during the year.

Stage 3: Rapport Building

Following successful negotiation of the introduction stage, the IECSE teacher and his or her ECE partner continue to move toward partnership in building a professional and personal rapport. This stage represents a distinct departure from the second stage. In the rapport-building stage, the IECSE teacher must move the relationship into a stage in which the ECE partner sees the relationship as proactive and empowering rather than remedial and short-term. Although key interpersonal communication skills are utilized in the introduction stage, the full complement of interpersonal communication skills will be necessary during this rapport-building stage.

Rapport describes a reciprocal relationship in which an initial level of trust and engagement has been established that can be facilitated by enhanced trust and diminished suspicion. In this stage, the IECSE teacher, through public and private conversation and, more important, through persistent and consistent professional and personal actions, has gained the confidence and trust of his or her ECE partner teacher. The IECSE teacher is seen as a confederate who is not judgmental and who has reaffirmed the competence of his or her partner teacher. The effective IECSE teacher, through his or her conduct with his or her ECE partner within the consultation process, his or her interactions with other adults and the children, as well as his or her respect for the confidential disclosures of the partner teacher, has earned the ECE partner teacher's respect. In effect, the IECSE teacher, directly or indirectly, has been tested at the most fundamental levels of trust and has "passed." It is not difficult to imagine the challenge of rapport building if the ECE partner teacher harbors suspicion and mistrust of his or her IECSE teacher partner. The outcome, in this case, might be a strained and dismissive relationship that is at the edge of professional courtesy. A more harmful outcome of failure to gain trust might be a demoralizing, passive-aggressive relationship characterized by polite exchanges without any commitment to implementation of recommended instructional practices or any evidence of professional growth.

There is a professional as well as a personal side of rapport building. At a minimum, the effective IECSE teacher must engage his or her ECE partner in child-focused dialog that results in intervention activities that may be situation-specific and time-limited. This is best addressed through public statements of the LEA supervisor to the ECE program director and letters of introduction from the IECSE teacher to the parents of the child, the ECE program supervisor, and the ECE partner teacher.

The more challenging aspect of rapport building is related to the parallel construction of a personal relationship with the ECE partner teacher. This is a much more demanding form of rapport and is subject to certain realities that may predispose both partners to developing personal rapport or serving as significant obstacles to the same. Establishing of personal rapport will be easier in some relationships than in others. Factors that may contribute to building of personal rapport include relative age of partners, extent or perception of imbalance in professional power, cultural and ethnic differences, socioeconomic differences, religious and personal values, political perspectives, personal and professional jealousies or insecurities, and other interpersonal dynamics. Limiting the extent to which these factors might undermine development of professional and personal rapport is a challenge that ECSE administrators and IECSE teachers must address in supporting the IECSE model of service delivery.

Stage 4: Comfort

This stage of consultation occurs as a result of the confidence and trust established during Stages 2 and 3. *Comfort* results from a combination of predictable behavior on the part of the IECSE teacher, explicit or implicit testing of the confidentiality assured to the partner teacher by his or her IECSE partner, evidence of competence in addressing the needs of the partner teacher, and systematic and selective use of specific interpersonal communication skills. This stage is perhaps the most critical one in the movement toward partnership. The ECE partner teacher must be assured that the IECSE teacher is focused on his or her professional needs in addressing the developmental agenda of the target child. The ECE partner teacher also must determine that the IECSE teacher is a strong advocate in supporting his or her professional development while being respectful of his or her personal needs and values. This is the stage in which a form of communication "art" becomes an essential element of interpersonal communication.

Stage 5: Partnership

The final stage of the coaching relationship is characterized as a *partnership*. The focus of this partnership is the advancement of the developmental agenda of the target child. Both the IECSE teacher and the ECE partner teacher are viewed as enablers of the child as well as each other. Through the progression of Stages 2, 3, and 4, the partners have come to develop trust and goodwill. In the progression of the coaching relationship, both partners have benefited from the experience and competence of the other partner. Also, in addressing their professional agenda over the course of this relationship, both partners have divulged information relating to their professional and personal lives. Although some partners may come to understand that they share similar experiences and values, other partners, while recognizing key differences between themselves, evidence genuine respect and optimism with respect to professional and personal goals and challenges.

It is important to note that, as a result of any number of factors that have been addressed in Stage 5, satisfaction with the outcome of the consultation and coaching process will vary. Some partnerships will be marked by strong personal and professional bonding, whereas others may result in mutual professional respect but guarded personal interaction. This is an important aspect of the coaching relationship. Not every relationship will develop into an energetic and vibrant partnership. It is reasonable, however, to expect that each consultation and coaching relationship will result in the empowerment of both partners in addressing the needs of the child in question. This is the minimum expectation for all IECSE consultation relationships.

Although the five phases of a coaching relationship are examined in this discussion, it is also important to note that there are dynamic interactions between and among these stages or phases. The initiation, fading, and establishment of these phases is best described in Figure 5.2, in which the transitory nature of certain stages of the relationship (e.g., cultivating awareness) can be seen versus the later development of rapport and the continuing attention to rapport building throughout the coaching relationship (Bolton, 1979; DeBoer, 1995; & Turnbull, Turnbull, Erwin, & Skodak, 2006).

Evaluation of Outcomes of Coaching

Many factors will affect the relative success of each IECSE partnership. It is apparent that some IECSE teachers enter the consultation relationship with formal preparation in ECSE or with extensive experience in ECE learning environments. Some IECSE teachers may be more comfortable or confident as a result of their age. Older teachers may have more personal maturity or more confidence in their personal or professional efficacy. Some IECSE teachers are less adept at interpersonal communication, whereas others might be described as *natural* communicators. It is important to note that requisite knowledge and skills, including interpersonal communication skills, can be learned. Furthermore, just as specific knowledge increases with experience and study, critical communication and organizational skills also will improve with experience and prac-

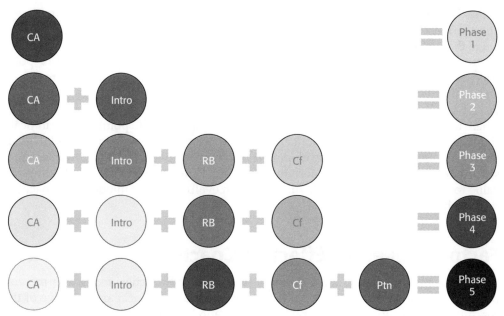

Figure 5.2. Progression of consultation partnership: A dynamic model. Fading or increase in intensity of shading within a circle indicates status of this stage in the five phases of progression. (*Key:* CA, Cultivating awareness; Intro, Introduction; RB, Rapport building; CF, Comfort; Ptn, Partnership) (*Sources:* Bolton, 1979; DeBoer, 1995; & Turnbull, Turnbull, Erwin, & Skodak, 2006.)

tice. Of course, this is more likely to occur when these skills are addressed with intention and shaped by reflection.

As a result of an awareness of variation in the nature of IECSE relationships, evaluation of the relative success of each IECSE partnership should be considered by IECSE teachers and their supervisors. A tool that is sensitive to differences in the professional preparation and experiences of the IECSE teacher as well as differences in the cultural and language experiences of both partners, includes information about the formal academic preparation and motivation of the ECE partner teacher, and acknowledges the potential impact of differences in characteristics of children is helpful in evaluating the relative success of each coaching relationship. It also is helpful in shaping an agenda for professional development for the IECSE teacher. A tool such as the Goal Attainment Scaling Model (GAS; Kiresuk, Smith, & Cardillo, 1994; Sladeczek, Elliott, Kratochwill, Robertson-Mjaanes, & Stoiber, 2001) can be helpful in evaluating the outcome of individual coaching efforts with respect to factors that may facilitate or hinder development of a partnership. The GAS approach assumes that in each instance in which an action would occur that is intended to result in a specific outcome there could be variation in success in realizing this outcome. The probability of a varying outcome is based on differences that exist before the action is undertaken as well as different responses of key factors or individuals to this action. It is, in effect, a covariance model that considers a range of factors that may influence the outcome or attainment of the objective. An example, in the IECSE relationship, would be an ECE partner teacher who holds an undergraduate degree in early childhood education. This partner might have more information regarding teaching strategies than an ECE partner without such training. As a result, it is possible that it may be easier to coach this ECE partner in providing the intervention necessary to move the target child toward meeting a preschool cognitive goal. Also, the learning environment might be more or less conducive to child development, the health of the child may undermine attendance in preschool, and other factors may have a negative influence on child development. The GAS model employs a numerical scale to judge the projected progress in attaining an objective as a result of a number of human, environmental, and related factors that could be anticipated. In some cases—on a 7-point scale, for example—the characteristics of the child, key staff, the learning environment, and so forth would suggest that the goal should be met, and the progress could be expected as movement from point 1 to point 7, or attainment of the goal. In another case, where the key factors are less positive, movement from point 1 to point 4 might indicate significant progress. The same model of analysis and prediction could be used in evaluating the prognosis for the development of partnerships in the IECSE consultation service delivery model. The underlying conceptual framework of this tool will be of value to IECSE teachers and their supervisors in evaluating consultation and coaching relationships.

Factors Linked to Effective Coaching

The nature of the coaching relationship is that the IECSE teacher, acting as a mentor, provides support to the ECE partner teacher, the mentee. The primary objective of the coaching relationship in IECSE services is to advance the knowledge and skills of ECE partner teachers so they can successfully address the IEP objectives of the target child in the absence of the IECSE teacher. A secondary objective is to improve the confidence and competence of the ECE partner teacher in generally supporting the development of young children with special needs. These objectives are best accomplished through a structured and systematic transfer of knowledge and skills. Some examples of the objectives of the coaching partnership include the following:

- Transfer of specific knowledge (e.g., the effect of use of American Sign Language in a simultaneous communication paradigm on development of speech) or general knowledge (e.g., how an IEP is developed)

- Motivation of the partner to seek and secure information in response to his or her inquiry or concerns (e.g., the effect of frequent bouts of otitis media on the hearing of children with Down syndrome)

- Teaching and modeling of new skills in curriculum planning (e.g., the use of matrix and embedded instruction models in addressing IEP objectives)

- Suggesting a modification of current teaching practices (e.g., the adoption of incidental teaching strategies as a complement to direct instruction)

- Creating forms to monitor child progress (e.g., an interval sampling form)

- Empowering the partner in seeking a more active role in planning for the instruction of the child (e.g., participation as contributing member of IEP team).

Specific actions are associated with effective coaching within the IECSE service delivery model. Effective IECSE teachers engage in intentional planning, use selected interpersonal communication skills, and adopt appropriate child-monitoring strategies in their systematic effort to assist their ECE partner in addressing priority IEP skills and behaviors. These organizational, curriculum planning, and interpersonal communication skills ensure the efficient and time-limited transfer of critical knowledge and skills to the ECE partner.

Interpersonal Communication Strategies and Content Knowledge that Support Effective Coaching

Three major knowledge and skill requirements are embedded in the process of coaching. To be an effective coach, IECSE teachers must demonstrate 1) knowledge of special education content and practice, 2) knowledge and selective use of primary interpersonal communication skills, and 3) awareness of resources that can provide content and support for skill development for the ECE partner teacher. Although this seems like a reasonable and manageable set of expectations, many IECSE teachers cannot demonstrate this content knowledge or skill set upon entering the profession. There are several reasons for this. Because few states recognize the IECSE service delivery model as a distinctly different component of Part B 619 services, preservice personnel preparation mandates specific to IECSE personnel in the United States are unusual. Although some IECSE teachers hold certification in special education, others may hold ECE licensure or may not be certified in any area of teaching at the time of their hiring.

The effect of this variation in preparation is that some IECSE teachers do not have basic content knowledge in special education or knowledge of best practices. As previously noted, the centerpiece of the IECSE relationship with the ECE partner teacher is that the IECSE teacher has specific content knowledge in the area of special education that is of particular value to the ECE teacher. To the extent that practicing IECSE teachers lack content knowledge and professional practice skills in special education, they need to address this through some form of remediation. Lack of content knowledge or knowledge of special education teaching practices is a serious challenge for the IECSE teacher and the school district. Depending on the professional development requirements of the state, some of these less-than-fully trained IECSE teachers will need to complete coursework and advanced degree programs in early childhood special education or special education as a way to become qualified. Practicing IECSE professionals also may be advised to develop personal professional development plans through the use of discipline-specific tools such as the PIECES, discussed in detail in Chapter 3 and available in Appendix C, and the *DEC Recommendations for Professional Practice* (Sandall et al., 2005). In addition, IECSE teachers also may organize collective professional development activities through local, regional, or statewide self-advocacy activities (e.g., DEC, NAEYC).

Awareness of interpersonal communication skills and specific training in their use is a challenge for almost all IECSE teachers. Few undergraduate or graduate programs leading to teaching licensure include content or skill practice in interpersonal communication. Although all education professionals could benefit from these skills, they are of particular importance to the IECSE teacher. These interpersonal communication skills empower IECSE teachers to establish rapport with their partners and to more precisely identify the needs of ECE teachers. It is important at this juncture to differentiate between *interpersonal communication skills* and *counseling skills*. It is neither recommended nor required that the IECSE teacher develop a level of interpersonal communication competence that is equivalent to the skill set of an accomplished counselor. The intent of adoption of a limited number of interpersonal communication skills is to assist the IECSE teacher in establishing a respectful and helping relationship. These particular skills, listed in Table 5.1, have been identified as basic strategies in communication that are helpful in engaging a partner in a time-limited and focused conversation in which fact and affect may be communicated (Horton & Brown, 1990; Wood, 2004).

Table 5.1. Basic interpersonal communication skills

Nonverbal and listening skills

  Physical attending

    Maintain eye contact with partner.

    Positive posture: Keep posture active and engaging. Sit upright, leaning in toward the partner instead of slouching away from the partner.

    Maintain an appropriate distance from the partner: Consider personal and cultural comfort and differences.

  Listening

    Use passive listening but active involvement through the following:

      1. Nonverbal attending skills

      2. Silence

      3. Minimal encouragement (e.g., head nodding, interested facial expressions, verbal encouragers such as "uh-huh" and "okay")

    Listen actively.

      1. Remain animated (facial expressions and/or movement).

      2. Comment on what your partner is saying.

      3. Question your partner.

      4. Share professional and personal experiences.

    Experience and express empathy.

      1. Keep language nonjudgmental; do not show agreement or disagreement with your partner.

      2. Keep conversation nonevaluative; respect your partner's values.

Verbal skills

  Further your partner's responses.

    Use minimal encouragers (e.g., "uh-huh," "I see").

    Use verbal following: Restate the main points of partner communication in familiar language.

  Paraphrase.

    Restate the partner's message. Emphasize factual information as opposed to the affective state of the partner. Respond to basic content of partner's message.

  Respond to affect.

    Attend not only to what is said but how it is said.

    Respond accurately and match partner intensity. This assures the partner that his or her message has been received and is accepted.

  Question.

    Closed-ended questions: Search for factual information—responses are "yes"/"no" or factual (e.g., numbers, objective information).

    Open-ended questions usually invite dialog: Involves "what" and "how" questions; responses of partner may reveal values, aspirations, and/or concerns.

  Summarization

    Restate most critical thoughts and/or feelings.

    Recall highlights, tie up info, and conclude discussion.

As a result of this focused communication, the IECSE partner may be able to provide information; demonstrate skills or techniques; or recommend resources to support the effectiveness, confidence, and comfort of the ECE partner teacher. The intent of adoption of selected strategies for interpersonal communication is not to manipulate the relationship but rather to add an element of efficiency and precision to the communication opportunity. This is particularly useful when opportunities for two-way communication are limited, as in the IECSE model.

Interpersonal communication strategies for an effective IECSE teacher include *verbal* and *nonverbal* strategies. Basic nonverbal strategies are related to face-to-face contact and body positioning or body language. Attention to these nonverbal aspects of communication should result in more respectful, attentive, and reciprocal communication. Making an effort to establish eye contact, with careful consideration of personal comfort and cultural traditions, assures the partner that you are alert and attentive. Sitting in a more erect and engaging posture (e.g., leaning slightly toward the partner) also can communicate attention and interest. Speaking without bringing your hands to your mouth and muting your conversation also is helpful. There also are a few recommendations for nonverbal responses to your partner's communication, such as occasional head nodding, that can serve to confirm that you are listening and understanding the communication. Head nodding in isolation or accompanied by a brief utterance (e.g., "uh huh," "okay") also encourages partners to continue their communication. Although these recommendations may seem to be common sense, it is only necessary to observe conversations to recognize that violations of these basic protocols occur quite often. Once these basic skills are identified, it becomes easier to understand how the absence of these skills can stifle or undermine communication.

Certain verbal communication skills also have been demonstrated to enhance communication (Table 5.2). These skills might be described as *active listening skills*.

These interpersonal skills involve helping partners focus or sharpen their concerns or questions as well as mirroring a partner's responses to ensure that you understand his or her question or concern. Another set of interpersonal skills is intended to sensitize the listener to the factual and emotional content of the communication. Initially, in the interest of confirming the objectives for interaction between the IECSE teacher and the ECE partner, use of verbal tactics such as confirmation of the content of the communication is important. It is necessary that the IECSE teacher understand the perspective,

Table 5.2.   Strategies for and characteristics of active listeners

Create a comfortable atmosphere.
   Find a quiet place to meet.
   Sit in adult-sized furniture.
   Provide support for limited release time for partner.

Evidence interest in your partner.
   Use an animated affect.
   Remember critical features of previous visits.
   Remember family events and activities the partner values.

Provide partner with your undivided attention.
   Turn cell phones off.
   Create a coaching area where children and other adults may not be present.

Provide eye contact and use positive body language.
   Sit near your partner.
   "Lean into" the conversation.
   Look at your partner (though be aware of partner's cultural norm).
   Keep hands away from face and/or mouth.

Encourage your partner to talk.
   Use "time delay" to limit your conversation.
   Use open-ended as opposed to closed-ended entrees or questions.
   Use nonverbal encouragers (e.g., head nod).
   Use verbal encouragers (e.g., "uh-huh").

Let your partner steer or direct conversation.
   Allow your partner to initiate conversation.
   Help your partner focus on child or professional issues.

concerns, or questions of the ECE partner. These communication skills include restating or paraphrasing the communication so that the ECE partner can clarify misinformation or any misinterpretation of the content or intent of the communication. In addition to this paraphrasing or restating of the communication, the IECSE teacher also should provide unobtrusive and minimal encouragement to the ECE partner to facilitate the conversation. In addition, during the communication or at the conclusion of an extensive exchange, the IECSE teacher should offer to summarize the key points of the conversation and to record these for further review or comment at the conclusion of the consultation or coaching session.

The most demanding interpersonal communication skill for the IECSE teacher is reflection of affective or emotional content that may be embedded deeply or barely disguised in the communication. Once again, IECSE teachers are not counselors, and the intent of their engagement with ECE partners is more in the nature of a business-oriented relationship rather than a therapeutic relationship. Nevertheless, frustration, anxiety, anger, or confusion might surface within the consultation or coaching session. It is important for the IECSE teacher to be attentive to and to recognize and identify any affective concerns that may have arisen as a result of the coaching relationship. If this aspect of the interaction is not addressed, the rapport and comfort that has been established in the coaching relationship may be undermined or eroded. Issues related to classroom management, strained relationships among professionals outside of the IECSE relationship, tension with parents, the demands of academic programs in which the partner is enrolled, conflicting communications with immediate supervisors, and personal and family problems can lead to stressful emotions. In these instances, the role of IECSE teacher is to recognize and address emotional issues that are within their control and to evidence empathy and concern for those aspects of their partners' lives that are outside of their sphere of influence.

On a positive note, ECE partners also may share enthusiasm, pride, satisfaction, and other celebratory states in their communication with their IECSE partner. In many instances, the help and direction of the IECSE partner may have been the source of this accomplishment. Situations such as this occur when an ECE teacher is approached by his or her peers and asked to share his or her recently acquired knowledge or skills or when parents praise the ECE teacher for his or her effectiveness with their child and share their satisfaction with the program administrator. Another example could be when the ECE teacher's comments and observations regarding a child are solicited by the coordinator of the IEP team prior to a pending IEP meeting, signaling that the ECE teacher is genuinely welcomed as a member of the IEP team. Evidence of positive effect also could be seen when an ECE partner teacher achieves an outstanding grade on an examination or assignment in a community college or university course related to young children with special needs. The role of IECSE teachers in these instances is to acknowledge these achievements, accept graciously any credit that is afforded to them by their partners, and congratulate their partners in attaining this recognition.

Ways to Improve IECSE Coaching

The effective practice of coaching requires the intentional application of organizational and communication skills. As Kinlaw stated, "Coaching is a real-time activity. What makes coaching successful is the quality of the coach's communication. Becoming a successful coach requires us to prepare, practice, and receive feedback on how well we are doing" (1999, p. 152–153). IECSE teachers need to assume responsibility for improving their professional skills as well as advancing the practice of consultation and coaching within the ECE community. Addressing these objectives can provide a platform for development of professional development activities. Some possible professional development activities are laid out in the following paragraphs.

1. *Evaluate the use of coaching logs (see Figure 5.3; also Appendix B) to plan the agenda and content for coaching sessions as well as to provide a template for reflection on the success of the coaching session:* The use of coaching logs also could provide evidence of purposeful and sequential progression in meeting the needs of the target child and his ECE teacher.

2. *Role-play and practice coaching via the use of case studies and prompt questions related to provision of coaching services:* These professional development sessions could feature content based on information provided in case studies and discussion of the personal and professional resources, needs, and motivation of ECE partner teachers.

3. *Practice selected interpersonal communication skills, as outlined in Table 5.1; this may include simulated coaching sessions, responses to scripted prompts allowing practice in the use of basic interpersonal communication strategies, listening to and critiquing of videotape samples of coaching sessions, and so forth:* Kinlaw (1999) described a simulated coaching professional development activity that could be useful in developing coaching skills. A group of three IECSE teachers would agree to meet to practice coaching skills. This activity also could be conducted with two people and a video camera. One participant agrees to serve as the IECSE teacher while the other assumes the role of the ECE partner teacher. The role of the ECE partner teacher could be scripted through the use of case studies of ECE partner teachers, including sample IEP objectives of target children, or the role play could be spontaneous. Prior to initiation of the mock coaching session, the IECSE teacher would review basic tenets of the coaching process, including use of specific interpersonal communication skills. The role players could agree on the stage of the consultation and/or coaching relationship (e.g., rapport building or establishing comfort) as well as the affective tenor of the encounter (e.g., discussion of intervention strategies, discussion of child progress, discussion of value of previous coaching sessions from the perspective of the ECE partner, resistance of ECE partner to modify practices or activities for target child). These simulations could be limited to 10-minute sessions to allow for practice of skills in multiple situations.

   Following the simulation session, the partners can review the videotape for evidence of use of basic physical and verbal communication skills. The use of a checklist that indicated which communication strategies were used by the IECSE teacher, whether that strategy matched the communication prompt of the ECE partner, and so forth could be helpful in analyzing the coaching simulation. If there were a third-party observer, discussion of his or her observations would replace the need for videotape review as the sole source of external feedback. The observations of the observer also could be informed by his or her use of a similar checklist. At the conclusion of the review of the simulation session, the participants could exchange roles. This is an example of a professional development activity that is specific to the practice of consultation and/or coaching and that might support development of skills that are essential to effective coaching.

Planning for Consultation Session: Sample A

Date of visit: 11/22/11   Location: Children's World

IECSE teacher: M. Stowe   ECE partner teacher: E. Ramirez

Session #: 6   Duration of session: 75 mins.

Child: T.C.

Focus of session:

☐ Prioritization of IEP objectives   ☐ Monitoring of child progress
☐ MATRIX planning to embed instruction   ☒ Discussion of transition to kindergarten
☐ Discussion of peer pairing   ☐ Discussion of transition to another program
☒ Monitoring of partner progress   ☐ Assessment of child

☐ Development of task analysis of teaching skill _____
☐ Modification of materials: _____
☐ Provision of information and/or media on disability conditions: _____
☐ Demonstration of incidental teaching skill: _____
☒ Demonstration of direct instruction teaching skill: Use of DRO/DRA procedure _____
☐ Review of Internet resources: _____

Supplies and materials:

☐ Materials: _____
☐ Toy(s): _____
☐ Microswitch: _____
☐ CD or video: _____
☐ Child monitoring form: _____
☒ ECE partner teacher monitoring form: _____
☒ Journal article: _____
☐ Other: _____

Reflection on coaching session (narrative / rating system)

☐ Objective(s) met   ☒ Objective(s) partially met   ☐ Objective(s) NOT met

Comments:

• Discussed T's progress in seeking peer assistance to secure items that he cannot access
without help or use of tools. E has been shown how to use LIMITED ACCESS and TIME DELAY in
creating opportunities for T to communicate with peers. E was able to describe activities and
opportunities she created.
• Left file for E that describes how to use DRO and/or DRA strategies to reward appropriate
behavior.
• Began discussion of T's pre-K skills. Did not complete. Left local education agency kindergarten
skills checklist for her to complete before next visit.

Date of next coaching session: 12/05/10

Focus of next session: Local education agency kindergarten skills checklist; feedback on use of
DRO/DRA Monitoring

Figure 5.3. Planning for Consultation Session: Sample A. (Key: DRO, differential reinforcement of other behaviors; DRA, differential reinforcement of alternative behavior)

4. *Discuss strategies that could be helpful in preparing for multiple coaching sessions within the same day and across the week:* Organizational strategies could include the use of images of the ECE partner teacher and child in a weekly or monthly schedule and other proactive organizers to prepare the IECSE teacher for pending coaching sessions.

5. *Use e-filing, personal organization software (e.g., iPhone, iPad, Blackberry), e-mail, Twitter, and other personal and social networking media in improving the efficiency of IECSE services.*

Coaches can assume the role of expert, facilitator, or both (Stroh & Johnson, 2006). As the appropriately credentialed professional under IDEA responsible for translation of the IEP into practice, the IECSE teacher must accept the perception of his or her ECE partner that he or she is operating in the role of expert. This is an expected and respected role. Depending on the previous experience of the IECSE teacher with this ECE teacher or the previous experiences of the IECSE teacher with other ECE teachers in the same center of the same system, the presumption of expertise may not be tested by the ECE teacher. However, if there is no "history," other factors may undermine the presumption of expertise of the IECSE teacher. Operating under a temporary teaching credential or being a novice teacher are examples of objective threats to expertise. The ECE partner teacher may test the novice IECSE teacher in order to gauge his or her expertise. This is natural in a consultation relationship and should be anticipated. If there has been poor proactive communication or no communication concerning the implications and expectations of the IECSE model or if the ECE teacher is resistant to the model, then some push back, subtle or otherwise, is likely. The IECSE teacher should not mistake this resistance or testing of the mettle as personal in nature. It is simply an artifact of any consultation relationship. Expertise is assumed and must be demonstrated, as expertise is inherent in any consultation relationship.

Some perspectives on the nature of the consultation relationship are more blunt. Asura (as cited in Stroh & Johnson, 2006) suggested that consultants must be subject-matter experts because the employing agency has hired them to provide services that their own employees cannot. This is certainly true in the case of many preschool and child care programs. Asura further stated that the employing agency does not have time for the consultant to "practice." Although education is often a more forgiving environment and although this presumption of consultation expertise may be viable in the open market, it may not be the case in the world of IECSE services. The IECSE teacher may be thrust into a role that he or she is, at best, not fully prepared to execute, and he or she will have no choice other than to "practice" his or her craft on the job. Asura also shared the perspective from the business world that the consultant must be "familiar with our business, philosophy, and history before they try to sell us services" (p. 19). This appears to be good advice for the IECSE teacher. Although the community-based program that has enrolled the target child is not "buying" IECSE services, per se, the IECSE teacher is certainly in the business of sales. It is incumbent that IECSE teachers investigate the norms and culture of those programs in which they provide services. Operating rules and regulations of agencies such as Head Start; private, not-for-profit preschool programs; and so forth may support or discourage some actions that may come under consideration in the coaching process. Increased awareness of the host agency policies and practices also demonstrates respect and professional commitment, both of which serve to enhance the coaching relationship.

As an expert, the IECSE teacher is expected to assist his or her ECE partner in implementing disability or IEP-specific teaching strategies. In this role, he or she also assumes the mantle of facilitator. The IECSE teacher, while assuming the role of expert, also must consider the culture of his or her ECE partner in helping him or her translate this expertise into practices that can be supported within the ECE environment. For example, it would be a mistake for the IECSE teacher to recommend a series of one-to-one instruction sessions during the day with the target child in an ECE setting where there may be 20 children, ages 4–5, in each session of a half-day pre-K program that is staffed by an ECE teacher, an aide, and a parent volunteer. Although the formula for instruction might appear to be a reasonable practice in a pre-K special education classroom with 12 children and two teacher aides, embedded instruction (McWilliam 1996a; Sandall et al., 2005) is a more viable recommendation for most community pre-K programs.

The role of facilitator is consistent with the primary objectives of coaching in the IECSE service delivery model. The IECSE teacher seeks to engage his or her ECE partner in recognizing his or her responsibility and his or her pivotal role in fostering the development of all of his or her children, particularly the target child. This engagement through the facilitation role is likely to be more successful in helping the ECE partner teacher to assume ownership for the developmental outcomes of this child (Stroh & Johnson, 2006). In order to engage the partner teacher in addressing the child's key learning objectives, the goals of consultation must be clear to both parties. Goals that are vague and not measurable invite confusion. The effective coach works with his or her partner to resolve this potential confusion. This is particularly important with respect to the role of the IECSE teacher in the coaching relationship and the projected outcomes for the ECE partner teacher and the target child as a result of this relationship.

Stroh and Johnson (2006) described a sequence of phases that they suggest are critical in achieving a successful consultation relationship. Although all of these seven phases are not pertinent to the coaching relationship outside of the business world, several phases are consistent with the stages of consultation model proposed in this chapter and address the key features of successful IECSE service delivery. These parallel phases include establishing expectation and goals for consultation, formalizing an agreement, developing the project or action plan, initiating the project (interventions), and concluding the project (or relationship). Also similar to the perspective presented in the stages of consultation, Stroh and Johnson (2006) proposed that the progression through these stages of consultation would vary depending on the needs and resources of the "client."

It is possible that some community programs that have been involved in IECSE services may be reluctant to participate in a new relationship. The agency may report that the previous IECSE relationship was not good. They may cite interpersonal problems, personality conflicts, failure to deliver on promises, unpredictable or unreliable schedules for visits, the IECSE teacher engaging in pull-out services exclusively, and other concerns. Unfortunately, a negative experience, regardless of which party was at fault, will require reconciliation. This reconciliation should assume the form of active listening, often without comment, as the aggrieved party describes the problems that occurred in the prior IECSE relationship. Even though the other IECSE teacher may be a colleague, it is imperative that the IECSE teacher who is seeking to repair the relationship not defend the actions of his or her colleague. The instructional aspect of this encounter is that the IECSE teacher should listen carefully and note the concerns of the aggrieved ECE teacher, the program director, and any other staff who weigh in on the situation. He or she should do so in order that he or she can evaluate the causes and consequences of the actions of all parties in an attempt to avoid similar violations as well as to develop sensitivity to the key beliefs or traditions of the program and the personal and professional needs and expectations of the staff. The IECSE teacher seeking to mend the relationship should focus on his or her expertise and commitment and his or her intent to avoid replicating this situation. If the IECSE teacher has established credentials with other community programs, he or she or his or her supervisor should provide key personnel with these references. Although the practice of consultation in the IECSE service delivery model is not a precise science, it must be elevated from an art form. Some IECSE teachers are better suited to the position and some IECSE teachers have developed better interpersonal communication skills and organizational skills than others. Some IECSE teachers are more likely to succeed where others have failed.

Preparing for and Following Up on Coaching Sessions

There are two aspects of preparation for coaching visits. One aspect is general preparation and involves consideration of improvement in skills that would affect all coaching sessions. The second aspect, specific preparation, is concerned with preparation for the next coaching session or series of sessions and includes proactive organization of an agenda; creation or gathering of activities and/or materials; and recollection of the unique characteristics of the target child, the learning environment, and the ECE partner teacher. As is suggested throughout this book, there is a distinct and critical set of knowledge and skills that are specific to IECSE teachers. This knowledge and these skills must shape the practice of IECSE service delivery. This can only occur as the result of intentional adoption of these skills and consistent application of these skills in professional practice.

The interim between coaching sessions should be the most productive period for the ECE partner. During this period, most often a week between visits, the ECE partner is able to practice new teaching strategies, monitor child behavior, and apply new knowledge in his or her interactions with the target child. The ECE partner teacher needs to understand that he or she is not out there on his or her own between coaching sessions. He or she needs to be assured that he or she can access resources or check on his or her progress with his or her IECSE partner. Although this is yet another demand for time, it is a necessary component of the partnership.

The resources that are necessary to support this professional development may be provided at the time of the visit or before the next visit via e-mail, attachments to e-mail, or posting of materials on the LEA or personal web site. The communication culture and resources of the IECSE teacher and his or her ECE partner guide how this information is provided to the ECE partner and in what format. Although some coaching dyads may rely on traditional methods of communication between visits (e.g., telephone messages, mailing of materials, photocopies of resources, daily or weekly logs, basic e-mail), other dyads may use cell phone technology to 'tweet,' attach files to e-mail, send digital videos or images, forward links to web sites, and so forth. Viable options for partner communication and planning are expanding at a lightning pace. Some IECSE teachers and their ECE partners, depending on their communications savvy, preferences, and resources, may wish to communicate across a spectrum of communication options. It is safe to say that some form of personal organizer and expanded options personal communication device soon will be the standard in IECSE services for communication, creation of files, data entry, record access, record transfer, and record storage.

Summary

IECSE teachers who serve as coaches face a number of challenges, but the relationship with their mentees—ECE partner teachers—can be extremely rewarding. It is important that IECSE teachers be prepared to become experts in their skill area, whether early childhood special education or special education, and understand the best practices in this area. In addition to these skills, however, being a good communicator is also important. Good communication begins with awareness of one's attitude and personality and comfort in the role of change agent. Interpersonal communication skills can be practiced and modeled. Difficult times between partner teachers may be inevitable, just as with any two people in a relationship; however, relationship difficulties can be overcome through openness, honesty, and a commitment to the success of the partnership. Coaching in an educational partnership can be one of the most effective means of successfully supporting young children with disabilities.

CHAPTER 6

The IECSE Teacher as Assessor

Among one of the most important and complicated roles that an IECSE teacher assumes is that of an assessor. It is an important role because all education and related service professionals must make informed decisions based on data and evidence. It is a complicated role because IECSE teachers work both directly and indirectly with children when they do assessments. Directly, they collect data through observation and examination of artifacts. Indirectly, they help others (e.g., general ECE teachers, parents) assume the responsibility of data collection. In any case, IECSE teachers must have a deep understanding of the principles and recommended practices of assessment so they can fulfill the role of assessor.

This chapter outlines major issues related to assessment. We identify assessment as it relates to the knowledge and skills of other adults as well as to assessing the quality of early childhood environments as important responsibilities of IECSE teachers. Accordingly, this chapter begins with a discussion of formal assessment and outlines recommended practices for formal assessment measures.[1] Next, we provide a discussion of informal assessment activities, including alternative/authentic assessments designed to plan instruction or intervention. Given the IECSE teacher's role in working with other adults, it is important to explore ways in which IECSE teachers use assessment procedures to best support the adults who work with children every day. Thus, we also discuss the IECSE teacher's role in helping other adults assess children and self-assess. We also address the importance of assessing the quality of early childhood environments.

The Purpose of Early Childhood Assessment

Early childhood assessment is the process of seeking information about a child's emerging and established knowledge, skills, and behaviors. There are five established purposes of assessment in early childhood intervention: 1) identifying children who may be at risk for a particular condition or disability (i.e., screening), 2) diagnosing a particular condition or disability, 3) establishing readiness for a particular learning context, 4) designing interventions and instruction that will support progress toward meeting developmental or academic outcomes, and 5) evaluating the success of a particular early childhood program (National Research Council, 2008). Panelists who participated in our Delphi study (Dinnebeil et al., 2006b) identified the role of assessor as one that was

---

[1]We assume that readers already have foundational knowledge of early childhood assessment. Readers who do not are referred to a basic textbook on early childhood assessment, of which there are many.

important for IECSE teachers. Specifically, they identified the following responsibilities of IECSE teachers who functioned as assessors: 1) engaging as members of a formal assessment team, 2) collecting data as part of informal assessment processes, 3) recording and organizing assessment information, and 4) writing progress reports.

Formal Assessments: The Role of Standardized Tests in Early Childhood Intervention

Formal assessment is a term used to describe standardized, norm-referenced tests that yield scores reflecting a child's performance in relation to his or her peers (National Research Council, 2008). Norm-referenced tests are formal assessments because they are conducted with standardized materials under standardized procedures and settings. The standardization process enables an individual to compare the scores of one child with scores of another child that has the same demographic profile (McLean, Bailey, & Wolery, 1996). The same standardization processes, however, limit the degree to which information from these tests is useful in terms of curriculum planning and intervention. Testing is done at a single point in time, which can only provide a brief snapshot of children's capabilities under these standardized conditions—conditions that are usually unfamiliar to the child, leading many to question the validity of results (Pianta, 2004). In addition, test items often represent skills that are educationally irrelevant (e.g., stacking three 1-inch cube blocks). However, norm-referenced tests do yield information that is useful for diagnosing problems and helping teams make decisions concerning the need for specialized services (National Research Council, 2008).

The IECSE Teacher's Role in Formal Assessments

IECSE teachers often find themselves on assessment teams and have responsibilities for conducting formal assessments (Dinnebeil et al., 2006b). Consequently, it is important that they are knowledgeable and skilled at administering norm-referenced tests. Some tests require special training or a license to administer (National Research Council, 2008). All members of the assessment team must have a solid understanding of the uses and limitations of norm-referenced tests and must understand basic psychometric properties such as reliability, validity, and standard error of measurement. The DEC (2007) encouraged all of those who work with or on behalf of young children with disabilities to understand three elements related to the psychometric properties of formal assessments. First, DEC cited the fact that, in the very early years, learning and development occurs at such an astounding and frequently unpredictable rate that test scores tend to be unstable and not reflective of children's actual abilities. Second, in addition to the potential error that early childhood growth and development introduces into some tests, the presence of a disabling condition or developmental delay also can contribute error and instability to test scores. Third and finally, many measures of early academic development lack predictive validity and may not be educationally useful in making decisions. For these reasons, DEC cautioned against the over-reliance on test scores to make educational decisions for children.

Understanding the benefits and drawbacks of certain norm-referenced tests and other assessment is a responsibility of IECSE teachers and other team members. However, all team members also should have a responsibility to appropriately interpret test scores, including percentile ranks, age-equivalent scores, developmental quotients, and other types of standard scores (McLean et al., 1996). Finally, IECSE teachers have an ethical responsibility to follow standard procedures for administering and scoring tests as well as interpreting results to parents and other team members (Bagnato & Neisworth, 2005). We discuss recommendations for organizing and writing assessment reports below.

Organizing and Writing Reports

Although testing, scoring, and interpretation of scores must follow standard procedures, IECSE teachers and other professionals can organize and report information in a way that is helpful to others, including individuals unfamiliar with testing and assessment. Bagnato and Neisworth offered the following recommendations regarding sharing information with others:

- Professionals report assessment results in ways that are easy to understand and useful. For example, reports should be as free of technical jargon as possible. When technical terms must be used, professionals should include definitions of terms appropriate for a layperson. Reports also should be provided in the family's primary language.

- Professionals report a child's strengths as well as concerns or issues revealed through the testing process.

- Professionals report the limitation of tests when sharing information with others. For example, professionals might discuss general limitations of norm-referenced testing or specific ways in which the standardized testing procedures affected the child's response.

- Professionals write reports that reflect the relationships of developmental domains as well as the relationship between the disability and test scores.

- Professionals organize reports by functional or developmental domains rather then specific tests.

- Professionals representing different disciplines (e.g., speech-language pathologist, educator, occupational therapist) collaborate to write an integrated report.

- Professionals make sure families have the time they need to review reports, ask questions, or express concerns before anyone uses the information to make decisions.

- Families are free to invite others to evaluation meetings or meetings to discuss their child's performance or progress.

Informal Assessments: Alternative and Authentic

Results from formal, norm-based assessments provide information about a child's performance relative to the performance of his or her peers. Notari-Syverson and Losardo (2008) argued that results from these assessments lack information about children's *functional* abilities—that is, what they *can* do in the context of everyday routines and activities. Data from norm-referenced assessments provide very little information about children's potential for learning or the kinds of supports they need to be successful. For this reason, Notari-Syverson and Losardo, along with other leaders in the field (Bagnato, 2007; Bagnato & Neisworth, 2005; DEC, 2007; Meisels & Atkins-Burnett, 2000; National Research Council, 2008; Snyder, Wixson, Talapatra, & Roach, 2008) strongly advocated for a focus on *authentic or alternative assessment*. Notari-Syverson and Losardo defined *alternative assessments* as those assessment processes that occur within the context of daily routines and activities. The benefit of these informal assessments is that they provide the data necessary to make decisions about curriculum and instruction. Some of the informal assessments teachers use are progress monitoring, observation (or "kid watching," described later in this chapter), embedded approaches, authentic approaches, and mediated approaches. The latter three forms of assessment can also be taken together as a comprehensive ecological model.

Progress Monitoring

Progress monitoring is a key activity of an assessment team. As the term implies, progress monitoring refers to an assessment system that takes place over time and allows team members to follow a child's progress toward achieving IEP goals and objectives. It involves the use of assessment tools (e.g., checklists, interview protocols, time-sampling protocols, narrative recording methods) to collect data concerning a specific skill or ability. Data collected through progress monitoring efforts provides feedback to teachers and other team members about the efficacy of the curriculum and intervention strategies (DEC, 2007). Progress monitoring efforts can help a team understand the conditions under which a child can perform a skill or ability. It also allows team members to understand underlying motivations or reasons children behave or perform in a certain way. Finally, progress monitoring efforts can help team members understand the amount and kind of support that children need to make progress. That is, in order to make sound decisions about curriculum and instruction it is necessary to have solid and valid information on which to base those decisions. Progress monitoring efforts are important to systems change strategies related to RTI as described by Fuchs and Fuchs (2006). To make informed decisions regarding implementation of child-focused intervention strategies, teachers and others need solid information about the efficacy of general and specialized teaching strategies. There are a variety of ways to collect and record data about children's performance during these routines and activities. Most of these approaches rely on the careful observations of IECSE teachers or other adults that work with children.

Observation

Observation (also called, informally, *kid watching*) and the ability to record observations is a skill that many teachers learn as part of their preservice preparation program. Early childhood teachers often are challenged to find the time they need to observe young children in action, but they must recognize the value in sitting apart from an activity and simply watching what happens when children interact with materials and peers in their environment. IECSE teachers can learn a great deal about a child as well as the child's learning environment by observing. In addition, IECSE teachers can advocate for the importance of observation as they work with general ECE teachers or other adults who are with children on a daily basis. In some busy early childhood classrooms, time spent observing may be rare. To compensate, the IECSE teacher may take over the general early childhood teacher's responsibilities or work to find an "extra pair of hands" that will free time for the general early childhood teacher to observe.

Observers record the information they learn as they watch children. It is important to consider the ways in which information is recorded because it defines the types of information or data that results. For example, observers can tally the number of times a child pushes or shoves another child or they can write a descriptive account each time they observe an incident of pushing or shoving. The resulting information can be used in different ways. A tally system yields a frequency count; but, unless one can also record the time of day or the event in which the incident occurred, the observer does not obtain further information. Conversely, a descriptive account also could yield some information that may provide clues as to why the pushing or shoving occurred.

It is important to consider the ways in which information is recorded. As an assessor, an IECSE teacher must consider the various recording methods and choose one that is both effective (i.e., yields useful information) and efficient (i.e., can be realistically completed in the child's environment). Each recording method has benefits and drawbacks—the IECSE teacher and his or her partner must decide jointly on the best method to use. For example, Liz, a general early childhood teacher, might decide that she just does not have the time or resources to collect exhaustive data about Tyrone's verbal language use. She and Karen, an IECSE teacher, decide to use a tally system to record the number of times Tyrone labels a toy or object in the classroom during center time. Primary recording methods include the use of checklists, portfolios, anecdotal records, and various kinds of time-sampling methods.

In recording the results of observations, teachers must be cognizant of the need to separate fact from inference. For example, Susan, a general early childhood teacher, might observe Kerry hit another child and infer that Kerry is angry with the other child. Susan must be careful not to infer certain emotions or behavioral states based on observed behavior. She can record what she observed as well as her inference, but it is important for Susan or any other teacher to explicitly state the fact that the inference is tentative. She might write, "Kerry hit Javon in the housekeeping area. I wonder if she did that because she was angry at Javon." Recording the observation in this way helps to separate the fact from a possible reason that the behavior occurred.

In the next section, we review major types of alternative assessments. Losardo and Notari-Syverson (2001) defined three primary types of alternative assessments: 1) embedded approaches, 2) authentic approaches, and 3) mediated approaches.

Embedded Approaches

Embedded approaches are alternative assessments rooted in the everyday activities and routines that comprise a young child's day. Losardo and Notari-Syverson (2001) noted that activity-based (Pretti-Frontczak & Bricker, 2004) and play-based assessments (Linder, 1993) are two primary types of embedded approaches to assessment. Both approaches are *naturalistic* in that they use the child's interest in an activity or the environment as the context in which to observe and record information about a child's skills and abilities (Rule et al., 1998). Embedded approaches differ in intent in that activity-based intervention is related to intervening to promote or enhance children's developmental or academic progress, whereas play-based assessment usually takes place during initial or ongoing evaluations of children's progress.

Using an activity-based approach involves embedding individualized instruction related to IEP goals and objectives within the context of activities and routines that interest children. Professionals and other trained adults capitalize on a child's interest in an activity or routine to create a learning opportunity associated with the child's goal. Once the child demonstrates interest in the learning opportunity, the adult provides systematic prompting to the child so that he or she can elicit an appropriate response. For example, Colleen knows that Evan enjoys playing with blocks. She uses that information to find opportunities in the block area for Evan to use language to request materials from others. Activity-based intervention relies on the use of naturally occurring consequences to reinforce behaviors. Because some children seldom display interest in learning opportunities, professionals may entice children into a learning opportunity by modifying the environment. Such modifications can include controlling access to a desired object, introducing novelty into a situation, or violating a child's expectations for an activity (Rule, Utley, Qian, & Eastmond, 1999). Finally, professionals keep track of the child's response to the learning opportunity through the use of various types of data collection tools.

Curriculum-based assessment (CBA) also represents an embedded approach to assessment (Notari-Syverson & Losardo, 2008). A CBA approach involves assessing a child's performance related to a specific skill, ability, or behavior (McLean et al., 1996). Within a CBA approach, professionals monitor children's acquisition and use of developmentally based skills. Items in a CBA system are arranged hierarchically and represent a functional approach to skill acquisition and development. Notari-Syverson and Losardo identified examples of CBA approaches in the *Assessment, Evaluation, and Programming System* (*AEPS*; Bricker, 2002, as cited in Notari-Syverson & Losardo, 2008), the *Creative Curriculum for Preschool, Fourth Edition* (Dodge, Colker, & Heroman, 2002, as cited in Notari-Syverson & Losardo, 2008) and the *Preschool Child Observation Record, Second Edition* (HighScope Educational Research Foundation, 2003, as cited in Notari-Syverson & Losardo, 2008).

Authentic Approaches

Notari-Syverson and Losardo define *authentic approaches* as assessments that "document children's skills and abilities through the completion of real-life tasks in real-life contexts" (2008, p. 169). They recognize performance assessment and portfolio assessment as two examples of an authentic assessment approach. Both of these models involve the use of adults' informed judgments of children's abilities based on their behaviors as well as their permanent products (e.g., work samples). Results from performance assessments can include anecdotal notes, video or audio clips, or actual work products.

Portfolio assessment is often used as a way to document children's interests, abilities, and progress. Included in portfolios can be samples of children's work that document their progress toward meeting IEP objectives. For example, an art project may result in a picture that a child draws demonstrating pre-emergent writing skills. Alternatively, a teacher may take a photo of a child's block creation that demonstrates persistence and engagement in a task. Both of these are work samples that could be included in a portfolio and enable teachers and other team members to monitor children's progress. The Work Sampling System (Meisels, Jablon, Marsden, Dichtelmiller, & Dorfman, 1994 as cited in Notari-Syverson & Losardo, 2008) and the Ounce Scale (Meisels, Marsden, Dombro, Weston, & Jewkes, 2003, as cited in Notari-Syverson & Losardo, 2008) are examples of portfolio assessment systems. The Ounce Scale may be particularly useful because it includes opportunities to include observations from parents and teachers.

Mediated Approaches

Mediated approaches are identified by Notari-Syverson and Losardo (2008) as the final alternative assessment approach. The mediated assessment approach is one in which "guided teaching is used to provide information on children's responsiveness to instruction" (p. 170). A mediated approach is focused on the types of support children need to demonstrate or use a particular skill or behavior. A dynamic assessment is an example of a mediated approach. Notari-Syverson and Losardo defined *dynamic assessment* as "a child-focused, flexible method of observation and questioning aimed at determining not only what children are able to do but also at determining children's individual interests and needs and what adults can do to support their learning" (p. 171). Dynamic assessments are useful in documenting incremental progress toward meeting IEP goals and objectives. They involve repeated observations and documentation of the kinds of help children need to elicit a desired response. Progress is demonstrated as children need less-intensive kinds of support (e.g., a verbal prompt as opposed to a model or demonstration) or fewer incidences of support to reach a particular goal. For example, Joseph is 5 years old and is learning to zip his coat. Joseph's IECSE teacher, Amy, and his classroom teacher, Lilla, decide to track how much help Joseph needs to zip his coat, reasoning that they can monitor Joseph's performance by noting the kind of help that Joseph needs (e.g., hand over hand, modeling, verbal) to zip his coat. Amy and Lilla know that Joseph is making progress because he needs less and less help to zip his coat (and get outside!).

Taken together, the use of embedded, authentic, and dynamic approaches to assessment compose what Notari-Syverson and Losardo term a *"comprehensive ecological model of alternative assessment"* (2008, p. 168) that can be useful in monitoring children's ongoing progress as well as making curricular decisions regarding instruction and intervention. A model such as this also satisfies recommendations from the field (Bagnato & Neisworth, 2005; DEC, 2007) that no single form of assessment be used to make instructional decisions on children's behalf. The following section outlines key features of tools that IECSE teachers and their partners can use in recording data about children's skills, abilities, and interests.

Recording Information from Observations: Tools and Protocols

IECSE teachers are responsible for ensuring that the assessment systems they use yield useful information. As stated earlier, they may or may not have direct responsibilities for data collection, but they always have responsibilities to make sure that useful information is collected that can inform the use of intervention strategies. It is important that these assessment systems are efficient and do not produce unrealistic work demands on itinerant teachers themselves or on other adults who monitor children's progress. For this reason, IECSE teachers must have a solid understanding of the ways in which they can preserve or record information.

Narrative Records

A *narrative* is a rich, written description of an event or incident. In a narrative record, the observer tries to capture in writing as much as possible about an event while maintaining a high degree of objectivity. A narrative recording method often is used when teachers or other adults know little about a particular behavior or when the context of the event is important in understanding the behavior. Four types of narrative recording methods are described below.

Anecdotal Records

In some instances, teachers interested in the context of a behavior may choose to write a descriptive account of a specific incident. For example, Jared's teacher might observe Jared's attempts to engage another child in play and decide that the incident is important enough to record. An anecdotal record is a narrative accounting (usually a few sentences or a paragraph in length) of an incident, written objectively, that reflects key components of that incident (e.g., where, when, who, how). Wortham (2005) explained that an anecdotal record provides an accounting of a noteworthy event. Teachers and others who record an incident using an anecdotal note should be careful to describe the incident as objectively and descriptively as possible, avoiding inferences about behavior (although the teacher may choose to write a qualitative comment or inference clearly separate from the anecdotal record itself).

Running Record

Another type of narrative recording method is a *running record* (Wortham, 2005). A *running record* is a rich, descriptive account of an event. Teachers use a running record when they want to record everything possible about an event—what was happening in the classroom, who was involved, what they were doing, and so forth. Just as with an anecdotal record, a running record is an objective accounting of an event—free from inference or suppositions. Frequently a teacher may read back the running record and include inferential comments in an attempt to analyze key features of the incident. However, he or she is careful to separate the description of the event from his or her inferences or comments about it.

A-B-C Record

An A-B-C (Antecedent-Behavior-Consequence) record is used when a teacher is interested in understanding the functional relationship between a particular behavior and its antecedent (i.e., what happened before that might have precipitated it) and/or its consequence (i.e., what happened after that might have provided some type of reinforcement). It is a narrative recording of an event that includes a description of the behavior as well as a description of what happened immediately before and after the behavior occurred. For example, Jenny's IECSE teacher, Linda, observes Jenny hit another child on a fairly regular basis. She uses an A-B-C record to determine the reason why Jenny might be hitting. Using this method, she realizes that Jenny is probably hitting a peer when she wants the toy the other child has. Hitting results in obtaining the toy. Linda and Steve, Jenny's classroom teacher, can use this information to help Jenny find alternative (and more appropriate) ways to request objects from others. Teachers may use this method when a behavior occurs infrequently but at generally predictable times. For example, a teacher may use this type of recording method to understand a toddler's biting behavior.

Record of Type of Assistance Needed

For many young children with disabilities, progress is incremental. Interventions do not yield significant progress quickly and may be difficult to detect. In these instances, monitoring the type of assistance a child needs to respond correctly can be an effective way of determining whether an intervention is working. Instead of monitoring whether a child responds correctly, the adult records the type of help (e.g., full physical prompt, partial physical prompt, verbal prompt, reminder) the child needs to respond correctly. Because most interventions involve some type of mediation or assistance, seeing that a child moves from requiring a more intensive type of assistance to less intensive assistance signals that progress is being made (Wolery, 1996).

Event Sampling

Although narrative recording methods can provide rich, descriptive accounts of important events, sometimes the IEP team is interested in the occurrence of the behavior—when it occurs, how frequently it occurs, its intensity, or how long it occurs. In these cases, an event sampling approach to progress monitoring may be appropriate. For an event sampling approach to be effective, members of the IEP team must identify key dimensions of the behavior ahead of time. This means that the behavior must be *operationally defined* so that anyone who is observing the child can reach the same conclusion about specific dimensions of the behavior (Wolery, 1996). Some specific approaches to event sampling are detailed in the following sections.

Frequency Count

The most common type of event sampling method involves tallying the number of times a certain behavior occurs. For example, a teacher may be interested in the number of times a child attempts to leave the classroom. Tallying the behavior across the day can provide information about the frequency of the behavior. Teachers or parents can tally behavior in many different ways—writing check marks on a piece of paper, using a golf counter, or placing a paperclip in a cup or a pocket.

Interval Sampling Methods

Counting the number of times a behavior occurs across a day may be realistic if the behavior occurs infrequently; but if the behavior occurs frequently, the IECSE teacher and his or her partner may want to consider some type of interval recording method. An interval recording method involves separating time into distinct intervals (e.g., 15-minute increments) and then tallying 1) the number of times the behavior occurs in that interval (e.g., the number of times a child hit another child between 9:00 a.m. and 9:15 a.m.), 2) whether the behavior occurred at all during that interval (e.g., whether the child responded to another child's initiation at all between 9:00 a.m. and 9:15 a.m.), or 3) whether the behavior occurred at a specific instant (e.g., whether a child was meaningful engaged with a toy or activity at 9:00 a.m.). Teachers may choose a time of day that may be related to the behavior (e.g., the teacher knows that the behavior occurs more often during unstructured times of the day) and then may record the frequency of the behavior across the specified time of day (e.g., for the entire 45 minutes of center time) or a portion of that time (e.g., for a 15-minute segment of center time). Members of the IEP team, including the IECSE teacher, partner teachers, or parents, must decide on the recording method that *yields the most useful information with the greatest efficiency.* This can sometimes present a challenge. Choosing a recording method that is the most efficient or easiest to use (e.g., check to see if a child's diaper is dry every hour) yields some information but may not be the most useful information. Alternatively, certain recording methods (e.g., checking a child's diaper every 10 minutes) may yield more useful information but may be prohibitively time intensive.

Converting Raw Data

Wolery (1996) provided a useful overview of how progress-monitoring data can be converted to either percentage or rate. The IECSE teacher can divide the number of times a child responds correctly by the number of opportunities the child has to respond (e.g., the number of times a child answers a question correctly), yielding the percentage of correct responses. Percentages are easy to understand and can help members of the IEP team determine whether progress is being made. However, using percentages might be misleading because the number of correct responses is dependent on the number of opportunities a child has to respond. For example, a child who responds correctly to two out of two opportunities is performing at 100% correct. Another child may respond correctly across 10 opportunities, also resulting in 100% correct. Even though both children produced correct responses 100% of the time, we have more confidence that the child who has responded correctly 10 out of 10 times has mastered a skill than we have for a child who has responded correctly twice.

Rate

Rate is another way of interpreting progress monitoring data and refers to the number of responses over a given period of time (Wolery, 1996). For example, a teacher may be interested in a child's ability to climb stairs, and monitoring that behavior may show that the child can climb three stairs in a 5-minute interval. That child is climbing stairs at the rate of .6 stairs per minute. The teacher can use that data to track progress if speed in climbing stairs is important. Wolery noted that rate may be more useful than percentage because rate is not dependent on the number of opportunities provided and is a more sensitive measure of progress then percentage.

Duration

Sometimes members of the IEP team are most interested in the duration of a behavior—for example, how long the child remains engaged with a toy or play activity, how long a child tantrums, or how long it takes a child to eat a snack. If this is the case, timing the behavior is key (Wolery, 1996). Although interventionists do not need to record duration to the nanosecond, they do need to have an accurate way of assessing how long a behavior occurs. For this type of recording method to work, the behavior of interest must have a discrete beginning and ending. A stopwatch can be useful in these instances; the adult who is monitoring behavior starts the stopwatch when the behavior begins and stops the stopwatch when the behavior ends, recording the amount of time (e.g., 3 minutes, 45 seconds) that the behavior occurred.

Latency

For some behaviors, the IEP team is most interested in the *latency* of a child's response, for example, how long it takes a child to respond to a request or a prompt to engage in a behavior. This may be particularly useful when the IEP team is concerned about compliance issues. For example, members of the IEP team may be interested in recording how long it takes a child to respond to a directive or a request. In this case, timing is also important, but the key dimension to record is the amount of time that occurs between the directive being issued (e.g., "Please clean up the blocks") to the child responding to the directive (e.g., begins to clean up blocks). Again, for this to be a valid measure, behaviors must have discrete beginnings and endings. A stopwatch is also useful in these instances.

Reliability Is Important

We strongly emphasize the importance of all members of the IEP team discussing and reaching consensus on an operational definition of a behavior. Convergent assessment (Bagnato, Neisworth, & Munson, 1997) is an important dimension of authenticity and refers to the validity of results across different situations or environments. For example, an IEP team may have greater confidence that a child can follow two-step directions if parents report that the child can follow two-step directions at home and the general early childhood teacher reports that the child can follow two-step directions in the classroom. For this to occur, everyone involved in monitoring progress must agree on a common definition of "following two-step directions" and use that definition to monitor progress. If different members of the team use a different definition of what it means to follow a two-step direction (e.g., with prompts versus independently), then the validity of the progress monitoring efforts will be suspect.

Checklists and Rating Scales

Another way that IECSE teachers and their partners might use to monitor progress involves using tools such as checklists or rating scales. Both of these tools involve ways of recording information with less specificity than the observational methods described above (Odom & Munson, 1996). These tools require adults to make judgments about the quality of a child's behavior or skill level and can be quite useful in tracking progress. Odom and Munson suggested that checklists and rating scales require adults to make more holistic judgments about behaviors or skills that occur over a longer period of time as opposed to recording the presence or absence of behaviors as they occur. Checklists and rating scales are discussed separately below.

Checklists

Checklists are commonly used to track the presence or absence of a set of behaviors. They include multiple items that are grouped hierarchically, that is, in some kind of meaningful order. For example, a developmental checklist may include items that reflect behaviors that occur at certain times during infancy and early childhood. These items may be grouped according to developmental domains (e.g., language, fine motor, gross motor) and may begin with behaviors that occur early in development or with more simple behaviors or skills that form the foundation for later, more complex behaviors or skills. Checklists involve a binary response (e.g., yes or no), although some checklists might also provide an opportunity to note whether a behavior or skill is emerging. Teachers or other adults can devise checklists that are useful in tracking progress for a group of children. Commercially developed checklists are also useful in understanding key behaviors that occur developmentally and can be useful in helping others understand the scope and sequence of development. For checklists to be most useful, statements or items must be worded in such a way as to ensure that anyone using the checklist would record the child's behavior in the same way.

Rating Scales

Both *rating scales* and checklists involve making judgments about a child's behavior or performance. They also both reflect the scope and sequence of a set of behaviors or skills. Rating scales differ from checklists, however, in the sensitivity of the judgment made. Although a checklist requires adults to simply note the presence or absence of a behavior or skill, a rating scale requires the adult to rate the quality of the behavior or skill, thus providing more specific information than a checklist. Rating scales involve the use of a numerical scale with numbers on the scale representing certain dimensions of that behavior. The scale can be more global (i.e., have fewer numbers on the scale) or more specific (i.e., have more numbers on the scale). The more numbers used on the scale results in a scale that can better discriminate progress. For example, a rating scale with five rating points will provide more information than a rating scale with three rating points. Key to a quality rating scale, however, are the descriptions that anchor each numerical rating. To be useful, these anchors must be descriptive and precise, enabling different members of the team to rate a behavior or skill consistently and reliably. These anchors form rubrics that delineate qualitatively different key features or dimensions of the behavior. IEP teams can develop rating scales or rubrics that reflect important behaviors or skills—having discussions to develop these descriptors can be useful in helping the team reach consensus about what is important.

Helping Adults Stay on Track: Monitoring Adult Behavior

In this book we argue that the best use of an IECSE teacher's time is helping other adults who work more closely with children learn to use intervention strategies that will result in enhanced academic and developmental progress. This belief is articulated by others as well (Jung, 2003; McWilliam, 1996, 2005) and emphasizes the importance of tracking adult behavior as well as children's behavior. The success of an intervention depends on its implementation, both in terms of quantity (i.e., frequency) and quality (i.e., fidelity). As such, an important task of an IECSE teacher is helping to ensure that interventions are implemented as planned, usually in his or her absence. This presents a challenge, that is, how to ensure that interventions are being delivered as planned in between itinerant visits.

Helping other adults keep track of their own behaviors (i.e., implementation of planned child-focused interventions) is another responsibility of IECSE teachers that falls under the role of assessor. For example, Mary, Jon's IECSE teacher, and Lisa, Jon's classroom teacher, both agree that it is important for Lisa to use a specific intervention during snack time on a regular basis. Mary helps Lisa develop a form that will give Lisa the opportunity to document each time she uses this intervention at snack time. This information provides evidence that IEP-focused interventions are being used. Many of the same strategies discussed earlier for recording the results of child-focused observations are also appropriate for tracking adult behavior; however, a key difference is that IECSE teachers must expect the adults with whom they work to self-monitor their implementation of a child-focused intervention strategy. Therefore, these monitoring strategies must be easy and nonaversive to use. In its simplest form, self-monitoring involves 1) identification of key behaviors that are targeted for change and 2) objectively recording the presence or absence of the key behavior (King-Sears, 2008; Mooney, Ryan, Uhing,

Reid, & Epstein, 2005; Suk-Hyang, Palmer, & Wehmeyer, 2009; Wilkinson, 2008). IECSE teachers can help adults with whom they work (e.g., general early childhood teachers, parents) learn to monitor their use of child-focused intervention strategies to ensure that these strategies are implemented as intended.

Self-monitoring is one component of a self-determination strategy that assists learners (e.g., general education teachers or parents interested in learning to implement child-focused intervention strategies) in incorporating new routines or behaviors into their daily routine. Kalis, Vannest, and Parker (2007) reported the efficacy of using a self-monitoring procedure to increase the amount of praise used by a high school teacher of students with emotional and behavior disorders. The researchers taught the teacher to monitor (i.e., identify and record the occurrence of) her use of praise statements in her high school classroom. They reported significant increases in the teacher's use of praise statements as a result of the self-monitoring strategies. In addition, the teacher who participated reported that the strategy was easy to use and helped her to become more aware of her behaviors in the classroom.

Summary

Making informed decisions about a child's educational progress is a primary responsibility of any teacher. Educational assessment takes many forms and is conducted for different purposes. This chapter focuses on informal assessments used to make curricular and instructional decisions. IECSE teachers and those they work with must work together to decide on the best ways to collect meaningful data to use for making good decisions. In the role of assessor, the IECSE teacher directly collects information and also helps those he or she works with to collect meaningful information. In addition to collecting data on child behaviors, IECSE teachers also can help other adults with whom they work to monitor their use of interventions and other instructional strategies in the IECSE teacher's absence.

CHAPTER 7

The IECSE Teacher as Service Coordinator

Through the Delphi study described in Chapter 3 (Dinnebeil et al., 2006b), service coordination emerged as a role for IECSE teachers. Participants in the Delphi study identified a range of activities (e.g., arranging transportation, coordinating related services, visiting other classrooms in preparation for transition) that can best be termed *service coordination.* Although these activities might not be directly related to educational strategies and interventions, they are important to support the child's success in his or her learning environment. Among their job-related responsibilities, IECSE teachers often are assigned to coordinate services identified on the child's IEP. This can include transportation services as well as related and supplementary services. Through the consultation process outlined in Chapter 4, IECSE teachers often find themselves helping parents and others identify and gain access to community resources that support the child's developmental and academic progress. Finally, IECSE teachers often are tasked with coordinating the transition process as children move out of preschool services and into school-age services. In this chapter, we discuss these responsibilities in more depth.

Service Coordination in Early Intervention

A definition of service coordination is essential to understanding how the IECSE teacher's role as a service coordinator can be put into place and made effective. Service coordination is provided to families of infants and toddlers with special needs who receive Part C services under IDEA 2004 (PL 108-446). Families enrolled in Part C early intervention programs are entitled to the assistance of a service coordinator who helps the family gain access to services and resources to which they are entitled under the state's Part C program.

Dunst and Bruder (2002) conducted a survey of early intervention professionals and consumers (i.e., parents whose families received early intervention services). The purpose of the survey was to identify desired outcomes of three Part C activities: 1) service coordination, 2) early intervention, and 3) natural environment practices. The results of their study indicated that six variables can be considered desired outcomes of Part C service coordination. Those variables include the following:

1. *Systems coordination*: Coordinating funding sources, collaboration among personnel across agencies, and integration of services into the child's daily routines and activities. For example, the service coordinator would file third-party billing reports so that Medicare funds could be disbursed on behalf of the child receiving services through an individualized family service plan (IFSP).

2. *Information and referral*: Providing information to families as well as referring them to relevant community resources. For example, the service coordinator might assist the parents of a young child with a disability in finding pro bono legal aid through a community law center.

3. *Family support and resources:* Providing resources and supports that positively affect family outcomes. For example, the service coordinator might make recommendations about good pediatricians for a family wishing to change doctors.

4. *Family-centered practices*: Providing information so that families can make informed choices, providing flexible services that meet families' needs, and being responsive to families' priorities and concerns. For example, the service coordinator might make recommendations to a family about the practical issues of providing services in the home to a child with a disability.

5. *Teaming*: Facilitating the communication and coordination of activities among agency professionals. For example, the service coordinator might need to help bridge a rift based on personal differences between a speech-language pathologist and an occupational therapist.

6. *Family satisfaction*: Helping to improve the family's overall satisfaction with child-focused as well as family-focused services. For example, the service coordinator might want to e-mail or call the family to check in (outside the purview of legally mandated contact).

Achieving these identified outcomes is accomplished by implementing a set of service coordination practices also identified by Dunst and Bruder (2006). Through extensive field-based research with professionals and family members, Dunst and Bruder identified 67 service coordination practices (i.e., tasks, activities, responsibilities) that fell into the following nine categories:

1. Providing IFSPs

2. Overseeing and monitoring early intervention service provision

3. Coordinating and facilitating early intervention services

4. Family participation and decision making regarding IFSPs and service provision

5. Providing information to families about early intervention and related services

6. Providing information to families about opportunities for children's learning

7. Planning for and assisting with the transition from early intervention to preschool services

8. Providing information and assistance regarding children's health care

9. Providing information and assistance regarding child care

Characteristics of Effective Service Coordinators

Not surprisingly, the same characteristics that contribute to effective consultation also contribute to effective collaboration between parents and service coordinators. Dinnebeil and her colleagues (Dinnebeil, Fox, & Rule, 1998; Dinnebeil, Hale, & Rule, 1996; Dinnebeil & Rule, 1994) conducted a series of studies focused on identifying variables that contributed to and detracted from effective collaboration between parents and service coordinators in early intervention. Even though the focus of these studies was on Part C early intervention programs, it is logical to assume that the results would remain valid for collaborative relationships between parents (and/or general education teachers) and IECSE teachers who coordinate services for families and teachers. Parents and professionals identified characteristics that contribute to effective collaboration between parents and service coordinators, such as

- Good interpersonal skills

- Interpersonal style

- General friendliness

- Patience

- Sincerity

- Open-mindedness

In addition, interpersonal practices such as timeliness, follow-through, and tact contributed to effective collaboration between parents and service coordinators.

Similarities and Differences Between Early Intervention and IECSE Service Coordination

Although the focus of this chapter is on service coordination for IECSE teachers and *not* early interventionists, it is helpful to consider the outcomes and practices identified above when thinking about how IECSE teachers can serve as service coordinators. Just as early intervention service coordinators help to monitor and oversee implementation of the family's IFSP, so does an IECSE teacher help to monitor implementation of the IEP.[1] Within Part C early intervention programs, service coordinators assist parents and family members. A key difference we are proposing is that IECSE teachers provide service coordination to other adults in addition to parents who work with the child—adults such as general early childhood teachers and child care providers. Helping parents and other teachers find information and gain access to resources to support the child's developmental and academic progress is an important role for IECSE teachers, as is coordinating related services such as speech-language, occupational, and/or physical therapy as well as logistical services such as transportation and child care. In addition, the

---

[1]We have often found that IECSE teachers resist the idea of indirect or triadic service delivery because they believe that "implementing the IEP" means they have ultimate responsibility for ensuring that intervention is provided. We argue that for children served by itinerant personnel, "implementing the IEP" means coordinating services and helping to ensure that team members are appropriately fulfilling their responsibilities.

IECSE teacher serves a vital role when it is time for the child to transition from a preschool to a kindergarten or other early childhood program. Therefore, we propose the following as service coordination responsibilities of IECSE teachers:

- Coordinating and monitoring the delivery of services as indicated on the IEP

- Providing relevant and helpful information to parents and other adults who work with the child

- Helping parents and other adults (e.g., general education teachers) gain access to community resources that will enhance child outcomes or make it easier to provide high-quality services in the LRE

- Helping the child and family when it is time to transition from a preschool program to a school-age program such as kindergarten

The tasks and responsibilities laid out above are discussed in more detail in the following sections.

Coordinating and Monitoring Services Indicated on the IEP

Under IDEA (PL 101-476) and its subsequent amendments (including IDEA 2004 [PL 108-446]), school districts or LEAs bear the ultimate responsibility for ensuring that services outlined on the child's IEP are delivered as specified. As such, it is important that school district personnel such as IECSE teachers monitor the delivery of services as indicated on the child's IEP. This can include ensuring that therapies (e.g., speech-language services, occupational therapy, physical therapy, audiological services) are being provided as planned and that the child has access to all of the services and supports indicated on his or her IEP. It also includes ensuring that these services and supports are provided according to timelines identified on the IEP and by individuals who are qualified to provide these supports. IECSE teachers who are responsible for coordinating and monitoring services must develop procedures and processes for checking in with other team members, including parents, to ensure smooth and effective service delivery. They are also responsible for monitoring paperwork (e.g., third party billing reports, indirect services logs) to make sure the district is in compliance with federal, state, and local regulations.

Communication across all members of the child's IEP team is essential for smooth and effective service delivery. Fortunately, access to e-mail and other digital tools can make collaboration and communication across team members easier. Professionals can use telephone calls, e-mail, instant messaging, text messaging, and even social media tools such as Twitter and Facebook to ensure productive communication. Many (if not most) parents have access to some sort of technology such as a computer, e-mail, or a cell phone and can use these tools, as well. Access to technology varies according to the size of the district. Some large districts operate online IEP systems that allow team members to gain access to the IEP and document service delivery via a web-based, password-protected system. Other smaller districts have yet to adopt these high-tech solutions but find creative and effective ways to ensure that everyone on the IEP team is "on the same page" when it comes to delivering high-quality services.

Providing Helpful and Relevant Information

The best IECSE teachers are information brokers. They are not only knowledgeable about a wide range of issues related to early childhood special education but also they know how to gain access to information that they can share with others. Again, the Internet has changed the way that we gather and share information. Online access to academic and professional journals is commonplace with tools such as *Google Scholar* and *Google Book*. In addition, federally funded organizations serve as information clearinghouses for early intervention and early childhood special education. A brief list of some of these organizations is provided at the end of this chapter.

Not only must IECSE teachers have access to a wide range of information, available in many formats, but they must also be able to match the needs of the consumer with the appropriate type of information in the appropriate format. For example, if an early childhood teacher needs information about a specific disability condition, then perhaps a two-page information brief from the National Dissemination Center for Children with Disabilities (NICHCY) is appropriate. However, if that early childhood teacher needs to learn how to use a specific intervention strategy, then a video clip or videotape of someone demonstrating the use of this strategy would be appropriate. In addition to choosing the format of the information (e.g., video-based versus print-based), IECSE teachers must consider the literacy and interest levels of the person who needs the information. Parents or early childhood teachers who have limited literacy levels might need written information that is provided in simplified form. IECSE teachers might have to take the same two-page information brief downloaded from NICHCY and rewrite it (providing appropriate attribution to NICHCY) in a simplified form so it is useful to unskilled readers. By the same token, the IECSE teacher might have to highlight relevant information from that two-page information brief for readers who are too busy to read through the entire document.

Gaining Access to Community Resources

Supporting early childhood inclusion is difficult yet rewarding work. In 1996, Hillary Clinton reminded us that "[i]t takes a village to raise a child," and the same is true for early childhood inclusion. For inclusion to work, most parents and teachers need access to community resources—resources that provide the extra support and additional help needed. This help might consist of an extra pair of hands to help in the early childhood classroom during a busy time of the day or someone who can modify a piece of equipment so that a child can use it appropriately. It might consist of a visit to another early childhood classroom to see an intervention strategy in practice. Whatever it is, IECSE teachers must be prepared to 1) know about the situation and 2) gain access to resources for the adults with whom they work. For this reason, it is important that IECSE teachers be aware of the different kinds of resources available in their communities. Under federal Part C regulations, communities must have in place local interagency coordinating councils (ICCs). LEAs are required to have representation on these councils, and IECSE teachers make good LEA representatives because of their knowledge of practice and because their schedules do not necessarily tie them to one location throughout the day. Local ICC meetings provide opportunities for ICC members to learn about new and existing resources in their communities and provide ways for members to meet and network with key individuals from social services organizations who might help them gain access to these resources. Examples of good community resources might include the following:

- Parent-to-parent support groups

- Child care resource and referral agencies

- Special education resource centers

- Early childhood behavioral health experts

- Private therapy providers

- Local and/or regional affiliates of the National Association for the Education of Young Children (NAEYC)

- Professors and instructors at local colleges and universities who work with prospective teachers or others interested in helping young children and their families

- United Way personnel

- Head Start personnel

Helping to Support Effective Transitions

Transitioning into a kindergarten or other early childhood program is an exciting, complex, and often stressful time for children, their families, and their teachers (Pianta & Kraft-Sayre, 2003). This is true for all children, regardless of ability levels, but can be intensified when the child has a special need and an IEP. Transitioning from one program should be a positive time, signaling that the child is growing and developing and ready for the next step in his or her educational journey. However, children, families, and their teachers can view transition as a bumpy road if careful planning and execution do not occur. It often falls on the shoulders of the IECSE teacher to make sure that transitions are smooth and positive experiences for everyone involved.

Rous and her colleagues (Rous & Hallam, 2006; Rous, Hallam, Harbin, McCormick, & Jung, 2007; Rous, Myers, & Stricklin, 2007) have studied the process of transition carefully and extensively and contribute much to what we know about high-quality transition practices. A key concept underlying successful transition is that of collaborative linkages between agencies and programs. Rous, Myers, and Stricklin (2007) argued that "transition is viewed as occurring within contexts where collaborative linkages are established between preschools, elementary schools and others in the community in ways that support congruency across programs" (2007, p. 2). Rous and her colleagues identified three key elements in a successful transition experience: 1) critical interagency variables (which include alignment and continuity, communication and collaboration, and supportive infrastructure); 2) child and family preparation and adjustment; and 3) standard transition practices, strategies, and activities. Each is briefly described in more detail below.

Critical Interagency Variables

Transitions will be successful when individuals from key agencies can work together effectively. One of the key aspects of early childhood programs that can make transitions difficult is that many are community-based programs that exist outside of LEA jurisdiction. Moving from preschool to kindergarten is much more difficult than moving from kindergarten to first grade because there are multiple agencies involved. For this reason, it is critical that LEAs work collaboratively with community-based early care and education programs (both publicly supported programs such as Head Start as well as private for-profit and not-for-profit centers) to ensure alignment and continuity for children and families. Over the past 20 years, there has been a growing appreciation of the importance of building an early care and education "system" in which birth-to-5 programs partner with school districts and LEAs to ensure continuity and curriculum alignment (Child Care and Early Education Research Connections, 2007). Increasing the strength of these partnerships is the key to smooth and successful transitions.

In addition to collaborative partnerships and alignment across programs, it is important that agencies have the infrastructure in place to engage in effective transition practices (Rous, Hallam, et al., 2007). That is, both programs (the sending and receiving programs) should have the support available to guide children and families through the transition process, whether that entails freeing teachers to accompany families on visits to other programs or organizing parent information meetings. Administrators must recognize the importance of smooth and positive transitions and should be willing to work with families to make this happen. Finally, all early care and education programs should be based on a philosophy of collaboration and the belief that one of the goals of an early childhood program is to prepare young learners to be successful in their next educational setting.

Preparing and Supporting Children and Families

Another key element in the transition process that Rous, Hallam and colleagues (2007) identified was preparing and supporting children and their families for a successful transition. Preparing and supporting children entails making sure that they have the foundational skills they need to be successful in their next learning environment. These include self-help, self-regulatory, and social skills (McClelland, Acock, & Morrison, 2006). For example, as Kenyon's IECSE teacher, Jamie is concerned about his successful transition to kindergarten in the fall. Jamie and Ruth, Kenyon's mother, visit three different kindergarten classrooms that could be options for the next school year. Jamie shares information with Ruth about what to look for in high-quality classrooms, and they both agree that Mrs. Clarke's classroom could provide a great learning environment for Kenyon. They, along with Kim, Kenyon's preschool teacher, meet with Mrs. Clarke to discuss her expectations for Kenyon's success. Mrs. Clarke emphasizes how much she appreciates having children with different abilities in her classroom and stresses that one of the things that will help Kenyon be successful is his ability follow simple directions and interact with other children appropriately. Jamie, Ruth, and Kim discuss what they can do to help prepare Kenyon for a successful kindergarten experience.

Fortunately, the importance of preparing children for success in kindergarten is a goal of many high-quality community-based early care and education programs. However, young children with disabilities may need support above and beyond what is usually provided to their typically developing peers. IECSE teachers must work with partner teachers to make sure that children with disabilities are appropriately prepared for success in kindergarten.

In addition to preparing children, IECSE teachers also are tasked with making sure that families are appropriately prepared for a transition to kindergarten (Rous, Hallam,

Table 7.1. Effective transition practices

Category of transition strategy	Effective transition practices
Preparing for transition	Teachers and families participate in meetings about transition
	Teachers and families share information
	Teachers and families participate in transition workshops
Program visits	Family visits
	Child visits
	Staff visits
Instructional activities	Programwide activities
	Child-specific activities
Community resources	Resources related to disability and/or parental rights
	Community and neighborhood resources
	Parent support groups

Source: Rous, Myers, and Stricklen (2007).

et al., 2007). Parents and family members need information about options for their child's next learning environment. This information can and should consist of written information that parents can read at their leisure, but it also means visits to classrooms to make decisions about the "goodness of fit" between the child's temperament and abilities, the teacher's skills and style, and the overall quality of the environment.

Transition Activities, Strategies, and Practices

Through the work of the National Early Childhood Transition Center (NECTC), Rous, Myers and Stricklin (2007) conducted a national social validation study that focused on identifying effective practices that teachers and administrators use to facilitate smooth transition between early childhood programs. Through this study, they identified a set of four categories of transition strategies and, within those categories, a set of practices validated as effective. These are included in Table 7.1.

Summary

IECSE teachers play important roles as service coordinators as they support high-quality inclusion in early childhood programs. As service coordinators, IECSE teachers ensure the smooth delivery of services outlined on the child's IEP and monitor the delivery of these services. They also share information with parents and general early childhood teachers—information related to children's disabilities as well as information about community resources. As such, IECSE teachers need to be "tuned in to" community resources that could support young children with disabilities and their families. They can do this by being active in cross-agency groups such as local interagency coordinating councils or other community-based networks. Finally, an important responsibility of an IECSE teacher is helping children, families, and staff to prepare for successful transitions into kindergarten or other early childhood programs. Successful transition depends on interagency collaboration; alignment and curriculum continuity across early childhood programs; and effective transition practices, which include helping children learn the skills they need to be successful in kindergarten, sharing information with parents and staff, and facilitating visits to receiving classrooms. The skills and dispositions that support effective collaboration between service coordinators and parents mirror those that have been identified as being associated with effective early childhood consultation.

Resources

The list below provides a brief sampling of the vast number of web sites IECSE teachers can provide to parents, partner teachers, and other interested stakeholders. A word of caution about the Internet: Although the web sites below are professionally oriented and widely cited and vetted, many Internet resources are *not*. It should be part of the service coordinator's role to make certain that he or she provides not only useful but also valid and accurate sources of information.

- Autism Speaks (http://www.autismspeaks.org)

- Center for Applied Special Technology (CAST; http://www.cast.org)

- Center for Early Literacy Learning (CELL; http://www.earlyliteracylearning.org)

- Center on the Social and Emotional Foundations for Early Learning (CSEFEL; http://www.vanderbilt.edu/csefel)

- Circle of Inclusion (http://www.circleofinclusion.org)

- Council for Exceptional Children (CEC; http://www.cec.sped.org)

- Early Childhood Research Institute on Culturally and Linguistically Appropriate Services (CLAS; http://www.clas.uiuc.edu)

- Division for Early Childhood of the Council for Exceptional Children (DEC; http://www.dec-sped.org)

- National Dissemination Center for Children with Disabilities (NICHCY; http://www.nichcy.org)

- National Early Childhood Technical Assistance Center (NECTAC; http://www.nectac.org)

- National Early Childhood Transition Center (NECTC; http://www.hdi.uky.edu/NECTC)

- National Institute for Early Education Research (NIEER; http://www.nieer.org)

- Pacer Center (http://www.pacer.org)

- Technical Assistance Center on Social Emotional Intervention for Young Children (TACSEI; http://www.challengingbehavior.org)

- What Works Clearinghouse (WWC) Early Childhood Education (http://ies.ed.gov/ncee/wwc/reports/topic.aspx?tid=13)

CHAPTER 8

The IECSE
Teacher as Team Member

Teaming in early childhood special education and early intervention is a highly valued activity and is a required activity under IDEA 2004 (PL 108-446). Individuals may decide to form any number of different educational teams—curriculum teams, grade-level teams, and intervention assistant teams (Friend & Cook, 2000), to name a few. In this chapter, we focus on one particular team—the IEP team. The purpose of this chapter is to briefly review models of team functioning and recommended practices for early childhood teaming and describe the IECSE teacher's role in early childhood IEP teams. This chapter also will describe a model of team process that has led to positive outcomes for students in inclusive general education programs.

Major Team Models in ECSE

Friend and Cook defined an educational team as a "set of interdependent individuals with unique skills and perspectives who interact directly to achieve their mutual goal of providing students with effective educational programs and services" (2000, p. 28). Central to the concept of teaming are the notions of *interdependence* and *collaboration*. That is, members of a team depend on one another to achieve the team's goals and to provide effective services to students with disabilities. The notion of *interdependence* is predicated on the assumption that team members collaborate with each other. Although collaboration is a somewhat subjective phenomenon, Friend and Cook (2000) described several characteristics that serve to define collaborative relationships. First, collaboration is a voluntary activity—team members work together without a directive or requirement to do so. School district personnel may require team members to work together, but only the individual team members can make the decision to collaborate. Secondly, successful collaboration relies on the belief that all members of the team have unique and necessary talents, skills, knowledge, and perspectives that will enable the team to reach its jointly identified goals. Third, members of a collaborative team share decision-making responsibilities and resources. Fourth and finally, in addition to sharing responsibilities and resources, collaborative team members share accountability in the outcomes achieved by the team. In a collaborative team, everyone can take pride in a job well done or shoulder responsibility when an outcome is not reached.

Individuals who effectively collaborate with each other are generally those individuals who have the sort of interpersonal style that promotes effective communication. It is the kind of interpersonal style we have already discussed that characterizes effective consultants, coaches, and service coordinators (see Chapters 4, 5, and 7, respectively). Successful collaborators are individuals who are good listeners and communicators. They are open to new ideas and do not seek to control a situation. They enjoy working with others and find ways to do so effectively. Successful collaborators are trustworthy and take their responsibilities to others seriously. They reliably follow through on assigned tasks and are consistently dependable.

A Look at an Effective Team

Caroline, Mark, Debbie, and Marian are all members of Kerry's IEP team. Caroline is Kerry's IECSE teacher, Mark is Kerry's father, Debbie is Kerry's classroom teacher, and Marian is Kerry's speech-language pathologist. These team members have been working together since August to support Kerry's success in Debbie's preschool classroom. Although they seldom have the opportunity to all meet at the same time, they try to communicate with each other on a regular basis. Marian visits Kerry's classroom on Wednesday afternoons to observe Kerry's in-class speech abilities, and Caroline visits on Tuesday mornings to observe Kerry's progress with IEP goals and to consult with Debbie. They document what happens during those visits and share those notes with everyone on the team. In addition to helping Debbie find ways to help Kerry in the classroom, Caroline, Marian, and Debbie provide Mark with information about things he can do to help Kerry at home. They try to make sure that they are using the same kinds of intervention strategies consistently with Kerry at home and at school and work with each other to make changes as necessary.

Recently, Mark reported that Kerry was having difficulty playing with her cousins when they visited every weekend. Debbie noted that Kerry sometimes has difficulty playing with other children in the classroom, especially if she has to share toys or materials. Debbie and Mark talk about things they can do to help Kerry play more successfully and decide that they also need to check in with Caroline (the IECSE teacher) and Marian (the speech-language pathologist) to see if they have other suggestions. Marian suggests using a visual reminder to help Kerry remember to share her toys with others. They agree to use the same visual reminder at home and at school to make it easier for Kerry to learn. Caroline also suggests tracking Kerry's success with the visual reminder so they all know if the strategy is working. They agree to e-mail each other on Monday mornings to report how well Kerry has done with sharing in the previous week.

The degree to which team members work together and depend on each other characterizes three major models of team functioning: 1) multidisciplinary teaming, 2) interdisciplinary teaming, and 3) transdisciplinary teaming (Jordan, Gallagher, Hutinger, & Karnes, 1988). According to Friend and Cook (2000), all three of these models share certain characteristics. In all of these models, team members are aware that they are a member of the team and operate under a set of shared norms and expectations for functioning. It is critical that all team members are aware of and accept these shared norms; the degree to which the team can reach its goal is compromised if one or more individuals operate outside of the team's expectations.

Multidisciplinary Teams

A multidisciplinary team is one that is comprised of a number of individuals who represent distinct disciplines and have unique skills, knowledge, and perspectives that help the team achieve its goal. In the field of early childhood special education, a multidisciplinary team can include an IECSE teacher, one or more parents, a general education teacher, and other related service providers (e.g., occupational therapist, speech-language pathologist) as appropriate. Multidisciplinary teams work together toward a shared goal or outcome, but team members function somewhat independently in providing services to children and families (Jordan et al., 1988). Members focus somewhat exclusively on their own areas of expertise and do not work to intentionally integrate their services (Friend & Cook, 2000). Consequently, one of the pitfalls of the multidisciplinary team is a somewhat isolated approach to service delivery that may be difficult for teachers and family members to implement.

Interdisciplinary Teams

Interdisciplinary teams share many characteristics of multidisciplinary and transdisciplinary teams (e.g., team composition, shared goal, common expectations). However, members of interdisciplinary teams more often coordinate and integrate services than their colleagues who serve on multidisciplinary teams (Jordan et al., 1988). Members of interdisciplinary teams are more likely to communicate with each other on a regular basis and base their recommendations and approach to service delivery with other discipline's services in mind. Consequently, service delivery to students and their families is more coordinated and discrete services complement each other. For example, an occupational therapist's service delivery plan may be based on the routines and daily activities of the general early childhood teacher.

Transdisciplinary Teams

Transdisciplinary teams represent the most sophisticated form of teaming and are characterized by close coordination of services and a more holistic approach to service delivery. Members of transdisciplinary teams blend discrete services and integrate them into the child's daily routines and activities. In addition to fully integrated services, transdisciplinary team members engage in a process known as *role release* (Jordan et al., 1988), a concept that is central to a consultative approach to IECSE service delivery. *Role release* involves combining two or more professional roles (Friend & Cook, 2000) to coordinate and improve services to students with disabilities and their families. Members of transdisciplinary teams share their expertise with others on the child's IEP team who provide direct services to the child. They are available as consultants to the primary service provider and offer advice and performance feedback as necessary.

For example, in a transdisciplinary model, the occupational therapist would, through a process of coaching and consultation, teach the general education teacher how to deliver interventions designed to improve a child's fine motor skills. The occupational therapist would be available to work with the general education teacher in refining or modifying the interventions as necessary, but the general education teacher would be the individual who delivers the interventions on a routine basis. As one might expect, successful transdisciplinary teams work closely together, sharing knowledge and expertise that will benefit the student and his or her family. This process of integrated service delivery is the approach most advocated by leaders in early intervention and early childhood special education (McWilliam, 1996a; McWilliam, 2005).

Key Elements of Effective Team Functioning

Regardless of the team model under which team members operate, certain practices predict effective team functioning. The DEC identifies a number of recommended practices that focus on interdisciplinary team models (McWilliam, 2005). These practices are summarized next and provide guidance about how teams should operate to best serve young children with disabilities and their families:

1. *Teams make decisions and work together to plan, deliver, and evaluate services. All team members participate in developing the IEP, from beginning to end.* Team members are respectful of others' schedules and function in ways that support trust and effective communication. For example, an effective team makes an effort to ensure that everyone on the team is available for meetings, regardless of how difficult it is to schedule.

2. *Professionals learn from each other and cross disciplinary boundaries to engage in role release.* They are also willing to accept responsibility to deliver services that are outside of their professional discipline. They work in a transdisciplinary fashion to make sure that the services they design are integrated and coordinated into a single plan that can be implemented by primary service providers (including family members). For example, an occupational therapist on an effective team might work with the general early childhood teacher, teaching her how to deliver occupational therapy services throughout the day when the occupational therapist is not there.

3. *Team members design individually appropriate and age-appropriate intervention plans based on the child's needs and the context of their environment, not on the services available by a particular LEA or school district.* Team members make sure to identify services that help the child to be successful in his or her primary learning environment and continually monitor the effectiveness of these services, changing them as necessary as the child's skills develop or the primary learning environment changes. Priorities for services depend on what the child needs to succeed in his or her environment, not what is readily available. Team members take into account children's individualized needs (and not simply the nature of their disability) when making decisions about supplementary aids and supports. In addition, team members jointly decide on the *most normalized* intervention that can be delivered as easily and unobtrusively as possible to ease the degree of disruption to the child and family's life. Finally, team members recognize the importance of consultation and indirect services delivery in meeting children's needs. For example, members of an effective team make it a point to understand the child's daily schedule at home and use that schedule to plan interventions.

4. *Team members recognize that primary caregivers and teachers as well as typical routines provide the most appropriate setting for service delivery.* They recognize the importance of what happens everyday, not just during times when the child receives specialized services. Team members recognize the importance of all team members, including primary caregivers and family members or whomever the child spends most of their time (McWilliam, 2005). Members of effective teams recognize how important

daily routines at home are to the child's well-being and success and work to provide suggestions and modify recommendations to accommodate those routines and activities.

IECSE Teachers and the IEP Development Process

The role of team member is an important one for IECSE teachers (Dinnebeil et al., 2006b). Very often, IECSE teachers are the ones with responsibility for coordinating the process that leads to the development of the child's IEP. For this reason, we discuss how IECSE teachers can best work with others to design an effective IEP that will provide guidance to the team and enable children to reach developmental and academic outcomes.

Because the IECSE teacher interacts so frequently with other team members (e.g., parents, general education teachers, related service providers), he or she is often called on to coordinate the development of the IEP (Dinnebeil et al., 2006b). Given this important responsibility, it makes sense to understand the process of IEP development as well as elements of an IEP that will support effective service delivery. Turnbull, Turnbull, Erwin, and Soodak (2006) outlined a set of 10 components that are required for an effective IEP development conference. We discuss these within the context of IECSE service delivery.

Preparing in Advance

Preparation is critical to a meaningful conference or meeting. Many of us have attended meetings that lack meaningful agendas or are unorganized or unfocused. Advance preparation is critical to a successful IEP conference. IECSE teachers can prepare in advance by contacting all members of the team and ensuring that the date and time of the meeting is satisfactory for everyone. Parents might need assistance with transportation or child care. General early childhood teachers might need to be released from their classroom. Translators or sign language interpreters might be needed for team members who have trouble speaking or understanding English (Turnbull et al., 2006).

In addition to taking care of logistical concerns, IECSE teachers who coordinate the IEP process also will need to make sure that team members are prepared to participate in the meeting. This can include making sure that all team members have a copy of the current IEP (if there is one) to review current goals and the student's progress toward meeting those goals. Participants such as parents or general early childhood teachers may need information about who will be at the meeting and the roles of these individuals. It might mean that some team members have "homework," including updating students' present levels of performance or conducting formal or informal assessments. If a student might be moving on to a different setting, being prepared might mean visiting potential new programs or classrooms (Turnbull et al., 2006).

Connecting and Getting Started

Turnbull and colleagues (2006) encouraged team members to create a positive and productive atmosphere for everyone. Many parents or individuals without formal training in special education might be nervous or uncomfortable about the meeting. As a former special education teacher, one of the authors of this book always made it a point to wait for parents outside of the room in which the meeting was taking place. Entering the meeting with the parent was more likely to help the parent feel comfortable and less intimidated. The same practice could be initiated for other team members who are not familiar with the process or might be easily intimidated. Team members might need nametags so other team members can identify their names and professional roles. Introductions are mandatory, including introducing the participant's role in the meeting. If he or she is the coordinator of the meeting, the IECSE teacher can clarify meeting "ground rules" and review the agenda. Turnbull and colleagues encouraged starting off on a positive note by describing positive experiences or incidences regarding the student. They also recommend providing snacks, if possible!

Reviewing Formal Evaluations and Current Levels of Performance

The first part of the meeting consists of reviewing current information about the student's progress in meeting goals and objectives outlined on the IEP as well as any results from formal assessments (Turnbull et al., 2006). IECSE teachers should make sure that people reviewing this information understand it. Participants should be encouraged to avoid educational jargon and highly technical terms. Without singling anyone out, IECSE teachers can ask for clarification on terms or information that they think might be confusing for participants. They can and should also invite other team members to ask questions or make comments regarding the information shared. As the meeting progresses to the next stage, there should not be any questions about the student's current levels of performance.

Sharing Resources, Priorities, and Concerns

At this time, it is appropriate for team members to share information about resources they can gain access to that can support the student's progress. It is also an appropriate time to share information about priorities for student progress and concerns that team members might have (Turnbull et al., 2006).

Sharing Visions and Great Expectations

Just as team members are encouraged to share their resources, priorities, and concerns, Turnbull and colleagues (2006) encouraged team members to share their visions or "great expectations" (pp. 260–261) that team members have for students. This serves to set the stage to develop an IEP that is guided by a vision for the student's success.

Considering Interaction of Proposed Student Goals, Placement, and Services

Before proceeding to identify goals or objectives, Turnbull and colleagues (2006) emphasized the importance of discussing how the vision and expectations that team members have for the student interact with placements and services.

Translating Student Priorities into Written Goals and Objectives (or Outcomes)

After the team members have discussed the student's current levels of performance as well as the dreams and visions they have for the student's progress, it is appropriate to develop written goals and objectives based on these priorities (Turnbull et al., 2006). All team members should participate in this process. If coordinating the meeting, IECSE teachers should ensure that goals and objectives represent functional skills (as discussed below) and that the criteria used to determine whether the student is progressing satisfactorily make sense and will yield useful information. It is also important at this point to discuss the role of team members as direct or indirect service providers. Everyone on the team should be in consensus as to individuals' responsibilities for implementing interventions outlined on the IEP.

Determining Placement, Supplementary Aids and/or Services, and Related Services

The team should only make a decision regarding placement *after* goals and objectives are identified. The team has a responsibility to determine the setting or LRE that can best meet the student's needs after discussing possible placement options. The team should consider characteristics of the setting (e.g., class size, geographic proximity to student's home, staff and peer characteristics) when making decisions about the best place to serve the student. If the team decides that IECSE services are warranted, there should be a full discussion about the nature of these services and the value of a consultative approach. This is also the time to discuss supplementary aids and services (e.g., augmentative and/or alternative communication devices, paraprofessional support) as well as related services (e.g., adapted physical education, occupational or physical therapy, speech-language therapy). All team members should remember that making decisions about placement and services should occur with a full understanding of what the student will need to gain access to the general curriculum. This is also the time to discuss the extent to which the student will participate in the general education program (Turnbull et al., 2006). If the IECSE teacher is coordinating the meeting, he or she should make sure that all team members clearly understand the outcome of this discussion and should strive to reach team consensus.

Addressing Assessment Modifications and Special Factors

If the child is entering a grade in which statewide assessments are mandated, the team should consider whether the child should participate in these assessments or if modifications are in order (Turnbull et al., 2006). In addition, Turnbull and colleagues advised that team members discuss whether other special services such as positive behavioral support, braille, or assistive technology should be available to the student.

Summarizing and Concluding the Conference

At the end of the meeting, the team should assign responsibilities for follow-up or other tasks that must be attended to. At this time, the IEP document may be written. The meeting coordinator should summarize major outcomes of the meeting and make sure that everyone understands these outcomes. The team needs to determine the date and time of the next meeting and make decisions for regular team communication. The team members should make sure that they understand parents' preferences for communication and should provide contact information as needed. Finally, the meeting should end on a positive note, citing the value of team partnerships and expressing appreciation to all team members (Turnbull et al., 2006).

Writing Functional Goals and Objectives

IECSE teachers are the special education generalists on the IEP team. As such, they usually have the primary responsibility for helping to craft IEP goals and objectives. Because people other than special educators and related service providers are likely to be addressing IEP objectives in general education classrooms or other natural learning environments, it is important for the IEP team to write goals and objectives that are functional, operational, and easy to understand. In addition, the IEP team must be able to develop evaluation criteria that make sense and allow team members to appropriately monitor the child's progress. Readers can find more information about progress monitoring in Chapter 6. This section will address the importance of writing functional IEP goals and objectives.

According to Jung (2007), functional IEP objectives are *SMART*—specific, measurable, attainable, routine-based, and tied to a functional priority. A *specific* objective is one that is written in such a way that everyone on the team has a common understanding of it. In other words, it means the same thing to the occupational therapist as it does to the general education teacher. All too often, IEP objectives can be interpreted in different ways, leading to confusion and rendering them useless. For example, writing "Evan will identify the letters in his name" can mean one thing to his parent and another to his IECSE teacher. However, writing "Evan will verbally name the letters in his name when an adult points to them" is much more specific and less open to interpretation.

Measurable objectives are those that are objective (as opposed to subjective) and include clear criteria that will allow team members to determine the student's progress (Jung, 2007). In addition, the team members must make sure that the criteria are easily assessed; in the case of a child receiving IECSE services, people other then the special educator or related services provider will be collecting data. General early childhood teachers cannot incorporate complex or unwieldy data collection systems into their schedules. For example, it is difficult for early childhood teachers to collect data related to children's responses to verbal initiations from peers across the day . . . there just is not enough time to do that. Instead, the team might consider choosing a window of time in the child's day that is likely to include opportunities for verbal initiations to occur (e.g., center time versus circle time) and then identify criteria that will allow the teacher to more easily collect these data.

High-quality IEP objectives are also those that represent *attainable* skills (Jung, 2007). The criteria used to identify success should represent incremental progress toward mastery as opposed to an "all-or-nothing" approach. It is far more gratifying for parents, teachers, and other team members to see small but measurable progress toward meeting a goal than it is to work on the same goal over months or perhaps the entire school year. Writing attainable objectives can involve the use of task analysis—a process that breaks down larger tasks into smaller, more manageable steps (Wolery et al., 1992). This allows the team to see success more often and provide the type of help that children need to learn new skills and become proficient using them. Task analysis also allows the team to understand hierarchical steps for mastery of skills. Pretti-Frontczak and Bricker (2000) emphasized the need to generate IEP objectives that represent a developmental or hierarchical approach to instruction. That is, before a child can zip his or her coat, he or she needs to be able to bring both of his or her hands to midline. This approach is especially critical in the early years when children are learning pivotal skills that are used in many contexts.

In identifying *routines-based* as an important element of functional IEP objectives, Jung (2007) echoed what others have emphasized (Grisham-Brown & Hemmeter, 1998; McWilliam, Ferguson, Harbin, Porter, & Vandiviere, 1998; Pretti-Frontczak & Bricker, 2000); that is, the importance of addressing skills that are generalizable and transferable across settings. Generalizable skills are those that a child can use in a variety of settings. These skills are best taught in the context of everyday routines and activities. They are skills or behaviors that permit the child to function fully and appropriately in his or her natural learning environment. For example, "using a pincer grasp to pick up small objects" is a generalizable skill because it can be used in a variety of settings and contexts. It is also a skill that children will need to function successfully at home or at school.

The *T* in SMART stands for skills that are "tied to a functional priority" (Jung, 2007, p. 56). Jung emphasized the need to write objectives that represent knowledge, skills, or behaviors that children will need to be successful in their natural learning environment. Jung contrasted this approach to the approach in which IEP objectives are tied to test results or assessment items that children miss. She states that although these objectives are generally specific and measurable, they are not useful in the sense that the child does not need to attain them to be successful in his or her environment. For example, "stacking three 1-inch cube blocks" might be an item on a test that a child misses; although it is specific and measurable, it does not represent a useful skill (unless the child is going to architectural school!).

The SMART framework (Jung, 2007) provides a useful approach to crafting IEP objectives that 1) result in academic or developmental progress for children, 2) are easy to incorporate into general education settings or natural environments, and 3) are easy for all team members to use and understand. Jung (2003) echoes our belief that by working directly with other adults who are with children throughout the day and across the week, IECSE teachers are exponentially expanding learning and instructional opportunities for children.

Handling Team Conflict

Unfortunately, even with the best of intentions, very few IEP teams are free from conflict. Conflict can arise when team members disagree on goals or when they disagree on plans to reach those goals. For example, Jen, Alex's IECSE teacher, believes that Alex's needs might be met best by consulting with Donna, Alex's general ECE teacher. However, Alex's mother believes that Alex is not receiving the services he needs unless Jen is actually working with him during her visits and believes that Jen is just not doing her job. This type of conflict can happen easily in the provision of IECSE services; therefore, team members need to discuss their perspectives and work hard to agree on a plan of action that everyone believes in. In addition, individuals can be internally conflicted when they doubt their goals or the course of action they have taken to reach those goals.

In a different example, Ellen, an IECSE teacher, might prefer to provide direct services to the children on her caseload as opposed to consulting with others because she does not feel as if she has the knowledge and expertise she needs to serve as a consultant. Discussing her perspective with her supervisor can help Ellen resolve this internal conflict. It might be that Ellen just does not have the confidence in herself to understand how her knowledge and experience can benefit others. Conversely, if Ellen is a new teacher, she may actually not have the knowledge and skills needed to be an effective IECSE teacher, in which case she and her supervisor might want to consider staffing changes. Any of these types of conflict will challenge the success of the team. Effective teams recognize that conflict is inevitable and find productive ways to deal with it. IECSE teachers may find themselves in the middle of conflict situations because they are the contact person for the parent, the general early childhood teacher, related services providers, and administrators. It is important that IECSE teachers are able to recognize conflict and find effective ways to address it.

Friend and Cook (2000) discussed various approaches that individuals use to respond to conflicts. Some individuals tend to avoid conflicts and, while that can help in the short term, it does nothing to resolve a situation. Some individuals aggressively address conflict and seem to take pleasure in "winning." Although this can be helpful in a few situations, such as one in which ethical concerns are present, Friend and Cook advised that this type of approach is not very useful and can actually serve to isolate an individual from others with whom they work.

Just as some individuals work actively to make sure that conflicts are solved in their way, other individuals seem to consistently set aside their own beliefs so that others can have their way. Although this can help to quickly resolve a conflict, in the long run, it can be detrimental because individuals who consistently accommodate to others may have good ideas that would be helpful ways to solve an issue or a problem. Friend and Cook acknowledged that two other conflict resolving approaches may be more effective.

An approach that may be more effective is one in which individuals compromise or negotiate to solve problems. Individuals who tend to compromise or "give in" on certain aspects of a problem or situation expect others to compromise on other aspects of the situation. Compromise can be helpful if the problem is minor, but can be detrimental if the compromise doesn't contain the essential resolutions that would more effectively solve the problem.

Finally, Friend and Cook (2000) acknowledged the importance of a collaborative style of conflict resolution. Within a collaborative approach, the solution to a problem is based on everyone's input and is more likely to engender "buy in" by individuals, although it generally takes more time to arrive at collaborative solutions.

Resolving or Addressing Conflict

Although it is important to be cognizant of the various ways in which people deal with conflict, it is even more important for IECSE teachers to know how to deal with it. Throughout this book, it has been stated that individuals who serve in itinerant roles should be experienced and "seasoned" teachers. IECSE teachers need a level of maturity that brings with it a sense of how to interact effectively with others. Friend and Cook (2000) identified ways that team members can best negotiate with others through conflict situations. These approaches are discussed next.

1. *Remember that conflict is about an issue, not an individual.* Effective IECSE teachers are those who can resolve conflict without having a team member or other individual feel attacked or personally compromised.

2. *When resolving conflict, start with the issues on which everyone can agree.* Finding common ground is an important concept, especially when conflict is a result of individuals' underlying beliefs or principles that are unlikely to change.

3. *Diffuse emotionally laden situations to address the issue that needs resolution.* IECSE teachers can use this strategy by responding positively or ignoring negative comments. In some cases, Friend and Cook (2000) advised that heavily charged conflict be avoided temporarily.

4. *If the conflict is serious and resolving it has serious implications, it may be advisable to seek outside assistance from a neutral party.* This type of mediation can be useful in helping everyone with a stake in the problem to reach an acceptable solution.

5. *Adapt to the issue or leave.* Friend and Cook (2000) advised that in few cases, the best solution might be to exit the situation. This can be the case when there is no way to resolve the issue. "Letting go" of the situation is one way to deal with conflict and might be the only viable solution if it is causing the team member undue stress or resolution is not likely.

Understanding Conflict and Resistance to Change

In many cases, conflict among team members is a result of an individual's reluctance to change the status quo (Friend & Cook, 2000). Change is disruptive and can cause some individuals a great deal of stress and anxiety, especially if they do not understand the change or feel as though they have no control over the situation. People also may become stressed if they believe that the change will negatively affect them personally. IECSE teachers can help to resolve conflict by understanding individuals' resistance to change.

Concerns About Change

Perhaps the most widely used model for understanding individuals' resistance to change is the Concerns-Based Adoption Model (CBAM) developed by Hall and his colleagues (Hall, George, Steigelbauer, & Dirksen, 2006). This model recognizes the fact that any type of educational innovation (e.g., early childhood inclusion or a consultative approach to IECSE service delivery) is subject to resistance by teachers because it represents a significant change in educational practice. Individuals resist change for a variety of reasons, and the CBAM helps others to understand concerns that teachers have about change. A description of the CBAM stages of concern is provided below because it may be helpful in understanding concerns that teachers have and how to best address them. Each stage is listed along with a short descriptor of teachers' primary concerns regarding change.

*   *Awareness*: At this stage, teachers are not really aware of the change or have only cursory knowledge about it.

*   *Informational:* Teachers at this stage are interested in learning more about the change and what it means for their practice.

- *Personal:* After they have learned about the innovation, teachers at this stage are concerned about their ability to implement the change as well as the impact the change will have on them personally.

- *Management:* Teachers may have some cursory experiences with the innovation and begin to be concerned about how to manage it and what it will involve in terms of logistics.

- *Consequence:* At this stage, teachers wonder about the impact of the change on their students and how they might modify the innovation to better meet students' needs.

- *Collaboration:* Teachers at this stage have accepted the change and are interested in helping others learn more about it.

- *Refocusing:* Finally, teachers are interested in making major modifications to the innovation or replacing it with something else.

IECSE teachers who work with team members who are resistant to change can use the CBAM framework (Hall et al., 2006) to understand resistance and help team members move toward accepting the change or innovation. Using the example of changing from a direct services approach to a consultative approach to IECSE service delivery, one can see how team members (e.g., a general early childhood teacher) might initially be very concerned about how the consultative approach would affect her personally as a classroom teacher ("How does anyone expect that I can do this when I have 15 other children in the classroom who also need me?"). If IECSE teachers understand what might be causing a concern, they can talk with their team members about it and help to address the concern or resistance.

Overcoming Conflict: The Powers of Persuasion

As we have suggested throughout this book, IECSE teachers have the power to be agents of change to support early childhood inclusion. With superb interpersonal skills and the ability to work with other adults effectively, they have the expertise that is critical to promoting early childhood inclusion. Supporting change often entails persuading others of their ability to take on a new challenge or adopt a new approach. Friend and Cook (2000) provided an excellent overview of the various ways in which team members can act persuasively to support productive change.

First, IECSE teachers can understand that individuals behave in a certain way in order to obtain or avoid something. IECSE teachers must understand the power of consequences—either positive consequences such as incentives or rewards, or negative consequences such as reproofs or reprimands. IECSE teachers can help those who resist change to become more familiar with the situation because familiarity with a situation increases individuals' comfort levels. In addition, it may be important for those with a negative perspective on a situation to find positive aspects of the change instead of focusing on the negative. Reframing the situation can help alter or modify one's perspective of a change. Effective team members acknowledge the importance of one's perspective, understanding that perceptions—even if they are inaccurate—form the basis for action. Individuals act within their own system of values and beliefs and it's important to understand another person's perspectives, including his or her values and beliefs, in order to help move the person from Point A to Point B.

It is also important to realize that humans strive for consistency between what they think and how they behave. IECSE teachers can help those with whom they work to identify discrepancies or inconsistencies between their thoughts and their actions. For example, an IECSE teacher might help her partner teacher see that her teaching approach is inconsistent with her beliefs about how children best learn. She may also create situations in which the resister is able to see the relationship between a proposed change in strategy or action and a desired outcome. Finally, the IECSE teacher may ask the resister to verbally commit to making a change, knowing that individuals are more likely to follow through with a change if they have stated so verbally (Friend & Cook, 2000).

Summary

The role of a team member is one of the most wide-reaching and complex roles that an IECSE teacher can undertake. In this chapter, we have reviewed basic models of team functioning and discussed key elements of successful teaming. We have discussed effective strategies for developing IEPs, including outlining a process for coordinating an IEP meeting as articulated by Turnbull and colleagues (2006). In addition, this chapter included a discussion of generating IEP goals and objectives that lead to academic and developmental success for students.

Teaming depends on effective interactions among team members. It is important to acknowledge that team process is generally not free from conflict. We have identified major sources of conflict and styles that exemplify how individuals respond to conflict. We have also shared information about the CBAM as articulated by Hall and colleagues (2006) and summarized information from Friend and Cook (2000) regarding approaches IECSE teachers can take when persuading others to adopt a change or innovation.

CHAPTER 9

A Model for
Providing Itinerant Services
*Gathering Information
and Planning for Intervention*

The purpose of this chapter is to describe a process that IECSE teachers and those individuals with whom they work can use to support children's developmental and academic progress in community-based preschool programs or other natural environments. The process begins with collecting baseline and background information about children, their everyday environments, and the other adults who work with them. Once IECSE teachers collect information, they can work in collaboration with other adults to plan intervention services that can be embedded into children's daily routines and activities. Throughout this chapter, we discuss how Heather, Maxi's IECSE teacher, uses this model to work with Maxi's teacher and mother to provide high-quality itinerant services. Chapter 10 continues this process by outlining the consultation and coaching process articulated earlier in this book.

Heather and Maxi

Maxi is 4 years old and loves going to preschool in Ms. Sherry's room. She especially loves playing with her best friends Helene and Addison. Maxi has been enrolled in Ms. Sherry's room for the past 3 weeks, ever since her mom went back to work. A special school bus comes to pick Maxi up every morning to accommodate her wheelchair. Maxi has cerebral palsy, which has caused limited mobility. She uses a wheelchair to get around but is slowly learning to use a walker. In addition to having cerebral palsy, Maxi has difficulty attending to everyday activities. She is easily distracted, especially when it comes time for large- or small-group activities.

Heather is Maxi's IECSE teacher. This is her fifth year providing itinerant services. She enjoys visiting other classrooms and says that she learns a lot by watching other teachers work with children. Although she started out providing direct services as an itinerant teacher, she is shifting toward more of a consultative approach. She visits Maxi's classrooms on Thursday mornings, usually from 9:00 a.m. to 10:30 a.m.

Sherry is Maxi's preschool teacher. Sherry has an associate's degree in early childhood education and this is her 12th year teaching young children. She is enthusiastic and energetic and wants to do what is best for Maxi. With that said, Sherry has never worked with a child who has cerebral palsy and is very nervous. She wants to do what is best for Maxi but is afraid that she is going to do something wrong and has asked if her classroom is really the best place to meet Maxi's needs.

Megan is Maxi's mother. She has just returned to work after staying at home with Maxi and her older sister for 5 years. She absolutely wants what is best for Maxi. In the past, Maxi has received special education and related services at home. The IECSE teacher would come to her home and work with Maxi on different skills. Megan also would bring Maxi to the physical and occupational therapists' offices on a regular basis. She knows that Heather's job really is to help Sherry work with Maxi, but she wants to make sure that Maxi receives all of the help she needs. She used to feel very confident that Maxi was getting the help she needed when the other itinerant teacher used to come to her home; and, although she likes Heather, she is not entirely sure that consultation is the way to go.

Gathering Information

Chapter 6 discussed the role of the IECSE teacher related to assessment—formal and informal as well as assessment of children, adults, and environments. In addition, Chapter 4 described ways in which IECSE teachers gather information that can assist them in establishing a productive consultative relationship with other adults. To make appropriate decisions on behalf of children and families, IECSE teachers must know as much as possible about the child who is receiving itinerant services.

Heather is looking forward to getting to know Maxi. At Maxi's IEP meeting, she talked to Megan and Sherry. She knows the itinerant teacher Maxi had before—the one who used to make home visits—but she has never met Maxi. Heather knows that if she is going to help Maxi be successful in Sherry's classroom, then she first has to get to know Maxi.

Who Is the Child?

Understanding the culture, strengths, challenges, interests, and abilities of a child who is receiving itinerant services is key to planning and implementing effective interventions. IECSE teachers are different from other adults who work with the child because they have limited contact with the child. Heather only sees Maxi once a week for about an hour and a half. Because, like in this example, these professionals sometimes only have limited contact with a child, it is important that IECSE teachers gather as much information about the child from a variety of sources, including the child's family, his or her teachers, school records (including the IEP), and direct observation. Heather has read through Maxi's school file and talked to her mom—once at the IEP meeting and once about a week ago. She has also spoken with Sherry twice—once at the IEP meeting and once over the telephone when she called to schedule the visit. McWilliam, Casey, and Sims (2009) described the Routines-Based Interview (RBI), a process for gathering information from family members and caregivers who spend large amounts of time with the child. Interventionists, including IECSE teachers, discuss the results of the interview with the parent or caregiver, helping to identify possible outcomes that may lead to enhanced development and meaningful participation in everyday routines and activities.

The director of Maxi's preschool arranged for a substitute teacher to help out in Sherry's room for Heather's first visit, which gave Heather and Sherry some time to get to know each other. Heather used the RBI (McWilliam et al., 2009) to find out about Maxi's day. Below is part of their conversation:

Heather: *Sherry, I'd like to talk with you about Maxi's day. Understanding what Maxi does each day will help me understand how I can best help her be successful in your classroom. Maxi is here in your classroom because her mom and everyone else on the IEP team thought it would be the best place for her to learn and prepare for kindergarten. You can do so much more for her during daily routines than I could in 90 minutes a week, and if you can share with me what her day looks like, then perhaps we can come up with a plan to best support her.*

Sherry: *Sure, I'd be happy to tell you about Maxi's day, but we really don't do anything special—just typical preschool stuff.*

Heather: *Well, it's that typical preschool stuff that's really going to prepare Maxi to be successful in kindergarten. Can you walk me through a typical day?*

Sherry: *Well, Maxi gets here at about 8:15 in the morning. The bus drops her off and the bus aide brings her into my classroom after she hangs up her things.*

Heather: *When you say, "she," do you mean Maxi hangs up her things or the bus aide hangs them up?*

Sherry: *The bus aide hangs them up. Maxi has enough challenges—I didn't think she needed to worry about hanging up her things.*

Heather: *Okay, maybe we can talk about that later. After Maxi gets into the room, what's next? What does she like to do?*

As the conversation above indicates, Heather asks Sherry to tell her about Maxi's day—the kinds of activities she engages in, what Maxi likes (and does not like), and what concerns Sherry has for Maxi's success. When she asks the questions about what concerns Sherry has, Sherry admits that although she thinks that Maxi is a great little girl, she worries that maybe her classroom is not the best place for her. Sherry does not know anything about working with children who have the kind of challenges that Maxi has; and the classroom is so busy, Sherry is afraid that Maxi is going to get hurt. We'll pick up on that concern a little later.

Another Way of Gathering Information

Wolery and colleagues (2002) offered a similar approach to McWilliam and colleagues' RBI approach (2009), which was discussed previously. *Congruence assessment* offers a process that IECSE teachers can use collaboratively to identify children's strengths and challenges as they relate to participation in classroom routines and activities. In addition to observing the child in a variety of contexts (e.g., participation in classroom activities, interactions with peers, engagement in routines with parents if appropriate), reading the IEP, and engaging parents and caregivers in focused discussions, these two systematic approaches provide effective ways to gather the baseline information needed to plan meaningful interventions for the child.

Using the example above, Heather asks Sherry to describe how Maxi participates in the different routines and activities in Sherry's classroom. In addition to asking her about Maxi's likes and dislikes, Heather also asks Sherry to identify concerns she has for the way that Maxi interacts. Sherry is quick to point out that circle time is difficult because Maxi just does not want to pay attention. Instead of participating in circle time activities, she tries to interact with the children sitting next to her. Sherry finds helping Maxi use the bathroom very difficult because Maxi needs so much help. Sherry is also worried that she is going to hurt Maxi when she picks her up or helps her move from one place to the other.

Who Are the Adults Who Work with the Child?

Again, because the primary responsibility of an IECSE teacher is to help the adults who spend the majority of time with the child to deliver specialized services in the IECSE teacher's absence, it is important that the IECSE teacher know these adults. As we have discussed previously, IECSE teachers and the adults with whom they work must learn to work together effectively and productively. Buysse and Wesley (2005) emphasized the importance of building effective relationships with consultees; to do that, consultants and consultees must get to know each other. Information about the early childhood teacher's experiences with young children, including young children with disabilities, will help the IECSE teacher understand the kinds of supports and resources he or she might need. Information about the parent's education level will help the IECSE teacher understand effective ways of sharing information. Consultants should be careful to engage their consultee in conversation around these questions as opposed to using a direct interview or "interrogation" method.

After Heather and Sherry had talked about everyday classroom activities, Heather asked Sherry to tell her a little bit about herself:

Heather: *Sherry, thanks for all of the information about your classroom. It seems like this is a great place for Maxi to learn! You must have been teaching forever! Can you tell me a little bit about your background?*

Sherry: *Thanks! I really don't have any special background. I've always known I wanted to be a teacher and really enjoy being around young children. In high school I used to help out in a child care center and knew that I'd found my place. After high school I enrolled in a community college and earned an associate's degree in early childhood education. I might want to go back to school one day, but for now, I'm happy doing what I'm doing.*

Heather: *I know what you mean about taking a break from school! I learned a lot, but all that studying and writing papers—I don't mind not having to do that again! Is Maxi the first child that you've worked with who has an IEP?*

Sherry: *I had a little boy a year ago who had a speech problem and another little girl who had behavior problems—they both had IEPs, but I never saw them. I had a class about working with kids who have special needs and sort of know what an IEP is, but I don't really know what to do with it. The other kids I worked with looked like typical kids— Maxi's the first child I worked with who's in a wheelchair.*

Heather: *It sounds like you're a bit nervous about working with Maxi—I know equipment like her wheelchair, walker, and her special chair can be a bit overwhelming at times. It seems, though, that you're really committed to doing what's best for Maxi and I hope that I can help you to feel more comfortable and confident. I know that Maxi loves coming to your classroom and between myself, the OT, and the PT, I also know that we can help you feel successful.*

Sherry: *You're right Heather—working with Maxi seems overwhelming. I mean, she's a sweet little girl, but I don't want to move her the wrong way or hurt her at all. If you think I can do it, I'm up for it—of course with your help!*

As the conversation continues, readers can see how much Heather has learned about Sherry—her education, experiences working with children with disabilities, and her trepidation in working with Maxi. Heather also shares some information about herself with Sherry—disclosing relevant personal information can help build rapport and confidence in the relationship. Below are some suggestions for questions that IECSE teachers can ask their partners:

- What kinds of experiences has the person had with young children, including young children with disabilities?

- What kinds of experience has the person had working with consultants or coaches?

- What does the person know about the child's disability or associated learning difficulties?

- What is the person's education level? How does she learn best?

- How much time does the person have to work with a coach or a consultant?

- How does the person feel about working with this child? What is he or she excited about? What is he or she concerned about?

- How does the person feel about working with a coach or a consultant? What is he or she excited about? What is he or she concerned about?

- What does the person expect from a coach or a consultant?

- What are the person's goals for the consultative relationship?

Understanding the Learning Environment

IECSE teachers such as Heather who are planning for consultation must have a solid understanding of the child's learning environment, which, in Maxi's case, is her preschool classroom. In Chapters 4 and 6, we have discussed the importance of the learning environment and its relationship to successful inclusive experiences. We have discussed using environmental rating instruments such as the Early Childhood Environment Rating Scale–Revised (ECERS-R) developed by Harms and her colleagues (Harms, Clifford, & Cryer, 2005; Harms, Cryer, & Clifford, 2003, 2007). Information gathered through these instruments can be very helpful in shaping the goals of the consultative relationship as well as identifying the kinds of intervention strategies needed to support children's learning. One of the things that Heather can do to become acquainted with Maxi's room is to use the ECERS-R to analyze its features. She can use the information she collects from it to help her and Sherry plan how they can best help Maxi. Instruments such as the ECERS-R are helpful because they provide a way of conducting a structured (versus a haphazard) observation. When Heather shares this information with Sherry, she needs to be sensitive to the fact that some early childhood teachers might become defensive or intimidated if the scores are not as high as they would think. In these cases, it is helpful for Heather to remind Sherry that high scores on an instrument such as the ECERS-R denote an excellent degree of quality that only few programs achieve. There may be factors outside of Sherry's control that cause lower scores on some items (e.g., furnishings and equipment). Alternatively, a low score on the ECERS-R might provide the impetus that Sherry and other preschool teachers need to improve the early learning environment.

Knowing the Ropes

In addition to identifying key dimensions of the child's learning environment, IECSE teachers also must have solid information about rules, regulations, policies, and procedures that govern a preschool classroom. Head Start teachers follow Head Start Performance Standards that provide guidance about classroom routines and activities (Administration on Children, Youth and Families, 2009). Other community-based programs that are licensed by the state operate under strict policies regarding staff–child ratio, health and safety procedures, or nutrition guidelines. Given the increase in the number of states that institute quality rating improvement systems (QRIS; Mitchell, 2009), IECSE teachers would be wise to learn about the policies under which quality-rated centers operate. For example, QRIS programs often are required to engage in assessment processes that can be helpful to the work of the IECSE teacher. They also provide guidance concerning curricular decisions, including stipulating time spent in certain areas such as emergent literacy or mathematics. They also may have policies and procedures related to working with children who have disabilities. Knowing these guidelines can help the IECSE teacher be prepared to effectively support the child as well as the child's teachers. Although Heather cannot be expected to know everything about how licensed early childhood centers work, she should know whom to ask or where to consult in case she has a question.

"Know Thyself"

Finally, IECSE teachers who enter into consultative relationships to support early childhood inclusion have to know their own strengths and challenges. Just as early childhood teachers need to feel confident, competent, and comfortable working with young children who have special needs, IECSE teachers need to feel confident, competent, and comfortable in their role as a consultant. Tools such as the PIECES (Dinnebeil & McInerney, 2011), already described in this book and included as Appendix C, will help IECSE teachers assess their own knowledge and skills related to a consultative approach. Acting on this self-assessment by engaging in continuous learning and professional development can help the IECSE teacher stay current in the field and help to strengthen his or her competence (thereby helping him or her to feel more comfortable and confident).

As you may recall, Heather has been an IECSE teacher for the last 5 years, but it was not until recently that she started serving in more of a consultant's role. At the end of the last school year, Heather decided that she needed to move in that direction—she knew that working with a child once a week on IEP goals did little to help the child. Although Heather has confidence in her ability to work with children (she was a classroom teacher for 7 years prior to becoming an IECSE teacher), she does not feel completely comfortable as a consultant. She has trouble giving feedback, especially if it is not positive feedback. She also struggles with demonstrating skills to others; she feels as though when she says, "Watch me" she's saying, "I'm better than you are!" Heather completed the PIECES over the summer and decided that she really needed to focus on her ability to share specific feedback with others and plans to work on that as part of her work with Sherry and Maxi.

Planning to Embed Learning Opportunities into Daily Routines and Activities

Successful IECSE services do not only depend on a positive relationship between the IECSE teacher and the other adults with whom he or she works. Children with disabilities will experience success in inclusive early childhood settings if the adults who teach and care for them have the ability and opportunity to offer specialized services during the day and across the week. The primary goal of the IECSE teacher becomes one of ensuring that adults not only have the knowledge and skills that they need to offer these services but also have opportunity to do so. Together, adults 1) make decisions about the IEP or IFSP goals that are of highest priority, 2) identify natural learning opportunities that occur during the child's daily or weekly routine, 3) identify intervention strategies likely to support goal attainment, and 4) decide how to best monitor the child's progress (Jung, Gomez, Baird, & Galyon Keramidas, 2008). As Heather and Sherry got to know each other better, their conversations shifted to focus on how they can best help Maxi.

Prioritizing Learning Goals or Objectives

The first step in the consultative process is deciding which IEP or IFSP goals should be addressed. Goals and objectives can be prioritized in a number of ways. McWilliam and his colleagues (2009) advocated using an RBI process to help parents and caregivers identify high-priority functional goals. As mentioned previously, Wolery and colleagues (2002) described a process whereby IECSE teachers and their partners use *congruence assessment* to identify high-priority routines and subsequent learning objectives. We describe the MEPI process, whereby IECSE teachers and their partners identify IEP goals and objectives that are likely to need *intensive and/or direct intervention* (I), as opposed to those goals and objectives that can be addressed indirectly by capitalizing on supportive *peers* (P) or *arranging environments* (E) or those goals and objectives that are likely to be resolved through *maturation* (M). Table 9.1 provides an overview of MEPI.

Using MEPI to Identify Maxi's Priority Objectives

Heather and Sherry used the MEPI approach to determine Maxi's priority objectives. They decided that one of the things that would really help Maxi be more independent was learning to use her walker and that she was unlikely to learn how to do it without some intensive instruction. She also needed to learn how to pay attention during large-group activities (such as the morning meeting) and small-group activities. Megan (Maxi's

Table 9.1.   Definition of MEPI

	Term	Definition/examples
M	Maturation	Is the skill or behavior likely to develop simply as a result of a child maturing? For example, certain fine motor skills improve as the child's muscles grow and develop. If this is the case, the individualized education program (IEP) or individualized family service plan (IFSP) team should monitor the goal as it resolves itself through biological maturation.
E	Environment	Is the skill or behavior likely to develop in a supportive environment? For example, deficiencies in vocabulary or other language skills might be the result of an impoverished environment. Enriching the environment through the addition of meaningful materials, contingent learning opportunities, and social interaction might be sufficient to support progress toward an IEP or IFSP objective.
P	Peer support	Is the skill or behavior likely to develop as a result of positive peer support? Children who learn through observation and imitation are likely to acquire skills simply by observing their peers. This can be true for social interaction skills or self-help skills. The IEP or IFSP team's role is to ensure that the child has the opportunity to learn via peer interaction and monitor goals and objectives that are likely to be affected by the presence of supportive peers.
I	Intensive/direct intervention	Is it likely that the only way a child will acquire a skill is through direct or intensive intervention? If so, then this goal or objective becomes a high priority for the itinerant ECSE teacher and her partners. In addition, some goals might need immediate intervention, as is the case for children who engage in aggressive behavior that hurts or threatens to hurt others.

mother) had mentioned that she really wanted Maxi to be prepared for kindergarten, and Heather and Sherry both knew that these skills were important. In addition, Sherry and Heather had also spoken with Ron, Maxi's physical therapist, and LaToya, Maxi's occupational therapist, about helping Maxi learn to move around more independently in the classroom. Ron and LaToya visited the classroom and showed Sherry and Heather how to help Maxi. Megan also knows how to help Maxi move from one spot to another and use her walker, and she volunteered to come to Maxi's room at lunch and after work to help out. All of these objectives (using her walker, moving around the classroom, and paying attention during group activities) were important for Maxi's success and were not likely to be achieved without some direct intervention.

Identifying Learning Opportunities

Once IECSE teachers and their partners have settled on the learning goals and objectives most important to target, the next step in the planning process is identifying naturally occurring learning opportunities that are part of the child's daily routine. If the goals and objectives targeted are functional (Grisham-Brown & Hemmeter, 1998; Jung, 2007; McWilliam et al., 2009), the job becomes comparatively easy. That is, functional goals and objectives are those that reflect important skills that children are likely to need to be successful in their learning environments. IECSE teachers and the adults they work with can identify key routines and activities that can support learning opportunities—activities such as snack or meal time, circle time, learning centers, or transitioning between activities.

In considering possible learning opportunities, IECSE teachers also must consider the work demands placed on the adults responsible for carrying out the intervention in the IECSE teacher's absence. For example, mealtime might present itself as a prime opportunity for learning to use a fork; however, it might be an unduly busy or hectic time for parents or caregivers. In Maxi's case, Sherry has indicated that transition times, especially going out to play, are really hectic times. Given this, Heather knows that it is best not to target this time as a time to help Maxi learn to use her walker or move around. They decide to develop an alternative plan for addressing these skills during a time that places fewer demands on the attention of Sherry and the other teacher. Although Heather and Sherry were able to identify other appropriate learning opportunities throughout the day for Maxi to focus on these skills, if they had not or could not have been able to find more appropriate times, then they would have to make plans to bring in extra help or classroom support so that Sherry could focus on Maxi's skills. Planning matrices are helpful tools that IECSE teachers can use with their partners to identify likely learning opportunities (Grisham-Brown & Hemmeter, 1998). Daily routines and activities are listed along the left-hand side of the matrix, and children's learning objectives are listed across the top of the matrix. Working together, the IECSE teacher and his or her partner identify several times during the day when it is probable that the child would have an opportunity to use a skill. For example, meal time is a natural time to help a child practice using a fork. Transition times offer natural learning opportunities to practice self-help skills such as zipping a jacket or following directions. Center-based learning activities are times when children are likely to engage in conversations with each other. If a child's environment is a high-quality learning environment *and* the goals and objectives are functional, then IECSE teachers and their partners should be able to easily find multiple times during the day to help the child practice skills. Figure 9.1 provides an example of a planning matrix completed for Ben, a preschool-age child with multiple disabilities. Ben's teachers (his IECSE teacher and his general classroom teacher) have identified multiple times during the day they can provide opportunities for Ben to learn and practice skills identified for intervention on his IEP.

Setting Up Learning Opportunities

Unlike their peers who are typically developing, young children with disabilities may be reluctant to voluntarily engage in meaningful learning opportunities (McWilliam & Casey, 2007). For example, although a child who is typically developing may eagerly ask for "more" cheese crackers at snack, a child with disabilities may not. Maxi may need a reason to pay attention for increasing periods of time during large- or small-group activities. Naturalistic intervention and incidental teaching strategies depend on engaging children in interesting learning activities that present naturally occurring opportunities to use a skill (Rule et al., 1998). Creating interest and motivation to engage in a learning opportunity becomes a task of the teacher or caregiver. Fortunately, adults who work with young children are creative and manipulative (in a good way!) and can devise many ways to entice a child into a learning opportunity (Ostrosky & Kaiser, 1991). For example, Heather and Sherry talked and found a number of ways that they can help Maxi pay attention during morning meeting. Check the strategies below and see whether you can determine which ones would work to help Maxi stay engaged in group activities.

- *Provide interesting or novel materials in the classroom.* Teachers can rotate familiar toys or materials that children are tired of and add new or novel toys or materials that can spark children's interest.

Daily schedule of activities	Objective 1 Making choices	Objective 2 Reach and grasp	Objective 3 Initiate social interaction	Objective 4 Cause/effect (use of a switch)
Center time	Block center or housekeeping?	Build tower with blocks.	Greet other children; vocalize or make eye contact.	Use switch to turn on toy (e.g., dump truck at the blocks center "building site").
Classroom chores	Water plants or feed fish?	Reach for and/or grasp the attendance slip—place on desk in the main office.	Initiate contact with office personnel	
Snack/cooking activity	Make pudding or milkshakes?	Reach for and/or grasp cooking utensils.	Make and maintain eye contact with peers, communicate when it is their turn to stir, and so forth.	Use switch to activate the blender or other appliance.
Small group: art	Decide which art materials to use.	Reach for and/or grasp the built-up paintbrush handle.	Initiate interaction with an adult; ask for assistance	
Outing: Going to park with parents	Slide or swing?	Reach for and/or grasp to hold onto swing or side of slide.	Make eye contact and/or vocalize to let adult know that he wants to be pushed.	Use switch to turn on the music box.
	# opportunities: 5	# opportunities: 5	# opportunities: 5	# opportunities: 3

Figure 9.1. Sample planning matrix for Ben.

- *Place a desired toy or object within the child's view but out of his or her reach.* Children become motivated to ask for help so that they can get the toy or the object. Placing a child's favorite truck on the top of the shelf encourages that child to ask for help in getting the truck. Heather and Sherry can use this strategy to encourage Maxi to move around the room. For example, instead of placing her favorite toys in front of her, they may place them out of her direct reach so that she needs to move on her own to gain access to them.

- *Provide just a little bit of a preferred material or activity so children have a chance to ask for more.* For example, the teacher might only give each child one cracker to encourage children to ask for more.

- *Provide children with opportunities to make choices between activities or materials.* For example, providing different things to drink during snack (milk or juice) requires children to make a choice and tell the teacher (or someone else).

- *"Sabotage" an activity by "forgetting" to provide all of the materials that a child needs or wants.* For example, "forgetful" teachers can give children paintbrushes and paper but no paint. Children love to remind the teacher what he or she has forgotten! A strategy such as this can help Maxi learn to pay attention during group activities.

- *Set up an absurd or silly situation that violates a child's expectations.* For example, serve blocks and plastic animals for snack and wait to see the children's reactions!

The purpose or end result of each of these strategies is to draw a child into a learning situation. It is important to remember that setting up an opportunity does not guarantee that a child will "take the bait." For example, the child's teacher might add some novel materials to the housekeeping area, but the child might not be interested in them—that is, he or she might not "take the bait." If the child is not interested in a situation, then it is difficult for the teacher to proceed any further with intervention. Sometimes it takes a creative teacher (with some fishing experience) to create meaningful learning opportunities for some children! "Setting up" opportunities to catch children's interest is like "setting out some bait." Fishermen increase the odds that they will catch a fish by using tantalizing bait to entice the fish. Teachers increase the odds that they can draw a child into a learning situation by providing interesting and fun activities; however, as all teachers and fishermen know, sometimes the bait does not work and you just have to try again another time.

Rule and colleagues (1999) also cautioned teachers against overusing a strategy as well as singling out a child by using one of the enticement strategies described above. Overusing a strategy can lead to a child's frustration or confusion (e.g., the child *always* has to ask to gain access to something, expectations are *consistently* violated). Singling out a child by only requiring her to ask for more although other children receive more of something without asking can threaten emotional development. In addition, cultural mores or upbringing may come into play, as is the case for a child whose culture requires that children be accepting of what they have (and not ask for more).

Using Child-Focused Intervention Strategies

Once the IECSE teacher and his or her partners have identified appropriate learning opportunities and have devised ways to pique children's interest, they must identify specific child-focused intervention strategies that are likely to support children's learning.

It is important to note that strategies focused on setting up learning opportunities as described previously are not child-focused intervention strategies. They simply help children to become interested in a learning opportunity. Once the child is interested in the learning opportunity, the teacher or other adult employs a child-focused intervention strategy to support the child's response. In Maxi's case, Heather and Sherry might use a system of most-to-least prompting to help Maxi learn to move or use her walker. Wolery (1994) described four classes of evidence-based, child-focused intervention strategies that are useful for supporting children's learning in routine activities. Wolery and colleagues (1992) also provided a thorough discussion of response-prompting strategies. Finally, the Interactive Collaborative Autism Network (ICAN, 2009; http://www.autismnetwork.org) includes detailed information about a range of academic, behavioral, communicative, environmental, sensory, and social interventions that outline procedural components and provides examples of their use. This online resource is especially useful for IECSE teachers who provide resources for other adults who work with young children who have disabilities. A summary of intervention strategies is provided in Table 9.2.

Making Decisions Concerning Child-Focused Intervention Strategies

Wolery (2005) provided recommendations concerning how child-focused intervention strategies should be implemented in early childhood settings. These recommended practices also provide guidance as to which strategies to use to help a child learn different types of skills (e.g., communication skills versus motor skills). In addition, Wolery emphasized the importance of understanding how phases of learning (i.e., acquisition, fluency, maintenance, generalization) affect decisions about the use of child-focused intervention strategies. Both of these considerations are important points of discussion between the IECSE teacher and the other adults with whom he or she works.

In making decisions about which child-focused intervention strategies to employ, the DEC's recommended practices related to child-focused intervention strategies, as developed by Wolery (1994) and detailed in Table 9.3 (Hemmeter, 2005), emphasize the importance of accuracy and consistency. *"Treatment integrity"* refers to the extent to which a treatment or intervention is implemented as planned (Wilkinson, 2006, p. 426). It is important for IECSE teachers to consider the degree to which general early childhood teachers or other adults *can* and *will* implement the child-focused intervention as it is intended to be used. Although some argue that even incomplete implementation of an intervention can result in some level of change (Rhymer, Evans-Hampton, McCurdy, & Watson, 2002), inaccurate or incomplete implementation can contribute to a lack of progress on the child's part and feelings of frustration and/or disappointment on the adult's part. There is some evidence to suggest that interventions that are similar to instructional strategies the teacher already uses may be more likely to be implemented consistently and correctly than interventions that are dissimilar to other instructional strategies the teacher uses (Riley-Tillman & Chafouleas, 2003). In any event, when making decisions about which child-focused intervention strategies to use, IECSE teachers and their partners must consider the importance of consistency and systematic implementation of the strategy across settings, time, and people. That is, the intervention strategy must be delivered consistently regardless of where it is used (e.g., at home, in the classroom), when it is used (e.g., weekdays, weekends), and who delivers it (e.g., the teacher, his or her assistant, a parent, another adult).

Table 9.2. Child-focused intervention strategies, from least intrusive to most intrusive

Class of strategy	Strategy name	Steps
Reinforcement	Positive reinforcement	1. Identify and define a focus behavior in measurable and observable terms.
		2. Identify a reinforcer (can be tangible or nontangible) based on the child's interests and likes.
		3. Deliver the reinforcer immediately after and contingent on each time the child produces the behavior.
		4. If using a tangible reinforcer, pair it with praise or a positive statement.
		5. Monitor progress to document whether the reinforcer is working (i.e., results in an increase in desired behavior).
		6. Once the behavior is established, fade tangible reinforcement so that the child is reinforced periodically for desired behavior.
		7. Continue to fade tangible reinforcers as well as praise if the behavior continues to improve.
	Response shaping	1. Identify and define a focus behavior in measurable and observable terms.
		2. Identify a reinforcer (can be tangible or nontangible) based on the child's interests and likes.
		3. Identify the degree to which the child can best approximate the focus behavior.
		4. Deliver the reinforcer immediately after and contingent on the child producing the most accurate approximation of the behavior.
		5. If using a tangible reinforcer, pair it with praise or a positive statement.
		6. Monitor progress to document whether the reinforcer is working (i.e., results in an increase in desired behavior).
		7. Once the child consistently produces this approximation, continue to train and reinforce only a MORE accurate approximation of the focus behavior.
		8. Continue reinforcing successive approximations until the child can produce the focus behavior accurately.
		9. Continue monitoring effectiveness of the reinforcer.
		10. Once the behavior is established, fade tangible reinforcement so that the child is reinforced periodically for desired behavior.
		11. Continue to fade the tangible reinforcer as well as praise if the behavior continues to improve.
	Differential reinforcement of other behavior	1. Identify and define a focus behavior in measurable and observable terms.
		2. Select another incompatible behavior that replaces the focus behavior (the behavior to be reduced).
		3. Identify a reinforcer (can be tangible or nontangible) based on the child's interests and likes. Pair the reinforcer with praise and positive feedback.
		4. Determine the time limits in which the other behavior must occur.
		5. Ignore the focus (i.e., inappropriate) behavior if and when it occurs.
		6. Reinforce the other behavior when it occurs within the time interval.
		7. Monitor the effectiveness of the reinforcer.

(continued)

Table 9.2.   (*continued*)

Class of strategy	Strategy name	Steps
		8. Once the behavior is established, fade tangible reinforcement so that the child is reinforced periodically for desired behavior.
		9. Continue to fade tangible reinforcers as well as praise if behavior continues to improve.
	Behavioral momentum	1. Identify and define a focus behavior in measurable and observable terms.
		2. Identify a number of other behaviors that have a high probability of compliance. These are behaviors that the child is likely to produce readily upon request.
		3. Identify a reinforcer (can be tangible or intangible) based on the child's interests and likes. Pair the reinforcer with praise and positive feedback.
		4. Request three or more high-probability behaviors in sequence.
		5. Request the low-probability behavior (or focus behavior).
		6. Reinforce the low-probability behavior when it occurs.
		7. Monitor the effectiveness of the reinforcer.
		8. Once the behavior is established, fade tangible reinforcement so that the child is reinforced periodically for desired behavior.
		9. Continue to fade the tangible reinforcer as well as praise if behavior continues to improve.
	Correspondence training	1. Identify and define a focus behavior in measurable and observable terms.
		2. Identify a reinforcer (can be tangible or intangible) based on children's interests and likes. Pair the reinforcer with praise and positive feedback.
		3. Ask the child to make a statement about his or her intentions to engage in the focus behavior.
		4. When the child appropriately engages in the focus behavior, provide reinforcement.
		5. Monitor the effectiveness of the reinforcer.
		6. Once the behavior is established, fade tangible reinforcement so that the child is reinforced periodically for desired behavior.
		7. Continue to fade the tangible reinforcer as well as praise if the behavior continues to improve.
Model	Expansion or commenting	1. Respond to a child's utterance by expanding on what the child says to 1) complete a sentence or model appropriate grammar or 2) add more information to what the child says.
		2. Do not make a request for the child to respond to the expansion.
	Model	1. Observe what the child is interested in and comment about it.
		2. If the child repeats the model, provide positive feedback.
	Mand model	1. Observe what the child is interested in and request that the child say or do something.
		2. If the child responds correctly, provide positive feedback. If the child responds incorrectly, prompt for a correct response from the child.
Response prompting	Time delay	1. Identify and define a focus behavior in measurable and observable terms.

Class of strategy	Strategy name	Steps
		2. Determine whether the child is able to wait for a prompt or help if he or she does not know how to respond to a request.
		3. Provide a cue to the child to use the behavior.
		4. If the child responds correctly, provide positive feedback and/or reinforcement.
		5. If the child does not respond to the cue, wait 3–5 seconds and prompt the child to respond correctly.
		6. If the child responds correctly after the prompt, provide positive feedback and/or reinforcement.
		7. If the child does not respond correctly, do not prompt and do not reinforce.
	Least-to-most prompting (also known as the system of least prompts or graduated guidance)	1. Identify and define a focus behavior in measurable and observable terms.
		2. Identify a reinforcer (can be tangible or intangible) based on the child's interests and likes. Pair the reinforcer with praise and positive feedback.
		3. Ask the child to do or say something.
		4. If the child responds correctly, provide reinforcement and positive feedback.
		5. If the child responds incorrectly or does not respond, provide a prompt that reflects the least amount of help necessary to respond correctly.
		6. If the child responds correctly, provide reinforcement and positive feedback.
		7. If the child responds incorrectly, provide another prompt that offers more help than the previous prompt.
		8. If the child responds correctly, provide reinforcement and positive feedback.
		9. If the child responds incorrectly, continue to provide higher levels of prompts that offer more support than the previous level of prompting.
		10. Monitor the effectiveness of the strategy.
	Chaining	1. Identify a focus behavior and break it down into component steps (conduct a task analysis).
		2. If using a backward-chaining method, complete all of the steps leading up to the final step and ask the child to complete the last step.
		3. If using a forward-chaining method, ask the child to complete the first step and ask the child to complete subsequent steps.
		4. If the child responds correctly, provide reinforcement and positive feedback.
		5. If the child responds incorrectly, prompt a positive response.
		6. If the child responds correctly, provide reinforcement and positive feedback.
		7. If the child responds incorrectly, continue providing increasing levels of prompts or supports until the child responds correctly, then reinforce.
		8. Continue the process by asking the child to perform increasing steps in the process until he or she can complete the task independently.

Table 9.3. The DEC's recommended practices for child-focused intervention strategies

Adults use systematic procedures within and across environments, activities, and routines to promote children's learning and participation.

Interventionists are agents of change to promote and accelerate learning; learning should be viewed in different phases that require different types of practices. Phases are 1) acquisition, 2) fluency, 3) maintenance, and 4) generalization.

Practices are used systematically, frequently, and consistently within and across environments and across people.

Planning occurs prior to implementation, and that planning considers the situation to which the interventions will be applied.

Practices are used that are validated, normalized, useful across environments, respectful, not stigmatizing of the child and family, and sensitive to cultural and linguistic issues.

Consequences for children's behavior are structured to increase the complexity and duration of children's play, engagement, appropriate behavior, and learning by using differential reinforcement, response shaping, high-probability procedures, and correspondence training.

Systematic naturalistic teaching procedures such as models, expansions, incidental teaching, mand-model procedure, and naturalistic time delay are used to promote acquisition and use of communication and social skills.

Peer-mediated strategies are used to promote social and communicative behavior.

Prompting and prompt-fading procedures (e.g., modeling, graduated guidance, increasing assistance, time delay) are used to ensure acquisition and use of communicative, self-care, cognitive, and social skills.

Specialized procedures (e.g., naturalistic strategies and prompt/prompt-fading strategies) are embedded and distributed within and across activities.

Recommended instructional strategies are used with sufficient fidelity, consistency, frequency, and intensity to ensure high levels of behavior occurring frequently.

For problem behaviors, interventionists assess the behavior in context to identify its function and then devise interventions that are comprehensive in that they make the behavior irrelevant, inefficient, and ineffective.

From Hemmeter, M.L. (2005). Recommended practices for child-focused intervention strategies. In S. Sandall, M.L. Hemmeter, B.J. Smith, & M.E. McLean (Eds.), *DEC recommended practices in early intervention/early childhood special education* (pp. 42–53). Missoula, MT: Division for Early Childhood; adapted by permission. For the complete DEC recommended practices, see Sandall, S., Hemmeter, M.L., Smith, B.J., & McLean, M.E. (Eds.). (2005). *DEC recommended practices: A comprehensive guide for practical application in early intervention/early childhood special education*. Missoula, MT: Division for Early Childhood.

Data Collection and Progress Monitoring Decisions

In addition to identifying effective child-focused intervention strategies, IECSE teachers and their partners also must decide how they will monitor children's progress toward meeting their targeted IEP goals and objectives. In Chapters 4 and 6, we discussed various ways to collect data and track children's progress. Progress monitoring tools differ and can include work samples, time sampling protocols, or event sampling protocols. In choosing an appropriate progress monitoring tool, IECSE teachers and their partners must decide on the most salient features of the behavior—that is, are they most interested in the frequency with which a behavior occurs or are they most interested in the behavior's duration or intensity? Are they most interested in the types of help or support a child needs to succeed, or are they most interested in the child's work itself (i.e., a work sample). Heather and Sherry decided that they were interested in the length of time that it looked like Maxi was paying attention during morning meeting. (It is impossible to tell conclusively whether someone is paying attention, but Heather and Sherry decided that if Maxi was watching the teacher or whoever was speaking and was actively participating in morning meeting activities, then she was paying attention.) In making decisions about how to best collect data that can effectively inform instruction, IECSE teachers and their partners must consider the following:

- Which progress monitoring tools offer the *most detailed and relevant information* about children's progress toward meeting IEP or IFSP goals and objectives?

- Which progress monitoring tools are the *most efficient* for general education teachers and/or parents to use within the context of a busy day?

- Which progress monitoring tools are general education teachers and parents *most likely to use* on a routine basis?

- *What kinds of support* does the general education teacher or parent need to appropriately use the progress monitoring tool?

Summary

By engaging in an effective consultative relationship, Heather and Sherry found ways to embed meaningful learning opportunities that address high-priority IEP goals into Maxi's daily schedule. Although IECSE teachers have challenging jobs that require the acquisition and use of sophisticated skills, their job is not impossible. In this chapter, we offer a process that IECSE teachers can use to gather information and plan for the intervention process, a process that includes 1) understanding important characteristics of the child, including his or her strengths, interests, and learning needs; 2) identifying important characteristics about the adults who work with the child; 3) identifying key features of the learning environment that will support or impede progress; 4) prioritizing IEP or IFSP goals and objectives that the IECSE teacher and his or her partner can address; 5) identifying daily routines and activities that can serve as appropriate learning opportunities; 6) deciding whether children need to be motivated to engage in appropriate learning opportunities; 7) implementing appropriate child-focused intervention strategies to promote learning; and 8) developing effective and efficient progress-monitoring processes. In the next chapter, we will focus on the process of consultation and coaching to implement the intervention plan IECSE teachers develop with their partners.

CHAPTER 10

A Model for Providing Itinerant Services

Coaching, Consultation, and Evaluation

IECSE services, whether they are direct or consultative, should provide developmental support leading to the acquisition of key skills identified in the IEP. This outcome only can be realized with systematic, planned, and intentional effort on the part of the IECSE teacher and his or her ECE partner. The charge of the IECSE teacher begins following the IEP team meeting during which developmental objectives and placement are determined. Following these actions, the wheels are set in motion for the development of a plan of action for addressing these learning objectives within a community setting. This includes determination of whether IEP services will be provided in a direct or consultative manner. This chapter presents a model for delivering itinerant services through either coaching or consultation.

Consultation and Coaching Roles: Similarities and Differences

Before we discuss the consultative or coaching service delivery model, the distinction between consultation and coaching should be drawn. Although much of the focus of this text, as well as other relevant texts (Buysse & Wesley, 2005; Case-Smith & Cable, 1996; Hanft & Place, 1996) and publications (Fialka, 2001; Harris & Klein, 2002, 2004), is on consultation, coaching is a logical and desirable extension of consultation, particularly in a task-oriented or goal-oriented relationship such as IECSE services. Coaching includes all of the elements of consultation; however, in addition to showing another person a skill or sharing knowledge, coaching assumes continuity of commitment to the partner as well as active motivation of the partner. Whereas consultation is often episodic or intermittent, coaching is consistent and persistent. Consultation also is often based on unequal levels of expertise and authority. The consultant may be hired to observe and comment on efficiencies (or inefficiencies); demonstrate the use of a new product, process, or procedure; or demonstrate specific skills with the intent of their adoption by the target audience. Although a consultant may schedule periodic consultation sessions, these sessions are usually not frequent. Several weeks or months may transpire between consultation sessions.

Another model of consultation is an intense version in which the consultant may conduct several consultation sessions within a single week or month or over a few months. The clear expectation for consultation, from the perspective of the consultee, is that the consultation process is not personal and is time-limited. In addition, failure to use new products effectively or to adopt new processes or procedures is usually viewed as a deficiency of the consultee, not the consultant. The consultation relationship is often that of the expert and the learner or client.

As discussed previously in this text, effective consultation and coaching within the IECSE model assumes that the IECSE teacher is the expert and the ECE teacher is the learner or client. In the IECSE coaching model, failure to improve the knowledge and skills of the ECE partner teacher is not viewed as a failure of the *partner* but rather as the outcome of ineffective *coaching*. The coaching session is always framed with the expectation that performance and commitment will improve as a result of the coaching process. Effective coaches do not provoke defensiveness, guilt, or loss of confidence. The purpose of coaching is to help partners become more than they imagine themselves to be (Kinlaw, 1999).

In both the consultation and coaching models, there is an acknowledged difference in skill or content information between the expert and the learner. In the IECSE model, this arises from differences in formal education, professional experience, and, usually, certification or licensure. The IECSE teacher should be expected to have a different set of skills (e.g., teaching strategies) and content knowledge (e.g., characteristics of children) that are specific to early childhood special education or special education. This is not an inconvenient problem or an unimportant distinction between partners but rather an essential element that creates the need for the consultation or coaching relationship. This inequality must be addressed skillfully. The task of the consultant is to move this dynamic relationship from that of static consultation to robust and empowering coaching.

Working with Partners to Choose Consultation or Coaching Strategies

Unlike consultation that occurs in response to a request for specific assistance or a request for demonstration of a product or skill set, the consultation model in IECSE services may be seen as a mandate under IDEA for the school district to carry out its responsibility to provide a FAPE in the LRE. As such, the consultee, or the mentee in the coaching relationship, is presumed to be interested in accepting this assistance. Although the perception of inequality in this partnership may cause some discomfort, it is an unavoidable aspect of the IECSE teacher–ECE teacher partnership. There are, however, specific strategies that can be adopted to address this situation. In Chapter 1, we discussed formal communication tools that can be used to describe the consultation model. Sample form letters that define the roles and responsibilities of the IECSE teacher and the IECSE model versus the classroom instructor model; and that also address expectations for cooperation between IECSE teachers, ECE partner teachers, LEA administrators, parents of children in IECSE services, and ECE program directors are included in Appendix A. These form letters provide basic content for a series of communications between key partners in the IECSE process. They explain the basic model of IECSE service delivery, focus on adult–adult communication, and provide clear assurances of support from LEA personnel.

In their face-to-face relationship, the IECSE teacher and his or her ECE partner teacher must come to terms with the interpersonal nature of their partnership, which should help in moving the partners from consultation to coaching. This process of coming to an agreement about respective roles and responsibilities is central to the success of the IECSE model of service delivery.

The Phases of Coaching and Consultation and Movement to Partnership

As in any relationship, partners must develop trust as the central element of the relationship. If trust between the partners is established, the benefits of the partnership can be realized. If trust cannot be established, however, the benefits of a partnership will not be realized. Trust begins in the first stage of the emerging partnership. To use a sales metaphor, IECSE teachers are salespeople, and ECE partners, depending on their awareness of the IECSE model, are informed or wary customers. IECSE teachers are selling improvement in knowledge, skills, competence, and confidence. The challenge is that some customers may not be interested in the product or are unaware of its value. Also, like many salespeople, IECSE teachers are very interested in repeat sales, particularly if their employers have adopted or seek to develop an affinity network of committed programs. So, IECSE teachers must employ certain skills and strategies to sell their product.

The phases or stages in the consultation/coaching relationship have been described, in detail, in Chapter 5. In this chapter they are repeated to show how a relationship might develop within the consultation model of IECSE services.

Phase 1: Cultivating Awareness

The initial phase of the consultation partnership is *cultivating awareness*.

Jen and Felicia are ECE teachers at a preschool and work together on a daily basis. Jen has been an ECE teacher for 10 years, whereas Felicia has just started work this year after getting her associate's degree in early childhood education. Although Jen is an experienced ECE teacher and a great mentor for Felicia, Felicia's recent college-based exposure to the great possibilities that exist in a consultative IECSE service delivery model may be a topic of discussion in their day-to-day conversations, particularly if the only experience with IECSE service Jen has had is through a direct services model. Felicia may be able to facilitate Jen's interest in the consultative IECSE model. Although she may not be able to be an expert resource, she could pique Jen's interest in the model.

Phase 2: Introduction

In the second phase, *introduction*, the roles and responsibilities of the IECSE teacher are personalized through specific and formal communications with the ECE teacher as well as during initial visits to the classroom or child care center. This agenda may describe the underpinnings of the initial four to six visits between the IECSE teacher and the ECE teacher.

In our example, Maria, an IECSE teacher, may visit Jen's classroom to introduce herself and describe her position. Maria may be somewhat reserved and offer to answer any questions Jen has rather than volunteering information. Maria may make references to letters of introduction to the child's parent (Sample Letter 5, Appendix A), the director of the ECE program (Sample Letters 1 and 3, Appendix A), and to Jen from the IECSE teacher (Maria) (Sample Letter 2, Appendix A), which detailed the consultative model and its potential benefit in the preschool environment.

Phase 3: Rapport Building

Phase three, *rapport building*, actually begins in the introduction phase and is refined throughout the consultation and coaching relationship. This phase is an interesting balancing act between personal and professional attention and interaction. In our example, Maria, the IECSE teacher, and her ECE teacher partner, Jen, may build rapport by talking about the similarities in their educational and personal backgrounds—both have been teachers for approximately 10 years and attended colleges in the mid-Atlantic area, both are married and have children, and both express some reservations about the mission of their school district and how well the superintendent is fulfilling his promise to revive the system.

Phase 4: Establishing Comfort

Phase four, *establishing comfort*, precedes the emergence of a complete partnership. Like the building of professional and personal rapport, establishing comfort is the result of long-term interactions between the IECSE teacher and the ECE partner. This phase of the relationship could be expected to entail months of visits and consultation and/or coaching interactions. In effect, establishing comfort is a process that evolves and does not occur at a particular point in time. In our example, Jen and Maria began their relationship in somewhat different ways—Jen not quite knowing what to expect from an IECSE teacher she had never met and a process in which she never had engaged, and Maria with hope and confidence that a process she was very familiar with could produce positive results in a new environment. Through repeated and respectful communication, dedicated professionalism, personal kinship, and interest in the futures of the children in the classroom, the two partners were able to begin to trust and respect each other, with a comfortable professional and personal relationship as the result.

Phase 5: Partnership

The final phase of the coaching process, *partnership*, is the culmination of the prior phases and verifies the success of the coaching process. This is the desired outcome of the IECSE service delivery model. This phase, or state, is characterized by an atmosphere of mutual respect, improved competence of both members of the team, genuine encouragement of continued professional and personal development of both parties, and a sense of friendship that transcends the relationship. Creation of a partnership is the result of planning and intentionality.

By the beginning of the following school year, Jen and Maria knew each other and understood their respective needs. Jen was comfortable having Maria in the classroom to evaluate the learning environment and the children with special needs on her case-load. She respected Maria's extensive knowledge concerning how to modify the pre-school curriculum for young children with disabilities. Jen was able to learn some new strategies for supporting the children in her classroom who had special needs. Maria, for her part, was very impressed with Jen's resilience and willingness to learn. She also found herself continually in awe of Jen's ability to work with a classroom of 16 children with such apparent ease.

Making a Difference in the Knowledge, Skills, and Attitudes of ECE Partner Teachers

The IECSE teacher can make a difference in enhancing the knowledge and skills of his or her ECE partner teacher in a number of areas. The IECSE teacher can provide his or her partner with basic information on the causes and implications of a developmental condition such as Down syndrome. By providing relevant information in the form of articles, descriptions of conditions, videos, web site resources, web links to videostreams, and even online courses, the IECSE teacher may improve the confidence of the partner teacher in his or her interactions with a child with a disability. The ECE partner teacher will have a better understanding of the primary and associated disabilities of the condition as well as informed expectations concerning the behavior and skills of the child. This information will allay fears as well as address the misperception or misinformation that often undermines inclusion. Lack of accurate and current information adds to the anxiety of some teachers who rightfully claim that they "don't have special training to manage these kids." As the IECSE teacher may have a number of different ECE partners, he or she must be aware of a range of options for transmission of information that matches disparate levels of formal education, literacy, and professional and personal motivation.

The IECSE teacher may provide information on a variety of topics that are relevant to the characteristics of a child who is the focus of this instructional relationship. Information provided by the IECSE teacher also may be responsive to the longer term personal and professional development interests of his or her ECE partner. Basic information on the causes and implications of conditions such as intellectual disability, hearing impairment, attention-deficit/hyperactivity disorder (ADHD), fragile X syndrome, orthopedic impairments, epilepsy, other health disorders, autism, and other disabilities may be helpful for many ECE teachers. This information also may be helpful in understanding child development and function. Many resources address this type of information in a variety of formats (e.g., podcasts, print resources, dedicated web sites, professional journals, web links to videos, newsletters). Teachers also may seek information on specific conditions or impairments linked to specific conditions such as conductive hearing impairment, strabismus, pharmaceutical management of epilepsy, aphasia, and so forth. ECE partner teachers also may request information that describes specific teaching skills (e.g., use of picture cues, Picture Exchange Communication System [PECS; Bondy & Frost, 1998], Social Stories™ [Gray, 2010]), hierarchy of prompting, or other strategies to support engagement in the classroom environment (e.g., peer buddies).

The IECSE teacher also can help her ECE partner become more aware of the power of the holistic learning environment in supporting the development of the child and in using a range of instructional factors to address priority learning objectives. The MEPI model (application presented in Chapter 9) is a conceptual model that can be employed to help in determining the intensity of instruction and priority of IEP objectives.

Young children with special needs often have IEP objectives that address skills or behaviors across a range of developmental domains. IECSE teachers may have responsibility for 12–15 (or more) children. This will require sophisticated management of a number of IEP objectives. In an effort to improve the efficiency of learning and teaching, it is recommended that the IECSE teacher determine—with the contribution of the IEP team, parents, and the ECE partner teacher—which IEP objectives may require more intense instruction and which IEP objectives may be expected to develop as a result of maturation, environmental factors, and peer interactions. The MEPI model is intended to provide a rationale for review of IEP objectives and determination of intensity of intervention. The MEPI model recognizes four factors that may influence student development. These four factors correspond with "questions" to shape evaluation of the potential contribution of these factors to child development and, more specifically, attainment of priority IEP objectives.

The first factor in the model is maturation (M). In considering the impact of maturation on development, the partners must consider whether any IEP objective may be a skill that will be significantly influenced as a result of biological maturation. For example, speech skills may improve as a result of practice (and opportunity) as well as development of fine motor and attention skills. Motor skills, such as improving reach and grasp, appropriate grasp and manipulation of printing or coloring tools, and improved fluency in self-help skills (e.g., buttoning, zipping) also may be expected to improve as a result of frequent practice of these or related skills, and improvement in coordination (i.e., praxis) of gross and fine motor skills. Improvement in some of these skills may be linked to biological development and maturation.

When assessing the impact of the learning environment (E) on child development, some IEP objectives or skills may be expected to be responsive to the demands of the learning environment. For example, a child with mobility impairment (e.g., moderate, spastic-diplegic cerebral palsy) will have opportunity and motivation to practice movement if frequent movement is an expected component of daily activities and/or the teacher creates motivation or expectation for additional movement requirements for this child. Movement also would be necessary in gaining access to learning materials, participating in classroom routines, meeting the expectations of peers (e.g., response to social bids such as "Come over here") and/or the use of naturalistic instruction and/or incidental teaching strategies (e.g., SPIES strategies). Cognitive skills also may be addressed by environmental expectations (e.g., the process of choosing centers before open play time, entry in journal before transition to next activity, placement of utensils for snack in role of "helper"). Systematic planning such as the rotation of clothing in the housekeeping area or arts area (e.g., smocks) will require children to practice buttoning, zipping, closing clasps, or tying. Restriction of access to favorite or necessary materials (e.g., in containers with burp lids, screw top lids, pull-out drawers) will necessitate fine motor skill practice and/or interaction with peers to request assistance and so forth.

Certain skills and behaviors may be responsive to peer-mediated strategies or peer support (P). As an example, the teacher may have to encourage peers to be less helpful to certain children or help peers be more aware of the communication attempts of some children and the importance of responding as soon as possible. The teacher also may teach some children how to demonstrate skills to their peers using a number of smaller tasks (e.g., task analysis). He or she also may teach certain peers to reward their friends for demonstrating appropriate behavior. These examples are, in a sense, a form of direct instruction that may be carried out by peers after some training by the teacher.

Intensive/direct intervention (I) may be required for certain high priority and critical skills identified in the IEP. Some skills that children will need to be successful in their immediate environment (e.g., home or school), or in their "next" environment (e.g., kindergarten) may be priorities for intervention. Acquisition of these skills and movement to fluency, maintenance, and generalization may require focused and concerted instruction. Adults must address some inappropriate behaviors (e.g., persistent physical aggression toward peers) immediately and consistently. This may require proactive teaching of appropriate skills via a commercial curriculum (e.g., *Skillstreaming*, McGinnis & Goldstein [1990]; *Incredible Years*, Webster-Stratton [1992]) and specific consequences for aggressive behavior. Expanding on-task behavior is another example of a skill that may require periodic intervention to maintain on-task behavior.

Some academic skills are addressed through group or individual instruction (e.g., identification of lowercase letters). It is important to note that academic skill instruction can be enhanced through embedded and longitudinal opportunities for learning and generalization. For example, placing word labels on common objects throughout the classroom to increase the probability of incidental learning, peer modeling, and peer mediation should facilitate discrimination and recognition of words and letters.

The primary benefit in the use of planning tools, such as the MEPI and curriculum planning matrices (Chapter 2), is to reduce ECE partner teacher anxiety, affirm the competence of the ECE teacher, and recognize the potential influence and richness of a high-quality early learning environment.

Evaluating the Effects of IECSE Services on Children's Development

The effect of IECSE services on children's development is not a secondary outcome. It is, in fact, the primary outcome of an effective IECSE relationship, and it can be achieved by consultative, indirect intervention on the part of the IECSE teacher instead of child-focused, direct instruction. The effect of IECSE services on child development can only be verified by monitoring the progress of the child with respect to priority IEP objectives. It is important to note, however, that the gains of a child who has been placed in a community-based setting may not be solely attributed to the effects of IECSE intervention. For many of those children placed in community-based pre-K programs, the effects of environmental engagement, peer expectations, and peer modeling are fundamental elements of the learning environment. These factors may be enough to support meaningful gains in some areas of development (e.g., social skills, expressive and receptive language, gross motor skills) without intensive teacher intervention. These are exactly the considerations that the IEP team must consider in evaluating the range of placement options as required by IDEA 2004 (PL 108-446).

Although the progress of the ECE partner teacher is the focus of the IECSE model, the effectiveness of the consultation or coaching is only evident in *child* progress. This is, for some administrators, the hazard in adopting the consultation model in IECSE services in lieu of intensive and episodic direct services. As discussed in Chapter 2, however, research evidence supports distributed instruction and practice as a more effective model for instruction and learning versus intensive and massed opportunity instruction. Regardless of tradition or preferred practices within the school district or state department of education, the child-focused, direct-instruction option does not appear to be a viable option for the IECSE service delivery model.

In adopting the IECSE service delivery model, and consultation practices in particular, it is necessary that a system for monitoring child development be negotiated during the consultation and coaching process. The effect of coaching can be seen in more efficient strategies for instruction, resulting in more opportunities for instruction and learning and, consequently, improvement of the child in key behaviors or skills defined in the IEP.

Informing Parents of the Success of IECSE Services

Unless the child is served in the home setting, effective communication with parents can be overlooked in the IECSE model. It is important to understand that, although parents are primary members of the IEP team, they may not fully understand the IECSE service delivery model. They may have particular difficulty understanding the rationale for adoption of consultation or coaching services versus providing one-to-one, child-focused instruction. From the perspective of the parents, special education services are the focus of their relationship with Part C or Part B 619 programs. This is a particularly delicate topic for many parents who have supported direct instruction and may have, in the past, elected center-based services rather than enrollment of their child in community-based services. It is no wonder that some parents who are actively involved in the IEP process may be unaware of the itinerant service delivery option in Part B 619 services. Some parents who may be aware of this option may be reluctant to seek placement in community-based programs out of fear of loss of significant one-to-one instruction time.

Parents who actively participate in the IEP process, including the IEP team meeting, can be expected to have a better understanding of the rationale for the recommendation for placement of their child in a community-based pre-K program. It is still prudent, however, to discuss the difference in how instructional services will be delivered in a consultation and coaching model instead of the more familiar direct instruction model. It is also important for the IEP team members to help the parents and other team members understand the role that maturation, peer expectations, and the characteristics of the learning environment will play in supporting the development of the child. This discussion is imperative when the IEP team determines that the child is likely to benefit from community placement and the parents are not active participants in the IEP process or are proponents of center-based special education services. Parents must understand the power of the community pre-K program with respect to facilitation of growth of their child. Parents must be reassured that IECSE services in community-based programs will be at least as effective as center-based services.

Parents whose children are served through IECSE services may gain a better understanding of the nature of the IECSE model through the sharing of planning and teaching tools used by the IECSE teacher and his or her ECE teacher partner. They should understand how the IECSE teacher, in conjunction with the ECE partner teacher, may use planning tools such as the MEPI and matrix planning to address where, when, and how key IEP objectives can be addressed in daily classroom routines and across activities.

Building on the Success of Coaching and Addressing Challenges to the Model

Expanding IECSE services, where appropriate, is contingent on the success of the consultation model. It is necessary for the school district to assume the leadership role in promoting the benefits of the IECSE model, particularly with respect to the effectiveness of consultation and coaching practices within this model. The school district, in conjunction with energetic ECE program partners, must provide public testimony regarding the positive gains of children and ECE staff as a result of the close working relationship that has been developed between the school district and engaged ECE program partners.

In an effort to heighten the awareness of ECE professionals and parents of the benefits of the IECSE model, the proactive school district might consider developing public information pamphlets. These pamphlets or brochures would be targeted toward parents and ECE program administrators and staff. The content would describe the LRE component of the IEP process and its link to the IECSE service delivery model. Similar content could be included in the following:

- Local school district web sites

- Local web site of the National Association for the Education of Young Children (NAEYC)

- Child Find web sites

- Brochures or fact sheets that are available at major area child care and preschool program sites, such as YWCA childcare programs, networks of faith-based providers, or similar programs

- Brochures or fact sheets that can be provided to parents of children transitioning from Part C to Part B 619 services

- Regional therapy services agencies that provide outpatient speech, language, physical, and/or occupational therapy services

- Regional or statewide special education resource center site

- Head Start web sites

- Local and regional parent support and advocacy group newsletters

- Other web sites that are visited by parents of young children with special needs, EC teaching staff and administrators, and child care program staff

The challenges to adoption of consultation practices within the IECSE model are best addressed by communication of the success of the model to current and potential constituents. Ensuring that the annual reports of the Head Start agency, the school district, and partner ECE programs include a summary of annual placement and service history specific to IECSE services is recommended. Featuring successful partnerships in local news venues, school district or program newsletters, and other more informal information vehicles also is recommended. These articles should include the personal comments of parents, ECE partner teachers, ECE program administrators and supervisors, and IECSE teachers that attest to the benefits of community placements of young children with special needs. These personal testimonies should focus on child gains, parent satisfaction with the IECSE model, and ECE partner teacher comments. The comments of ECE partner teachers should attest to the benefits of the coaching model for the child, as well as the professional and personal benefits of the consultation and/or coaching process in enhancing the competence and confidence of the ECE partner teacher.

Summary

Consultation and coaching are powerful strategies for imparting skills to other professionals. Nevertheless, initiating an effective consultative or coaching-based IECSE service delivery model requires considerable effort. The phases described above lay out a rough outline of what is necessary to make the consultative model work well in a school or district where this model has not been used before or where the model may be used inconsistently or infrequently. Evaluating the effectiveness of the model—based on the developmental progress of the child—needs to occur continually and must include the investment of all stakeholders; evaluation and assessment of child gain and testimony of ECE partner teachers concerning improvement in competence and confidence are integral to helping parents and other laypeople (e.g., guardians, grandparents, other involved family members) to regard the model positively. Positive and proactive strategies, as described above, should be considered in addressing the causes of resistance of school districts, ECSE and ECE professionals, or parents to the adoption of the consultation model in IECSE services.

CHAPTER 11

Pulling It All Together
A Case Study

The purpose of this case study is to illustrate how IECSE teachers would work with other adults to provide high-quality services to young children with disabilities. All of the names used in this case study are fictional.

Andrea, Siri, and Mallory

Andrea pulled up to the Stones's apartment building, listening to her stomach grumble and complain. Breakfast had been a long time ago! She couldn't wait for lunch. By agreement, she ate lunch at the Stones's house on Mondays. That was because one of Siri's IEP goals was using a spoon and fork to feed herself. She and Mallory, Siri's mom, had decided that eating lunch together would provide a good opportunity not only for Siri but also for Andrea and Mallory to work together to help Siri. At first, Andrea had brought her lunch; but soon Mallory had insisted on fixing lunch for all of them, so sometimes Andrea brought dessert.

Siri had just turned 3 years old, and Andrea had only been working with her for about a month. Siri was a sweet little girl who, because of her age, was sometimes slow to warm up to others. She had spent a lot of time in the hospital and was understandably wary of unfamiliar people. Siri was small for her age and had many undiagnosed fine and gross motor difficulties in addition to delays in receptive language. She was also a "germ magnet" and seemed to catch every cold that was going around. For that reason, Mallory had decided on home-based itinerant services for Siri. Because she stayed home with Siri, Mallory also provided child care in her home for two other children. Jacob was in first grade and was in school during the day, but Jacob's little sister, Avery, was 4 years old and was a perfect playmate for Siri. Avery was an active preschooler who got into everything. In addition to the extra income, Mallory was glad to have Avery because Siri adored her. She woke up in the morning asking about Avery, and her eyes sparkled when Avery arrived every morning. Having two very young children to care for was a challenge, but Mallory enjoyed it—especially when she managed to get both girls down for a nap at the same time so she had some time for herself! Being a single mom, she enjoyed Andrea's visits; it wasn't very often she had time to spend with other adults.

As Andrea walked up the stairs to the second-floor apartment, she smelled macaroni and cheese and smiled. She knew it was the girls' favorite (the elbow kind, not the shell kind), and, secretly, it was her favorite, too! Mentally, she reviewed last week's visit, realizing that she had forgotten to pick up the flyer about children's storytime at the library around the corner. She had told

Mallory that she would find out more details and it had slipped her mind. She was glad, though, that she had remembered to bring the data collection chart and DVD about supporting children's language. Mallory did not have an Internet connection but did have a DVD player. Andrea would often download video clips and other printed materials onto a DVD that Andrea could either watch on her television or from her computer.

At 21 years of age, Mallory was a young mother who was devoted to her daughter and committed to her future. She had given birth to Siri shortly after graduating from high school; and although she had attended the local community college sporadically, she didn't have any firm career path. Siri's father was not in the picture, but Mallory's parents were helpful in many different ways. Mallory also had an older sister and a younger brother. Her older sister had a family and invited Mallory and Siri over often, and her brother loved to babysit his young niece. Although Mallory wished her circumstances were different, she was grateful for her family and friends. Determined that Siri was going to go to college, she almost tried too hard, purchasing ABC flashcards and other school supplies for Siri. She was frustrated when Siri wasn't interested in them, especially when she sat down with Avery and Siri for "school" every morning. Andrea was capitalizing on Mallory's enthusiasm by helping her find other developmentally appropriate ways of supporting Siri's and Avery's learning.

Andrea knocked on the door, hearing the girls' footsteps as they ran to greet her. A few seconds later, Mallory answered the door, greeting Andrea with a cheerful "Hi!"

"Hope you like mac 'n' cheese!" Mallory exclaimed, "I know we had it last week, but the girls wouldn't stop asking for it! I have some peanut butter and jelly, too, if you'd rather have a sandwich."

"You know that mac 'n' cheese is one of my guilty pleasures, Mallory!" Andrea laughed. "How about next week you let me bring lunch? I make a mean bowl of Spaghettios!"

"Well, we'll see. I was actually wondering if maybe you'd want to meet me at McDonald's for lunch next week—there's one around the corner that has a playground," Mallory explained.

"That would be great—the girls would have a blast, and it would be a perfect way to help Siri with some of her gross motor skills that Char had mentioned."

Char was Siri's physical therapist, who, along with Oscar, the occupational therapist, provided these related services to Siri. Although Mallory brought Siri over to Maplewood School to see Char and Oscar twice a month, it was Andrea's job to consult with Char and Oscar so she could help Mallory assist Siri at home. In addition to Char and Oscar, Andrea also worked with Sue, Siri's speech-language therapist, to help Siri expand her vocabulary. Storytime at the library had been an idea that Sue had suggested to Andrea. In addition to providing a good, language-rich experience for Siri (and Avery), there was also a lot of information about how parents can support their children's emergent literacy at home. Also, there were other moms there who Andrea thought Mallory might like connecting with, remembering how much Mallory needed to have friendships with other women her age. Andrea reminded herself again to bring the storytime flyer when she next saw Mallory.

"So what are you going to teach Siri today?" Mallory asked.

Andrea sighed inwardly. It was hard for some parents to understand that Andrea's time was best spent working with them—not working with their children. In an hour, Mallory could do very little "magic," she tried to explain. However, parents and other caregivers who were with their children 24/7 could find many opportunities to help their children meet their goals. They just needed some help figuring out how to do it, and helping them figure out how best to help was Andrea's job. Over the years, Andrea had come to understand that some parents knew this instinctively, and

Andrea could only marvel at how they were able to accomplish so much. Other parents refused to accept this philosophy, adamant that their children deserved Andrea's full attention. Some even went so far as to leave the room when Andrea arrived. One mom had even tried to leave the house until Andrea had told her that she had to stay. Still other parents doubted their own ability and believed that their child needed the help of an "expert." Mallory fell into this last group—doubting her own abilities, sure that she could never give Siri the kind of help that she needed. Over the month they had worked together, Andrea had come to realize that Mallory needed a lot of reinforcement and confidence building.

"I'm not going to teach Siri anything, Mallory! Remember, you're the one who can best help Siri learn what she needs to learn," Andrea exclaimed. "Let's take a look at our notes from last week's visit to see what we should be doing this week."

Andrea pulled her notebook out of her bag. She had already reviewed last week's notes on the way over to the apartment and knew what was on the schedule. However, referring to the notes instead of simply reminding Mallory what was on the schedule was more tactful and respectful.

"Well, in addition to helping Siri eat lunch, our notes said that we were going to talk about ways to help Siri use language more effectively. Siri's just 3, so she's pretty young for school stuff, but there are lots of ways that you can help her learn what words mean. That's one of her IEP goals, and it's really important for success in kindergarten. Let's have lunch with the kids, and then we can talk about how you can help Siri. Does that sound okay?" Andrea asked.

"Sounds good," Mallory answered. "The mac 'n' cheese is getting cold!"

Andrea helped Mallory get Siri and Avery ready for lunch. Avery was a great little peer model for Siri, Andrea thought. Being a year older then Siri, Avery was Siri's hero. She wanted to do everything just like Avery did, which included eating what she ate. Because Avery liked macaroni and cheese, so did Siri. As Mallory put Siri's bib on, Siri studied Avery eating with her "big-girl" fork. It didn't take much prodding to get Siri to pick up her "big-girl" fork too; and although Mallory needed to help her use it, providing hand-over-hand assistance, she managed to consume lunch with a minimum of mess. Andrea watched Mallory helping Siri and remembered that when she had first started coming for lunch, Mallory had seemed pretty helpless—preferring to feed Siri instead of helping her learn to feed herself.

"Wow, Mallory—look at Siri use her fork! You're doing a great job helping her. Before long, she'll be doing it herself. In fact, maybe next week we can talk about how to back off a little bit and give Siri a chance to use the fork herself."

"Thanks," Mallory said, smiling and inwardly proud of Siri's accomplishment. "She certainly makes a bigger mess this way, but I guess it's worth it!" Avery was done with lunch, and it looked like Siri was just about done too, finishing off the last of her apple juice. Mallory wiped off the cheese from Siri's face (it was *all* over the place) and helped both girls wash their hands.

"You know, Mallory," Andrea said as they were cleaning the kitchen, "just talking with Siri and Avery about what you're doing is a great way to help Siri learn language. When she hears your words describing what you're doing, she learns what words mean. Pretty soon, she'll be using those words herself. In fact, that was one of the things I wanted to talk with you about today—using your words to describe what's happening. For example, you could tell her what you're doing using simple words like, 'Let's wash your face.' As you wash her face, she begins to understand what *wash* and *face* mean."

"I guess that makes sense," Mallory said, "but Siri doesn't really talk yet, and it seems like I'd just be talking to myself all of the time!"

"Well, you're sort of right," Andrea admitted. "But hearing you use language will provide a good model for Siri, and pretty soon she'll be repeating what you say and then telling you what she's doing. Didn't you say that the girls' favorite television program was on now? We could all watch it together and I could show you what I mean."

"That sounds like a good idea," Mallory said, as she gathered the girls on the couch in front of the television. "Maybe after that, it will be time for their nap!"

Mallory turned on the television and found the program, which was just starting. Andrea told Mallory that although preschoolers shouldn't watch very much television, watching a television program *together* was sort of like reading a book together. Adults could comment about what they saw on the program, and the language they used could help children understand what the words meant. However, with young children, the comments that adults made should be simple and easy to understand—not too many words, with an emphasis on the key words in the comment. To help Mallory understand what she meant, Andrea commented on what was happening on the show by saying, "Wow, that horse runs *fast*!" The girls turned their heads and nodded in agreement. "Horsie runs *fast*!" Avery said.

"See what I mean?" Andrea asked. "I knew that they were watching the horse, and by saying, 'That horse runs fast' I was putting into words what they were seeing. Avery did just what we want Siri to do—repeat what I said. How about you try it, Mallory?"

"Okay," Mallory said. As she watched what was happening, she said, "The girl is jumping rope." Turning to Siri, she said, "Now you say it. Say, 'The girl is jumping rope.'" She looked expectantly at Siri, and when Siri just nodded her head, Mallory turned to Andrea. "Okay, now what? She won't say it back to me."

"Well, Siri doesn't have to say anything to be learning. Avery's at a stage in which she likes to repeat back what someone says, but not all children do that—especially younger kids like Siri. I wouldn't worry about Siri repeating what you said or asking her to repeat it. For now, she's learning just by hearing what you say. I bet after a while, though, she'll start responding back to what you say—sort of like having a conversation. Want to try again?" Andrea asked.

Mallory nodded her head and said, "That's a *big ball*," as a big ball appeared on the television screen. Avery nodded her head, and Siri, looking first at Mallory and then at Avery, nodded her head too.

"That's great Mallory! Did you see how Siri acknowledged what you said by nodding her head? Pretty soon she'll be responding to you and using words to tell you what she sees," Andrea exclaimed. Mallory looked satisfied with herself, and she and Andrea took turns commenting on what was happening on the rest of the show.

Glancing at the clock, Andrea said, "We have about 15 minutes before I have to go, Mallory, and I wanted to share some information with you about helping children learn language. The girls look pretty comfortable—it looks like it's almost naptime. Maybe we can let them watch television for a few more minutes so we can talk." Andrea pulled out a blank form and a DVD. "I was hoping that we could use this form to identify some times during the day when you could use the commenting strategy we just practiced. What do you think about this activity—watching television with the girls after lunch? The girls have been pretty interested in the show and it's sort of a relaxing activity before naptime."

Mallory nodded her head in agreement and suggested that she could also try the commenting strategy when she took the kids for a walk during the day and maybe when they were playing with toys in the morning. Andrea agreed that those were great times of the day and asked whether grocery shopping would be a good opportunity to use commenting.

Mallory shook her head vehemently. "Oh, not shopping!" she exclaimed. "I have all I can do to keep the girls next to me and get the things I want! If I had to add that in, I'd go crazy!"

"No problem—I know that grocery shopping can be kind of a trial with two little kids in tow." Andrea looked at the matrix and asked, "What about getting dressed in the morning? You could talk with Siri about what you're doing and the kind of clothes she's wearing. You know—'blue shirt,' 'green pants'—that kind of thing. The most important thing is that you talk to her about what you're doing so she starts to understand the importance of language for communication."

"Sure, that sounds like a good idea," Mallory said. "I could probably do it when I'm fixing lunch too, although that can get a little busy. Maybe breakfast would be better—Avery doesn't get here until after breakfast, and it's a little bit more relaxing with just Siri and me."

"Well, let's add breakfast in and see how you do. If you can't do all of this, that's okay." Andrea completed the matrix and showed it to Mallory. "We've identified four different times of the day when you can comment about what you're doing. If breakfast doesn't work, then maybe we can figure something else out."

"Mallory, one of the things that's important is to keep track of how often you use this commenting strategy. There's a lot of research about the benefits of commenting in supporting children's language use, and I think if you could just document when you use it, we'll have a record that will be helpful in making decisions about what to do next. All I'd like you to do is to put a check mark in the box when you use the commenting strategy. For example, if you do it tomorrow morning when you're helping Siri get dressed, just put a check mark on that box. Next week, we'll have a record of how often you used it. I know life gets busy and you might forget to comment once in a while, and that's okay. You might also forget to mark the box once in a while, but if you realize that you forgot, you can just go back and mark it off. What do you think about using this system?" Andrea asked.

"I think I can handle it. Maybe I'll put it on the refrigerator to help me remember," Mallory said.

"That's a great idea, Mallory!" Andrea exclaimed. "I think that once you get in the habit, it won't be too much of a hassle. Maybe in a few weeks we can talk about how you can record what Siri did in response to your commenting—that would be a good step."

"Sounds good," Mallory said.

"One more thing before I go. I have this DVD that shows how adults can help children learn to use a fork and a spoon. I really like it because it shows you exactly what to do and say. I thought that I could leave it here for you and you could watch it. We can talk about it next week. I think that Siri's ready to start using a fork and a spoon by herself, and this video is good at explaining how to do that."

"Okay," Mallory said. "Maybe I can watch it after Siri goes to bed tonight."

"That would be great," Andrea said as she was filling out the Visit Log. "I'm looking forward to next week at McDonald's! It will be fun to go out with you and the girls. I also wanted to tell you that I think you're doing a great job working with Siri. I really admire your commitment to her and your willingness to try new things—Siri's a lucky girl!"

Andrea stooped down to say good-bye to Avery and Siri and handed Mallory her copy of the visit log and the matrix. She put her copies of the forms in Siri's folder and put on her coat. Giving Mallory a quick hug, she left the apartment knowing that she had the rest of the afternoon in her office to work on paperwork.

Andrea, Jackson, and Jen

Andrea was running late; not surprising, considering that she had to stop for gas this morning and stop at the office before her first visit of the day. To top that off, her supervisor, Maggie, had wanted to talk with her about the transportation schedules for the kids on her caseload. So when she pulled into the parking lot at The Hillside Center, she had to stop, catch her breath, and think about her visit to Jackson's classroom. She took a minute to pull out a binder—Jackson's binder, which contained the consultation logs, instructional matrices, and his IEP. All of this paper! Andrea wondered if it were time to invest in one of those small laptops—it certainly would make her life easier and save some trees! As she quickly reviewed last week's log, she was glad that she was working with Jen, Jackson's teacher.

Jackson was 4½ years old and had just been diagnosed with autism spectrum disorder (ASD). After observing Jackson at home and in his classroom, Andrea had expected it. Jackson seemed to be off in his own little world. He spoke very little and avoided both children and adults. The only thing that seemed to interest him was a bucket of little dinosaurs that was in the corner of the block area. Every morning he would make a beeline to the block area, dump out the bucket of dinosaurs, and start lining them up. He would do this uninterrupted until Jen, his teacher, gently guided him over to the circle where the day began. The same thing happened at home, except that at home he was fixated on his blocks. He loved to dump them out and stack them up and would spend hours in a corner of the family room, seemingly isolated from the rest of the world, including his older sisters Brit and Madison. His mom and dad joked that they were hopeful he was getting ready to build the world's highest skyscraper; but behind their jokes, they were worried about how Jackson was ever going to be ready for kindergarten.

Jackson had been attending The Hillside Center since he was a baby, and his older sisters had attended that school, too. Jackson's parents, Mr. and Mrs. Evert, both worked—he was a financial advisor and she was an office manager for a busy doctor's office. The Everts were happy with their children's child care center. They had done their homework, researching child care centers and learning how important a high-quality early childhood program was. They had visited many centers before deciding on The Hillside Center, a bright, cheerful place that had once been an old house. Hillside served 70 children from infants through preschool, with a school-age program in the summer. Every room had at least two teachers, one of whom had a bachelor's degree. James, the director, was proud of the center and especially happy to be partnering with the local school district to serve young children with disabilities like Jackson. In addition to Jackson, Hillside served six other children who had either an IFSP or IEP. Two of the teachers, Jen and Abbi, were in graduate school, completing a licensure program for early childhood special education. James was keeping his fingers crossed that he could convince them to stay at Hillside once they had graduated. He knew how tempting a public school teacher's salary and benefits were to his teachers, who he couldn't afford to pay very much.

Andrea was buzzed into the center and signed the visitor's log at the front desk before heading down to Jackson's room. As she stopped to admire the latest artwork, Scott came out of one of the classrooms, ready to step in for Jen so she could work with Andrea and Jackson. Scott was enrolled in the local community college and was excited to have been hired as a "floating" substitute at Hillside. He liked the fact that he was able to interact with all of the children in the center. He filled in for teachers who were absent and was the "extra pair of hands" when Hillside classrooms had visitors such as Andrea. Scott and Andrea exchanged greetings before entering Jen's classroom.

As Andrea walked into Jen's classroom, she reminded herself again how lucky Jackson was to have such a great learning environment. Andrea wished that all of the children on her caseload could attend preschools like Hillside! Jen's classroom was divided into learning centers, with small furniture and equipment serving as room dividers—high enough to give the children some privacy but low enough for teachers to monitor the kids' activities at all times. There were quiet areas for reading books and playing with small manipulatives, a dramatic play area decked out as a veterinarian's office, a block area complete with props and accessories to promote literacy, and an area for children's storage. Andrea spotted Jackson in the block area, as usual, playing with the dinosaurs. She was happy to see that, even though he was playing by himself, he was sitting on the floor next to two other children who were building a block structure. Given Jackson's love of blocks at home, she wondered if she and Jen could coax him into playing along with the children.

Jen got up from the dramatic play area where she was holding a stuffed bear for examination by Kiley, this morning's "vet." She signaled to Andrea that she'd meet her outside in a few minutes. Andrea used that time to say hello to Jackson and talk with him briefly about his day. Although Jackson didn't look up from the dinosaurs when Andrea walked over, he nodded his head when Andrea asked him if he was having a good day. At least that was some response, Andrea thought.

Jen and Andrea met in the small office adjacent to the classroom. They were lucky to have this adult space where they could discuss what had happened last week and talk about today's work. Andrea pulled out the consultation log from last week to review what they had discussed. She was glad that she had remembered to download the handout about transitioning strategies because this was one of the difficulties that Jackson and Jen faced every day in the classroom. She pulled it out of the folder and talked with Jen about some ideas they could use. They were both optimistic about using a picture schedule in the classroom. Andrea explained that a picture schedule was kind of like an agenda or organizer for a child and was very helpful to a child like Jackson who had difficulty with change. After Andrea explained it, Jen remarked that there were probably other children in the classroom who could also benefit from a picture schedule—especially some of the younger children. They decided to build the schedule as a wall chart that could be posted in the central area of the classroom. They also decided to use photos of the different classroom routines so they would be as realistic as possible for Jackson and the other children. Introducing the picture schedule to the whole class would be a good way to support Jackson without singling him out, and Jen decided that she could probably get it done in a week or so. Andrea volunteered to take the pictures. Both were eager to try out this new communication tool and discussed the possibility of Jackson's parents using something similar at home.

After they had talked about the picture schedule, Andrea and Jen reviewed Jackson's learning matrix for the coming week. With his IEP objectives across the top and the classroom routines along the left-hand side, the matrix provided a pretty easy way to identify some good learning opportunities throughout the day. Leaving Jackson's name off, Jen usually posted it on the wall by the sink so that she and the other teachers could easily refer to it. With 13 other children in the room, staying organized was important to Jen.

Jackson's motor skills were fairly normal, but, as is true for many individuals with ASD, Jackson had a lot of difficulty with communication. His learning matrix reflected this emphasis in communication, especially responding to others' requests or conversational initiations. (In addition, Jackson needed help expanding his vocabulary as well as increasing the number of words he used in a sentence.) Finally, Jackson needed help handling transitions. From a behavioral perspective, this was probably the most problematic. If he wasn't prepared for a transition, Jackson would have what his mom called a "meltdown," falling on the floor and crying. If that happened, it usually took about 10 minutes to get him calmed down to the point that he could make the transition. Andrea had emphasized with Jackson's parents and teachers that the key to dealing with this was prevention. If Jackson was adequately prepared for a transition, he would comply. Although he would need to learn how to deal with unanticipated transitions, the adults in his life could help by preparing him properly. This was one of the reasons for the picture schedule.

Andrea knew that one of Jen's challenges was providing these learning opportunities to Jackson while at the same time meeting the needs of the other children in the classroom. They discussed ways of making sure Jen or one of the other teachers in the room had the time they needed to help Jackson during these routines. For example, transitions were difficult for other children besides Jackson and arrival and/or departure times were challenging for the teachers. They decided that extra help during these times would be wonderful. Jen volunteered to talk with James about having Scott come to help for about 15 minutes each day during these transition times. Knowing that having a "Plan B" was a smart thing to do, Jen and Andrea also discussed making use of some of the parent volunteers who helped out at Hillside. With both of these options available, Jen was fairly confident that she would have time to help Jackson learn to transition on his own.

After talking about the logistics involved in getting some extra help during transition times, Andrea talked with Jen about a specific intervention strategy they could use. Andrea had done her homework and thought that perhaps *time delay* would be a good intervention strategy to use with Jackson during transition times in addition to the picture schedule. Earlier in the week, she had downloaded an implementation checklist from the Ohio Center for Autism and Low Incidence (OCALI; http://www.autisminternetmodules.org/mod_list.php) about how to use time delay. The checklist was great because it broke down the intervention strategy into discrete steps and could remind Jen and the other teachers exactly what steps they should take to make sure they used the strategy correctly. Andrea liked to use these checklists as a coaching tool as well as a great reminder to leave behind in the classroom. Last week, she had used a similar implementation checklist with another teacher. She and the teacher reviewed the checklist to make sure that the teacher knew all of the terms. Then she asked the teacher to watch her use the intervention with the child ("Make sure I complete all of the steps correctly!" she told the teacher), checking off each step as she saw it. Then they talked about what Andrea had done—making sure to address any questions the teacher had. Finally, they switched roles, with the teacher trying out the intervention and Andrea checking off the steps. Again, they debriefed, and Andrea provided some feedback to the teacher about what she saw ("It was great how you waited for Tyler to look at you before you gave him the instruction," and "Remember to be specific when you give him some praise"). Andrea agreed to come next week right before Jackson was ready to leave so she and Jen could use the checklist.

Glancing at her watch, Andrea saw that she still had about 25 minutes before she had to leave. Great! She needed to spend some time with Jackson updating her assessment records. Even though Jen was great about keeping track of Jackson's progress, Andrea needed to collect some data during her visits too. She usually conducted "probe" sessions with Jackson to see how his communication skills were progressing. Basically, that meant that she would join him in whatever activity he was engaged and use whatever opportunities presented themselves to evaluate his progress toward meeting his IEP objectives.

Although today Andrea was going to spend time interacting with Jackson, she also spent time just observing, or "kid watching." It was important to see, in general, how Jackson interacted with the other children and how he responded to Jen's instruction. Andrea chuckled to herself when she

Implementation Checklist for Time Delay

Instructions: The Implementation Checklist includes each step for implementing time-delay procedures. Please complete all of the requested information including the site and state, teacher being observed, and the learner's initials. Within the table, record a 2 (*implemented*), 1 (*partially implemented*), 0 (*did not implement*), or NA (*not applicable*) next to each step observed to indicate to what extent the step was implemented/addressed during your observation. Use the last page of the checklist to record the target skill, your comments, whether others were present, and plans for next steps for each observation.

Site: _____   State: _____

Teacher/practitioner: _____   Learner's initials: _____

Preparing for the time delay									
	Observation	**1**	**2**	**3**	**4**	**5**	**6**	**7**	**8**
	Date								
	Observer's Initials								
Step 1. Identifying target skill/behavior(s)		**Score**							
1. Teachers/practitioners define the target skill/behavior in terms that are observable and measurable.									
2. Teachers/practitioners identify the target skill/behavior as being either a:									
a. Discrete task									
b. Chained task									
3. Teachers/practitioners define learner response behaviors.									
Step 2. Determining current skills									
1. Teachers/practitioners assess a learner's current skills by directly observing the learner during daily routines and activities.									

Figure 11.1. Sample page of Implementation Checklist for Time Delay. (From Neitzel, J., & Wolery, M. [2009]. *Implementation checklist for time delay*. Chapel Hill, NC: the National Professional Development Center on Autism Spectrum Disorders, FPG Child Development Institute, The University of North Carolina; adapted by permission.)

remembered what one of the other teachers she worked with said about "kid watching". Not all teachers understood the value of observation, and this teacher had chided Andrea for "goofing off" during her visits to her classroom. Although Andrea laughed it off (she had thick skin), the next week she brought the teacher a handout explaining the importance of teacher observations and showed her the notes she had taken during the time she was goofing off. She also chided herself for not doing a better job explaining to the teacher beforehand what she was going to do and why she was going to do it!

Andrea and Jen completed the consultation log, noting what they had talked about and how they had to prepare for their next visit. Pressing hard on the top sheet, Andrea made sure that the other copies of the log were legible. One copy went in Jackson's book bag to take home, Jen kept a copy, and Andrea kept a copy. Andrea and Jen both filed their copies once they were finished with them so there was a good record of their work together. Although paperwork was never fun, at least this paperwork helped Andrea and Jen keep track of what they had done and their plans for the weeks ahead. It was also an easy way to keep Jackson's parents "in the loop"!

Heading back into the classroom, Andrea joked with Jen about the growing difficulty she was having getting up and down from the floor. "You know, these knees certainly aren't what they used to be! I'm going to have to start bringing along knee pads!" she exclaimed. Jen laughed in response, heading off to the art area where she saw that Ben had just dropped his paintbrush full of red paint. Andrea glanced around the room, spotting Jackson, as usual, in the block area with the dinosaurs. She quickly joined him and two other children who had just wandered over.

"What do you think about building a zoo for the dinosaurs?" she suggested to the children.

Although the other two children nodded their heads in excitement, Jackson looked down at the dinosaurs. Andrea was determined to engage Jackson in this activity. Suggesting that the children start building cages for the dinosaurs, she asked Jackson if she could borrow the Stegosaurus. She knew Jackson was well-versed in the names of the dinosaurs; and when she picked up the Tyrannosaurus Rex, she was pleased but not surprised when Jackson glanced up at her and quickly shook his head "No!" Taking the Tyrannosaurus Rex from her hand, Jackson handed over the Stegosaurus.

"Thanks, Jackson! I always get those guys mixed up!" Andrea said. "Jackson, would you put the Stegosaurus in his cage?" she asked. She was hoping she could draw him into the activity so he would have opportunities to interact with the other children. Jackson nodded his head ever so slightly and put the Stegosaurus in the "cage" the other two children had built.

"That's great, Jackson—maybe you could be the zookeeper and Kira and Peter could be the builders," Andrea suggested. "When Kira and Peter finish building a cage, they can ask you to put a dinosaur in! What do you think about that?" All of the children nodded their heads, including Jackson, Andrea noted. "If you need help, I'll help you, but otherwise I just want to sit and watch. Is that okay?" Andrea asked the children. Kira and Peter nodded their heads, while Jackson kept lining up the dinosaurs. "Okay! Better get started—those dinosaurs look like they might want to run away!" Andrea exclaimed (keeping her fingers crossed that Jackson would stay engaged in the activity).

Crossing her fingers must have worked, because Jackson did stay engaged in the activity—for nearly 7 minutes! Granted, he needed some help. Although Andrea mainly watched and kept track of what he said or did in response to Kira and Peter's requests, for three of their six requests, Andrea had to verbally prompt Jackson to respond. She made sure to note that on her observation form, thinking to herself how pleased his parents would be to learn that he had played with the other children today. Even the assistant teacher wandered over to the block area, catching Andrea's glance with a "thumbs up" sign. Soon, Jen was playing the "clean up" song. Andrea was glad she had remembered her camera. She pulled it out to take a few pictures of Kira, Peter, and Jackson cleaning up (well, sort of!).

Cognizant of the difficulties that Jackson had with transitions, Andrea pulled Jackson aside, reminding him that after everything was cleaned up, it would be time for snack. Jackson squirmed away from her, looking upset; but, thankfully, Jen rescued Andrea. Suggesting that if Jackson put two dinosaurs away, then she would put the rest away, she guided Jackson by the elbow as he dropped the Brontosaurus in the bucket.

"Good job, Jackson! Hmmmm ... I wonder which other dinosaur you'll choose to put away! How about the Stegosaurus?" Jackson looked upset, but complied with Jen's request. Jen quickly put the other dinosaurs in the bucket and put the bucket on the shelf. "Great job, Jackson! It's time for snack, now. I think Miss Sarah has cheese crackers for us. Yum! You need to wash your hands and go to the snack table; think you can do that? I bet Miss Andrea will help you if you need it."

Andrea nodded her head, and Jen moved away, letting Andrea take over. Andrea gave Jen the camera, quietly asking her to take a few shots of Jackson and a few other children washing their hands and a few shots of the snack table. Hopefully she would soon have the pictures she needed for Jackson's picture schedule.

Noting that Jackson was having a really good day, Andrea reluctantly started to pack her things. She had to be at Siri's house in about 30 minutes and needed to get going. She waved good-bye to Jen and the other teachers and, before she left, stooped down to tell Jackson good-bye. Again, she was surprised and pleased when Jackson looked at her and said, "Bye." She would remember to put that in her notes as well!

Andrea, Natasha, and Kate

Andrea checked her watch. It was almost 8:30 a.m., and she was due at Loving Hearts to see Natasha at 9:00 a.m. Andrea sighed. Visits to Loving Hearts were not high on her "wanna do" list. It was always difficult to see what was happening (and not happening) in Kate's classroom. Despite her best efforts to work collaboratively with Kate, Andrea often felt at a loss as to what to do. She had tried building a positive relationship with Kate, but most of the time, her efforts were met with resistance. It wasn't that Kate didn't want to do what was best for Natasha—it's just that she had such different ideas from Andrea about "what was best." However, Andrea had an idea last week that she was planning to share with Kate—an idea that she hoped Kate would like and that could perhaps open the door to them working together.

Natasha would soon be 5 years old and everyone hoped she would be headed to kindergarten next year. She had started receiving early intervention services shortly after birth. Natasha had Down syndrome. Consistent with other children who have Down syndrome, Natasha had delays in all areas of development. She also had a history of heart problems and had already undergone two surgeries to address heart defects. Natasha's older siblings had attended Loving Hearts as children too, primarily because it was close to home. Natasha's mother and father worked downtown and usually dropped Natasha off around 8:00 a.m., coming to pick her up at 5:30 p.m. Consequently, Natasha spent long hours with Kate at Loving Hearts.

Natasha was a handful! Whoever said that children with Down syndrome were kind and loving didn't know Natasha! Andrea thought. Of course, Natasha could be a sweetheart when she was with other adults. She liked to read books and help the teachers set up for snack. She loved the Disney princesses, the color orange, apple juice, and raisins. However, Natasha had problems sharing adults' attention with other children. When another child was playing with Kate or one of the other teachers, Natasha usually tried to push the other child aside so that the teacher would talk with her. She would also interrupt other children when they were working or playing, pulling toys away or pinching them. As a result, the other children steered clear of her, providing her with few opportunities to engage appropriately with them or "play nicely," as Kate said.

Given Natasha's difficulties with interacting with other children, her IEP focused on the development of prosocial skills such as turn taking, engaging in child–child interactions, and following directions. Also included on the IEP were goals related to name and letter recognition as well as vocabulary building and concept awareness.

Kate had been Natasha's preschool teacher for the last 6 months, ever since the director at Loving Hearts decided that Natasha needed to be in a different classroom. Kate was fast approaching

50 and had worked in child care all of her life. She had graduated from high school and landed a job as a teacher's assistant shortly thereafter. Although she had completed all of the requisite in-service trainings, she had never pursued higher education, feeling that her experiences as a mother and a teacher were all that she needed to be successful. Kate took pride in the fact that there had never been a child that she couldn't work with, and she wasn't about to ruin her record with Natasha! Although it was great that both Kate and Andrea believed that Natasha could be successful in the classroom, that's where their shared beliefs ended.

The Classroom Routine

Kate strongly believed that children needed teachers who had high expectations for them and that they needed to be schooled in the basics to be ready for kindergarten. In her room, play was a reward for hard work—hard work that consisted of completing worksheets, puzzles, or games targeting letters, numbers, colors, and shapes. Every morning the children gathered for a 40-minute circle time during which Kate reviewed calendar basics, the weather, and the day's upcoming schedule. Then it was time for work. The children participated in structured small-group activities that reinforced the skills Kate had covered at circle time. Teachers at the center did not use a specific curriculum but had access to preschool activity books with reproducible pages. In addition, each classroom had basic manipulatives including puzzles, small blocks, and a bookshelf containing about 20 children's books. Kate's room had a small housekeeping area in the corner and a sand table that was covered and used to display science materials. Finally, there was an art easel in another corner of the room and a small bookshelf with art supplies (primarily crayons and pencils).

Kate believed strongly in fairness, and in her mind, fairness meant that everyone did the same thing in the same way. She also believed that children should help their friends, so she expected the children in her mixed-age classroom (3–5 years) to help each other with their work. After small-group time ended (usually around 10:00 a.m.), the children were able to play for 20 minutes; it was during this time that Kate and her assistant prepared and set out the snack. After snack was over, it was time to go outside for 30 minutes and then back inside to have storytime and get ready for lunch and nap. The children were expected to nap for 90 minutes; and after nap was over, Kate completed a large-group activity with the children (usually emphasizing some preacademic concepts). After that, the children had free time to play until their parents picked them up.

Behavior Management

In keeping with her "fairness doctrine," Kate used the same behavior management system for all of the children. There was a time-out chair that children were directed to when they misbehaved. After spending 15 minutes in time-out, the children were expected to apologize for their transgression and return to the classroom activity. Children also were awarded stickers for good behavior and could choose a small toy from the treasure box after collecting 15 stickers. Natasha usually inhabited the time-out chair at least twice a day, and her "good behavior" chart that was posted on the wall was largely devoid of stickers.

Andrea and Kate

Andrea had been working with Natasha since the school year started—about 3 months. Andrea was a strong believer in the consultative approach to itinerant services—her motto had always been "two heads are better than one." She was easygoing and approachable and liked the other teachers she worked with to view her as a resource and support to them. This approach worked fine with most of the teachers and parents, but not with Kate. Kate believed that Andrea's job was to help Natasha individually. She argued that Natasha couldn't really pay attention in the classroom and was always getting into trouble. She wanted Andrea to help Natasha learn her manners and get ready for kindergarten but not necessarily in the classroom. She had set up a "learning station" in a small storage area attached to the classroom. She expected Andrea to use that space with Natasha; Kate used the space to work individually with children who were struggling, as well. Andrea visited Kate's classroom at 9:00 a.m. on Thursdays, and Kate excused Natasha from circle time to work with Andrea when Andrea arrived. Although Andrea had tried to schedule time when she and Kate could work together, nothing really ever worked out. Kate was busy from the time Andrea entered the classroom to the time she left, and Loving Hearts didn't have the staff that could fill in for Kate while Andrea visited. Naptime was sacred to both Kate and her assistant—it was during that time that they took a break and planned activities for the upcoming week. It didn't seem as if there was any time for Andrea and Kate to meet and work together on Natasha's behalf.

Last week, though, Andrea had a thought. The local community college had a large early childhood education program and, as part of the curriculum, offered two courses designed to prepare preservice teachers to work with young children who had disabilities. Andrea had wondered if it might be possible to recruit a student from the program to help out in Kate's classroom and provide that "extra pair of hands" Kate needed to spend time with Andrea. It was worth a try, Andrea thought. She decided to mention it to Kate at today's visit.

The Visit

Andrea signed in at the front desk and walked down the corridor to Kate's classroom. She paused at the door and peeked in. Circle time was late this morning, and Kate was just calling the children to join her on the rug. "Great!" Andrea thought. Maybe she could have a minute or two to talk with Kate about her idea.

She entered the classroom and walked over to Kate. "Hi, Kate! How are you? I know you're busy, but I wondered if you had a minute to talk with me about an idea I had." Kate's eyes swept the room, and she said, "Okay, but just a minute."

"Great—thanks so much for giving me a few minutes of your time. I honestly don't know how you manage this classroom day in and day out!" Kate looked pleased at the remark and said, "Well, after all of the time I've spent teaching, I've learned a thing or two. What do you want to talk about?"

"Well, I'd like to talk to you about the possibility of bringing in another pair of hands to help during my visits so you and I have some time to talk. I know that your time is precious, but it would be so helpful to me to work with you—I think if we teamed up a little bit more, we could really make sure Natasha is ready for kindergarten in the fall!" Andrea didn't want to give Kate a chance to shut her down, so she hurriedly added, "You know, I only see Natasha for about 45 minutes a week, and I really need your help to work with Natasha during the times I'm not here. I just don't think that 45 minutes a week is helping Natasha to reach her goals. If there was any way that you could work on some of them during the week, too, I think she'd make some real progress." Kate didn't say anything, so Andrea took the opportunity to add, "I met one of the instructors of the early childhood program from the community college last week, and it started me thinking about the possibility of recruiting a student who could come once a week—or possibly more. She could fill in for you, and you and I could have some time to talk. I know this is the time you do circle, so I could rearrange my schedule so that I could come sometime when you're not as busy—maybe when the kids are playing? What do you think?"

Kate's first inclination was to say no, but the thought of having an extra pair of hands once a week sounded inviting—she could use some time away from the daily routine. She liked the way that Andrea had recognized her skill as a teacher and had to admit that Natasha's behavior frustrated her. Andrea seemed like a nice person. She was always friendly, and Natasha loved her. "Well, that might be a possibility, although any student who comes here on a regular basis would need a clear background check and would have to do things the way they need to be done. I do suppose that spending time in a classroom would be good for a future teacher—I bet I could teach her a thing or two!" Kate glanced around the room, watching the children fidget and seeing her assistant give her a questioning look. "I have to get going, but let's give it a try as long as you can recruit someone and she fits in the classroom."

"No problem, Kate!" Andrea exclaimed. "I also thought that I'd do something a bit different today. I really need to see how Natasha's doing in the classroom, and it's really difficult for me to do that when I'm working with her one-to-one. If it's okay with you, I was thinking that I'd observe today and take some notes about Natasha's interactions with the other children. Maybe that will give us a sense of how to start our work together. Does that sound okay?"

"Sure, if you want to take a day off from Natasha, I certainly understand." Kate winked. "Everyone needs some time off now and then!"

Although Andrea certainly didn't consider observation time as "time off," she swallowed the comment and said, "Thanks!" She was just happy that she had made some headway in changing her approach in Kate's classroom. She knew that she would have to approach a consultative relationship with Kate sensitively because Kate had such different ideas about each of their roles in supporting Natasha's inclusion in the classroom. She was hoping that she could identify some instances in the classroom in which she could offer some help that would result in a "quick win" so that Kate would buy in to a collaborative approach.

As she settled into the corner of the room, Andrea noticed Natasha pushing another child away from her in the circle. Kate noticed it too but apparently decided not to address it by sending Natasha to time-out. Andrea took out her consultation log form and started noting what she had just observed. She usually used the log form to report on what she and Natasha had worked on and then shared a copy with Kate. She also mailed a copy to Natasha's parents. If her idea about having the community college student help out worked, that would change what she used the log form for, Andrea thought.

Natasha wasn't used to being in circle time when Andrea was there and kept glancing over to see what Andrea was doing. About halfway into the circle-time activity (while Kate was explaining the difference between *yesterday, today,* and *tomorrow*), Natasha pushed the child next to her so that she could sit closer to Andrea. Kate noticed the pushing and sent Natasha to time-out. It was interesting, Andrea observed. Natasha certainly seemed nonplussed about the request, because she walked quickly over to the time-out chair and sat smiling and waving to Andrea. Andrea wrote down what she had seen while thinking about how she was going to share this information with Kate. She knew that Kate took pride in the way she managed her classroom and had said on more then one occasion that "fairness" was important. How was Andrea going to start a conversation about the need to individualize for children as opposed to having the same expectations for everyone? She knew that conversation would be difficult and started thinking about some information that she could share with Kate. Even though she had been visiting Kate's classroom for 3 months, she felt that this was probably just the beginning of establishing a working relationship with Kate. She knew that she would have to earn Kate's respect and her trust and wondered how she should go about doing that. Her mind wandered just a bit from her task as she thought about the approach. Perhaps she could spend some time helping out in the classroom. This would give her a chance to demonstrate to Kate that she had credibility and would also give her more first-hand knowledge about Natasha's strengths and challenges. Having another pair of hands in the classroom during this time would certainly help, because it would give Kate a chance to step out of her role as a teacher and see the big picture. Andrea wondered how Kate would react to all of this—it certainly was a change in the way she ordinarily did business. She knew that Kate took pride in her ability as a teacher, especially in the fact that she knew how to work with all children! "That's a plus," Andrea thought. It meant that Kate was determined to be successful with Natasha and that she took responsibility for Natasha's learning. Andrea thought that Kate was going to have to broaden her concepts about what was important to learn, though. It wasn't just ABCs and 123s that were important. If Natasha was going to have a chance in kindergarten next year, she was going to have to learn how to get along with other children. Maybe that was an approach she could share with Kate, Andrea thought.

Circle time was nearing its end, and Kate was dismissing the children to their work groups. Natasha was still in time-out and still trying to get Andrea's attention. Natasha smiled and squirmed in her seat as Kate approached her to talk about not pushing other children. Even though it was supposed to be a reprimand, Natasha smiled and patted Kate's arm during the whole interaction. When Kate was finished talking to Natasha, Natasha gave Kate a hug and went over to her assigned seat. Andrea thought how interesting it was that Natasha almost eagerly accepted going to time-out. Going to time-out meant time to spend talking with the teacher (and getting out of circle time). Although it was clear to Andrea that time-out didn't seem to be working to reduce Natasha's disruptive behavior, she wondered if Kate realized that.

Glancing up at the clock, Andrea saw that it was almost time to go. She finished completing the log form, noting that she was going to be contacting the instructor at the college to find out about recruiting a student to help out in Kate's classroom. Andrea knew that would probably take a few weeks, but she was happy that the wheels were in motion and that she might have a shot at working with Kate after all. Before leaving, she asked again to speak to Kate.

"Kate, sorry for interrupting again, but I just wanted to say thanks for considering a change in how I'm helping Natasha. Next week, I was hoping that I could come when the children are having free playtime and just observe some more. I have a lot to learn about how Natasha interacts with the other children in the classroom; and even though we might not have the student lined up yet, I think it would be worthwhile to observe some more. In fact, if you want me to help with anything during that time, please let me know. I know how busy you are, and I don't want to be an imposition," Andrea said.

"Well, it will certainly be a change in the way things have worked in the past," Kate conceded, "but I'm willing to give it a try. All of my kids have been ready for kindergarten, and I'm not going to let Natasha ruin my record! I'll see you next week!" Kate turned away to the group of children she was working with, leaving Andrea to gather her things and leave the consultation log on Kate's desk. Andrea smiled as she left, thinking that perhaps the time had come for a change!

CHAPTER 12

Logistics of Providing Itinerant Services

Instruction within the IECSE model of service delivery is demanding. The effective IECSE teacher must know about special education intervention strategies, as well as exercise facility in interpersonal communication skills. In addition to this knowledge and skills, the effective IECSE teacher also must develop personal and professional organization skills. These expectations for competence underscore the differences between preparation as a classroom teacher and preparation for a career as an itinerant teacher. Although a certified or licensed teacher should be assumed to be a competent manager of a classroom learning environment, competence in the role of consultant should not be presumed.

An Overview of IECSE Service

A number of specific tasks must be executed in discharging the responsibilities of an IECSE teacher. These tasks are the platform for effective and efficient IECSE service delivery, and failure to address these elements will result in ineffective intervention.

Managing Travel

A manageable schedule of site visits, whether these are weekly, biweekly, or monthly, presents a challenge to the IECSE teacher. This schedule will need to reflect the needs of the child, the progression of the consultation and partnership process, the need for a different schedule for visits depending on the date during the school year when the child enters the program, the health of the child, and other pertinent factors. The schedule also must minimize travel time while maximizing opportunity for consultation and reflection.

Reducing travel time is, perhaps, the most important aspect of scheduling. Travel time can be reduced by limiting the number of sites that the IECSE teacher is required to visit, assigning IECSE teachers to sites that are in the same community or service area, and considering fewer visits per week or month with more time spent on site per visit. Reduction in distance between sites through zone coverage of sites also can reduce travel time. In some situations, travel time may be affected by ease of access and mode of travel (e.g., use of mass transit in urban areas). Travel in rural areas can consume an inordinant amount of time. This is a significant problem that must be addressed. Less frequent visits that are of longer duration (e.g., 2–2.5 hours) may be appropriate. Complementary consultation, in addition to biweekly or monthly visits, may be planned via Skype Internet interaction, web site access, e-mail communication, and audio and/or video conferencing with multiple ECE partners. These are creative options that have been used in more remote geographic areas (Barretto, Wacker, Harding, Lee, & Berg, 2006).

Patterns of Attendance of Children Receiving IECSE Services

In addition to geographic variables that shape the schedule of service delivery, the attendance of children in community-based programs will affect scheduling of coaching visits. Some children, because of the nature of their disability or particular challenges facing their family, may be at greater risk for absence. In situations in which there is an established pattern of erratic attendance, assignment of the IECSE teacher to multiple children in the same center may provide an option for last-minute rescheduling of site visits or reallocation of ECE program staff members. These accommodations could facilitate a more efficient schedule of service delivery. If an IECSE teacher is scheduled to visit a child and is notified of the child's absence by his or her ECE partner, either in advance of or upon his or her arrival at the center, the IECSE teacher might be able to shift his or her visit to another child on his or her caseload who also is in the same building. If there is not another child on his or her caseload, and advance planning for this contingency has occurred, the IECSE teacher may have access to a temporary office with Internet access where he or she can address organizational or record-keeping tasks. Although shifting attention to another child on the caseload may be prudent, this scheduling scenario may be disconcerting for some IECSE teachers and their ECE partner teachers. Understanding that this shift may be helpful in maintaining the integrity of the IECSE teacher's schedule may reassure the ECE partner.

If the visit is focused solely on consultation with the ECE partner teacher, the effects of the child's absence would be minimal. If the intent of the consultation were to model a teaching skill with the target child or to model a strategy and tool for data collection, the child's absence would be a significant problem. If a child is at high risk of absenteeism, the IECSE teacher and his or her ECE partner could also develop backup plans to engage in a consultation session if the child is not present. This could be part of the proactive planning of the IECSE teacher and would be understood as the default option by both parties. Within the consultation model, the presence of the ECE partner teacher and his or her availability to engage in consultation are the key elements in the process.

Assignment of IECSE Teacher Caseloads

Because the logistics of IECSE services are so demanding and necessitate considerable planning and travel time, some IECSE professionals have suggested that strict attention should be paid to assignment of caseloads. In Ohio, under regulations in effect in 2010, the current caseload for a full-time IECSE teacher is approximately 16–18 children, with a maximum caseload of 20 children. This schedule is highly variable; some IECSE teachers have a full-time caseload of more than 18 students, whereas other IECSE teachers combine classroom teaching responsibilities with part-time IECSE activities. Also, because children "age in" and "age out" of Part B 619 services at ages 3 and 5, respectively, caseloads may ebb and flow during the year. If this caseload allocation also is typical in other states, then the management of the number of visits per week is critical in shaping efficient IECSE services.

Some models for assignment of caseload merit further consideration. The most obvious option would be to limit caseloads to a more manageable number such as 12. Within a 35–40 hour week, this would allow approximately 3 hours per visit including the time used for planning, travel, consultation, and reflection. When the requirements of effective consultation are considered, even dedication of 3 hours per visit may be inadequate. Consider, however, that this model assumes 10–12 independent site visits as well as interaction with 12 different ECE partner teachers or parents. This is probably not the model adopted by most school districts. There are balanced and rational options for assignment of caseload that attempt to address travel distance, caseload size, requirements for a minimum number of consultation visits per week or month, and the number of adult partners associated with the caseload.

Zone or Regional Models for IECSE Service Delivery

One option to better organize the caseload is to consider a *zone assignment model*. In this model, IECSE teachers are assigned to visit children in one location or area without particular regard to the children's ages, type or severity of disability of the children, or strengths or weaknesses of the IECSE teacher with respect to his or her knowledge of special education practices or his or her experience and skills in special education instruction. The caseload also can be developed without attempting to match the personal and professional maturity of the IECSE teacher with his or her ECE partner and without evaluation of the interpersonal communication skills proficiency of the IECSE teacher. Finally, the ethnic identity and non–English language speaking skills of the IECSE teacher could be disregarded in creating partnerships. Although some school administrators would choose not to adopt this model, it is the most time- and cost-efficient model with respect to travel and mileage reimbursement. Unfortunately, that may be a significant factor for some districts. As an example, the difference between annual travel of 80 miles per week (for 36–37 weeks) versus 130 miles per week, based on current IRS reimbursement rates of approximately .50 per mile, results in an additional $1,000 per year in travel reimbursement expenses for that IECSE teacher. If this example is applied to multiple IECSE personnel, the additional costs could become burdensome.

A *regional model* of IECSE services also may be considered by school districts. This model may be particularly appropriate for rural regions, although the model also is used in urban and suburban districts. In a regional model, a county agency (e.g., intermediate school district) or a multidistrict coordinating agency (e.g., regional office of education) assumes, through a formal contract with representative school districts or the state department of education, the responsibility for IECSE service delivery for a number of districts within a region. The zone model or regional model can be even more time- and travel-efficient if IECSE personnel are regionalized rather than being required to report to a central location for purposes of planning, communications, and resource materials storage. Adoption of a regional or zone system of IECSE service delivery also could address the need for discipline-specific professional development opportunities as well as offer opportunities for mentoring of novice IECSE teachers.

The Affinity Network Model in IECSE Services

An *affinity network model* is another option in consolidating and organizing caseloads. The affinity network model seeks to develop long-term relationships with local child care and preschool programs that have a reputation for quality and a commitment to enrollment of young children with special needs. These programs may be widely recognized by the general community and members of the child care and early education profession as exemplary. Some programs may have been certified by a state or national agent (e.g., NAEYC accreditation, state licensure agency). These programs may have distinguished themselves by virtue of past and current enrollment patterns, public statements of program administrators and teaching and/or child care professionals regarding their support of inclusion, and parent recommendations.

The affinity network model is an interesting and proactive option for delivery of IECSE services for a number of reasons, including the following:

- Development of an affinity model results in public recognition of the child care or preschool program as a partner in inclusion. Affinity programs receive the professional attention of licensed ECSE teachers; physical, occupational, and speech-language therapists; and other related services personnel. This attention may raise morale among preschool staff, improve their knowledge and skills in ECSE practices and curriculum development, and add to their confidence and competence as early educators.

- Through the development of affinity networks, the ECE partners of IECSE teachers are better informed of the intent and focus of the consultation model and are more inclined to become active participants in the process. In addition, because these formal relationships are negotiated and maintained by child care, preschool, and LEA administrators, the challenges and expectations of the consultation model can be addressed prior to engagement of the IECSE teacher and his or her ECE partner. The development of formal partnership agreements such as the examples in Appendix B between LEA personnel and child care and preschool personnel also offers reassurance to parents that their child will receive services consistent with his or her IEP.

- ECE personnel in affinity networks may extend their commitment to personal and career development as a result of the attention and encouragement of their school district partners. Improved knowledge of special education conditions and their implications for child development, established proficiency in the use of basic special education teaching strategies, and demonstration of acceptable skills in evaluation of individual child progress would be reasonable outcome expectations for staff in an affinity network program.

- The affinity model provides the school district with an opportunity to collaborate in creation of a comprehensive professional development agenda with local child care and preschool staff. Selected child care and preschool members of the affinity group could serve as the focal point for comprehensive professional development activities for staff in other affinity group programs as well as the broader child care and ECE community in the region. In-service learning programs could be developed, and participation in these programs could be linked with 2- and 4-year college credit options. Selected sites also could serve as host sites for regularly scheduled parent information and education programs.

- An affinity network child care or preschool program could be the host storage and circulation site for ECSE and ECE learning resources (e.g., videos, software, journals) that could be available to staff of affinity group programs or the entire child care community. Selected child care and preschool programs also could be active partners with school districts in securing state and foundation grants to support innovative curriculum models.

- The use of the affinity model could help to develop links with local Head Start programs. Head Start programs are required, by statute, to include children with disabilities in their programs. Establishing a formal relationship with the school district and with IECSE teachers and related services personnel could provide a local Head Start with the impetus to enroll children with different and more challenging disabilities when appropriate. Developing a formal relationship between administrators of Head Start, LEA staff, and child care or preschool staff within an affinity group model could be very helpful in creating a mutually beneficial network.

- An affinity group model might be of interest to local colleges and universities. Institutions of higher education may be interested in placing students seeking licensure or certification in affinity group programs for student teaching or practicum experiences.

Before leaving this topic, it is necessary to consider the liabilities of an affinity model. Adoption of an affinity model would result in a perceived restriction of placement options. Encouraging parents to consider programs within the affinity network could present a problem for parents with respect to higher tuition fees, ease of access to child care and preschool programs from home or place of employment, restricted operating hours of some programs in the affinity network, and preference for specific religious affiliation of a program. Although restriction of parent choice is not the objective of an affinity model, the presence of an affinity network may shape parental preference. Of course, in most cases, a school district typically would not specify which child care or preschool programs are appropriate for children with IEPs. Despite the promulgation and support of an affinity network, as the result of a constellation of factors, most of which are out of the control of school district personnel, some parents may decide to place their child in a child care or preschool program that is not highly regarded within the ECE community, even with the most encouraging support of the IFSP or IEP team.

Another potential objection to an affinity group network is the focus of attention on selected child care and preschool programs within the community. Challenges such as congregation of children with special needs in selected centers and proportional enrollment of typical children and children with special needs must be considered.

Another liability associated with development of affinity networks is the concern that "the rising tide will not lift all boats." Some would argue that the presence of an IECSE teacher and related services personnel in *any* child care or preschool program—not just an affinity program—would inform the practices and dispositions of the ECE program administration and staff with respect to the value of inclusion. This could result in improvement in the quality of these programs for all children as well as improvement in the knowledge and skills of the ECE partner teacher. The now empowered ECE teacher could assume a leadership role within his or her program in advocating for enrollment of children with special needs. Also, even if that ECE teacher were to leave the program, he or she would be in a position to exercise his or her skills and influence in another child care or preschool program within the community or in another community. In other words, this partnership could be considered an informal vehicle for professional development of ECE personnel.

Although all of these expectations related to the immediate and long-term effects of the IECSE relationship are laudable, they also are very optimistic. There is no empirical evidence that supports these scenarios, and, it must be reiterated, the primary focus of the IECSE relationship is the advancement of the child. Although systems change is a desirable outcome of the IECSE relationship, the affinity network model is a more coherent and efficient approach to effecting system change while ensuring high-quality intervention services for the child as well as promoting improvement in services for all children.

Key Factors that Affect Planning for Consultation

The process of consultation is dynamic, particularly so with respect to IECSE service delivery. To be effective, the IECSE teacher must consider these factors in planning for consultation:

* Logistics of travel and scheduling of consultation visits

* Personal history and characteristics of ECE partner teacher

* Formal education and previous experiences of ECE partner teacher

* Preferred mode of learning of ECE partner teacher

* Support of consultation model by child care or preschool administrators

* Quality of the early learning environment in which the child receives services

* Stage of skill development of the child (acquisition, fluency, maintenance, or generalization)

* Phases of the consultation relationship

Key Logistics in Delivery of IECSE Services

The primary challenges in managing a caseload and establishing a schedule for consultation visits already has been examined. The following sections will examine these critical aspects of service delivery in greater detail. Some states have rules and regulations that define minimum service obligations under the IECSE model. For example, IECSE services must be provided for a minimum of 4 hours per month. In practice, some IEP teams sign off on instruction plans that have translated this 4-hour minimum requirement per month into 1 hour per week of instruction. This 1-hour-per-week schedule appears to be standard practice in some states, whether services are delivered in the child's home or in a community child care or preschool program.

There are inherent advantages and disadvantages of the 1-hour-per-week model. Some of these advantages and disadvantages are related to personal and professional organization, whereas others are logistical or relational. An advantage of the 1-hour-per-week model, particularly in the consultation approach, is the predictable nature of the relationship. The ECE partner teacher, with rare exceptions (e.g., holiday breaks, inclement weather), is guaranteed a weekly visit from his or her IECSE partner. This can be reassuring to some ECE partners, particularly in the beginning stages of the consultation relationship. The weekly visit also can be very helpful in instating instruction strategies, because the weekly visit presents consistent opportunities for modeling and observation as well as review of child progress. Conversely, weekly visits could reinforce the expectation of the ECE partner for pull-out and direct-instruction services, which could present a challenge to the development of a consultation relationship.

With respect to time management, the weekly visit schedule may be less time-effective. The personal and professional organizational requirements for weekly visits may be more demanding than adopting a less intense (e.g., 2-hour-long biweekly visits) schedule. With a weekly visit schedule, the IECSE teacher will have to prepare a plan for consultation, including planning for transfer of knowledge or skills via sharing of materials, modeling, evaluation of child response to instruction, and so forth. Executing this plan for consultation, including discussion with the ECE partner teacher as a primary vehicle of consultation, may be very difficult to navigate within a 1-hour window. If the IECSE teacher and his or her administrator were to adopt a biweekly or variable schedule for consultation, this might be more efficient for both the IECSE teacher and his or her ECE partner teacher. A biweekly plan would allow more time for planning of consultation activities as well as execution of a comprehensive consultation plan. Biweekly visits also would be less demanding for the ECE partner teacher and the program administrator, specifically with respect to planning for dyadic consultation time, including arranging for a substitute when requested in advance. This expectation for dyadic consultation interaction should be an integral element of the consultation agreement.

The nature of the consultation relationship between the IECSE teacher and his or her ECE partner also is pivotal in determining the schedule for consultation. The visitation schedule should be expected to differ based on the stage of consultation. It would be reasonable to expect more frequent (e.g., weekly) personal contact during the early stages of consultation (i.e., September through December) than during the later stages (i.e., April through May) for those children who begin the community program school year in August or September. Of course, this is more likely with 4- and 5-year-olds than with 3-year-olds who can enter Part B 619 services at any time following their 3rd birthday. Caseloads that include entering 3-year-olds will require departure from the September to May consultation schedule model. ECE partner teachers who have a child with an IEP entering their classroom in January, for example, may require intensive consultation scheduling through most of the remaining school year.

The previous experience of the ECE partner teacher with young children with special needs also may affect the intensity of consultation services and the frequency of visits. With an experienced ECE partner, the IECSE teacher might not need to focus his or her attention on modeling special education instruction skills but rather on the use of peer models or environmental accommodations. Previous experience in a consultation model with another IECSE teacher also might affect the schedule for visitation. A professionally mature ECE partner may not need the same attention as a novice ECE teacher. However, an older ECE partner teacher may require more assistance in adopting specialized instruction than a recent graduate of an inclusive teacher education program.

The confidence and self-efficacy of the partner teacher also must be considered when scheduling visitations. Some ECE partner teachers may be more confident in their teaching abilities than others. Some ECE teachers also may be more self-efficacious and see themselves as able to effect change in children, in general, and children with special needs, in particular. Other ECE teachers may be less confident, more easily intimidated by any number of factors, and less organized than their peers. The personal dispositions and professional characteristics of the ECE partner teacher must be considered in determining the intensity, frequency, and duration of consultation visits. This is a particularly dynamic and sensitive issue. Many administrators and parents view the effectiveness of IECSE services as directly related to opportunity for one-to-one instruction provided by the IECSE teacher. Of course, this is not the focus or expected outcome of consultation services in a triadic model. It is appropriate and, indeed, recommended that IECSE teachers consider calibration of consultation time and effort. Factors that should be considered in developing individual schedules for consultation visits include attempting to "match" the professional experience, motivation, and skills of their ECE partner teacher; acknowledging the stage of learning (i.e., acquisition, maintenance, fluency, generalization) of the child; and reflecting on progress across previous consultation sessions (i.e., beginning, middle, or end phase of the consultation process). The response of the partner teacher to indirect consultation strategies such as responses to e-mail, text messages, and visits to dedicated web resource sites supported by the LEA or the IECSE teacher also should be considered in scheduling.

Preparing for Site Visits

The objectives of the consultation site visit will vary depending on the duration or stage of the consultation relationship. Addressing these objectives will require the following planning activities:

- Review of child progress in meeting priority IEP objectives

- Review of intermittent communications (e.g., telephone conversations, e-mail, discussion board postings) with ECE partner teacher that occurred since last site visit

- Planning specific consultation activities (e.g., sharing of child assessment results, modeling of teaching skills, sample modifications of materials, recommendations for environmental accommodations) that will instate or expand the skills of the ECE partner teacher, particularly as these skills relate to priority IEP objectives

- Review of the daily and weekly schedule of the ECE site to determine, via the use of *matrix planning*, when and where priority IEP objectives can be addressed

- Securing professional development resources for the ECE partner teacher and planning how to provide the ECE partner access to these materials via handouts, journal articles, web site addresses, loan of videotapes or texts, and so forth; in addition, planning for how instructional materials or professional development materials will be transported to the site (e.g., place in plastic travel file at office and leave in car) to ensure they are not left behind, inadvertently)

- Planning for ECE partner communication regarding child progress and the ECE partner's progress in addressing priority IEP objectives

- Planning to communicate with the child's parents regarding the child's progress in addressing IEP goals, with the active collaboration of the ECE partner

- Planning for review of the ECE partner's professional growth plan as developed by the IECSE teacher and his or her ECE partner

• Planning for discussion of the progress of consultation and other relevant topics (e.g., date of next visit and need for substitute) with the program administrator, lead teacher, or owner and/or operator of the ECE program (as approved and supported by the school district supervisor)

Preparation for a site visit is necessary to improve the impact of consultation. A template will ensure intentional planning by the IECSE teacher as well as create expectations for the consultation process on the part of the ECE partner teacher and other key stakeholders (e.g., parents, administrator of the child care center or preschool supervisor, school district administrator). Public definition of the roles and responsibilities of the IECSE teacher will shape expectations for the form and function of the service delivery model. This reciprocal dynamic will support an active and productive consultation relationship. Again, development of formal agreements (see Appendix B) with the child care and preschool programs in which IECSE services will occur is highly recommended and will be examined further in this chapter.

It is important to note that failing to provide concrete information that describes the nature of the consultation process and the key activities of the IECSE teacher allows key stakeholders an opportunity to develop misperceptions of their reciprocal responsibilities and their roles as partners in this process. Without this information, parents may come to expect that IECSE services will focus on one-to-one instruction of their child by the IECSE teacher. The roles and responsibilities of the IECSE teacher, within the consultation model, also should be discussed in the IEP or IFSP meeting. Examples of typical activities that would occur in a site visit should be provided during IEP or IFSP team deliberations. Divulging the typical activities of an IECSE teacher should inform the decision on how to provide Part B 619 services in the natural environment or what would constitute the LRE recommendation for the child. Public awareness of the roles and responsibilities of the IECSE teacher also serves to drive administrative planning for appropriate professional development of IECSE staff. In addition, the school district supervisor is provided with a set of expectations for IECSE teacher performance that will inform appropriate supervisory review and support for individualized professional development. The PIECES, a model professional development instrument that can be used by IECSE teachers as a self-assessment tool and also by administrators to guide professional development and mentoring, was discussed in Chapter 3 and is provided in Appendix C.

Effective preparation is essential to effective interaction with the ECE partner. "Seat of the pants" consultation is a poor substitute for thoughtful, proactive, organized, and skillful consultation. Informal consultation, however, appears to be prevalent in the IECSE model. In an attempt to observe and verify that consultation occurred in IECSE teacher visits, Dinnebeil et al. (2006a) shadowed a number of IECSE teachers as they provided IECSE services. These IECSE teachers also completed a self-assessment of their allocation of time and effort in delivering IECSE services. Most of these teachers indicated that they spent significant time engaged in "consultation." The results of the shadowing study, however, indicated that consultation was often reactive, not clearly focused on instructional strategies, and idiosyncratic. Also, the IECSE teachers had clearly overestimated the time they had spent engaged in consultation and underestimated the time they spent in direct instruction or "miscellaneous" activities. It cannot be overstated that the effective practice of consultation requires the *intentional* adoption of specific planning methods and the *selective* use of interpersonal communication skills. It is unlikely that high-quality and effective consultation occurs in the absence of detailed and advance planning.

Planning for Consultation and Monitoring of Child Progress in Meeting Priority IEP Objectives

Based on direct observation of child skills or information provided by the ECE teacher or the child's parents, the IECSE teacher may need to plan to model specific special education strategies or specific features of special education strategies that have been shared previously with the ECE teacher. The IECSE teacher also may need to locate professional development resources (e.g., links to web sites, videotapes, journal articles) that either describe the teaching skill that is an appropriate match for the target skill or that provide information on a new skill that will be modeled in the next consultation session. The IECSE teacher also may need to prepare modified learning materials to demonstrate the link between the current skills of the child and recommended learning materials. It also may be necessary for the IECSE teacher to review the matrix planning forms to discuss opportunities for direct and incidental instruction with the ECE partner teacher. The IECSE teacher will need to identify, prior to the site visit, specific teaching skills that will be necessary for the ECE partner to instate or expand the skills of the child. He or she will then need to determine the content and key activities for the next consultation visit.

The IECSE teacher also must review, at least monthly, the progress of the target child in achieving or approximating priority learning objectives that are specific to the IEP. Active evaluation of child progress determines the direction and focus of consultation efforts and is the most important gauge of the effectiveness of IECSE services. Indications of progress in key areas of development support the effectiveness of consultation efforts. Concerns for rate of progress or failure of the child to master prerequisite skills or subskills should trigger evaluation of primary instruction strategies being used by the ECE partner teacher, consideration of additional adaptations of learning materials, modification of the learning environment, and engagement of peers in supporting learning. Evaluation should result in a plan of action that will shape immediate and future consultation.

Review of Intermittent Communications from ECE Partner Teachers and Parents

In building trust, a process that is paramount in a consultation relationship, the IECSE professional must maintain active communication with his or her ECE partners and the parents of those children he or she serves. The IECSE teacher also must address communications from ECE partner teachers and parents that occur between site visits. Setting aside time to manage these tasks is a priority for the IECSE teacher. As is often the case, encouraging individuals to communicate more actively often results in exactly that outcome.

In meeting the expectations of ECE partner teachers and parents, it is advisable to develop a formal communications policy that specifies effective modes of communication (e.g., telephone, e-mail, discussion board postings) as well as time lines for responses to communications. A formal policy for communication, which appears in the sample Letter of Agreement Appendix A, is another proactive tool that will foster trust between the IECSE teacher, his or her ECE partner teacher, and the child's parents. This policy also will be very helpful to the IECSE teacher in maintaining personal and professional organization that is essential in effectively discharging his or her responsibilities. A formal policy not only will include identification of preferred modes of communication but, equally as important, it also should include specific timelines for a response from the IECSE teacher (e.g., within 2 days for e-mail, 3 days for telephone messages, unless determined to be an emergency).

With respect to telephone and e-mail communications, the IECSE teacher should consider the relative merits of providing an office telephone number with voicemail capability, business e-mail account, business or social network, and/or text message contact information. If the IECSE teacher decides to release his or her home telephone number or cell phone number, he or she should inform ECE partner teachers and parents of appropriate hours for contact. It is a reasonable expectation that an educator will maintain his or her personal and family privacy. In addition, designating selected sources for communication will be very helpful in management of communications. Maintaining separation between personal and business communications will ensure more efficient management of business communications and serve to ensure timely responses. There is one caveat, however. The nature of IECSE service delivery may require the IECSE teacher to provide a cell phone number to his or her ECE partner teachers so they may contact him or her in transit if there are last-minute complications related to a consultation visit (e.g., child absent or becoming ill during the day). Specifying a mode of communication is an opportunity for the IECSE teacher to indicate his or her respect for the ECE partner teacher and the parent, as well as to ensure timely responses to communications.

After a communication policy has been developed, it is imperative that the IECSE teacher honors the guidelines. This will require specific allocation of time to management of communications. This should not be viewed as a secondary responsibility of the IECSE teacher. Failure to respond to communications in a timely manner will erode the confidence and trust of the ECE partner teacher and the child's parent. In short, with respect to communication, the IECSE teacher should not promise what he or she is unable or unwilling to deliver with respect to communication with partner teachers. While being sensitive to the needs of the ECE partners and parents, the IECSE teacher must establish a system for communications that is manageable. Failure to establish and promulgate a process for effective and respectful communication can result in damaged relationships, loss of confidence in the IECSE teacher, withdrawal from the consultation process, and undermining of the relationship.

Documentation of Site Visits and Progression of Consultation

The requirements for reporting and documentation may vary across LEAs and state education agencies (SEAs). Certainly, the IECSE teacher will need to document the dates and times of consultation visits as well as the mileage associated with each site visit. Periodic notes or data collection entries related to child progress in meeting IEP objectives also will be necessary. Notes related to the consultation process should include comments related to preconsultation planning for each visit as well as a brief exit summary. Planning notes and postconsultation reflections are key professional development activities of the IECSE teacher. Periodic evaluation (e.g., semiannually) of professional development with the use of a self-assessment tool such as the PIECES (Dinnebeil & McInerney, 2011) also is recommended.

Other requirements for documentation may include summary notes on related services personnel site visits, key issues raised in parent and/or ECE partner and IECSE teacher conferences, Medicare or third-party reimbursement forms, and other miscellaneous or mandatory local or state reporting forms. As is the case with communications, the IECSE teacher must establish a schedule that includes planned and appropriate opportunities for completion, filing, and storage of pertinent information, including e-filing and e-transmissions. In addition to "protected" office time, improved efficiency of record keeping via creation of common forms or templates, use of laptops and personal organizers, as well as filing of forms via e-mail may streamline record-keeping taks. There are a number of emerging software programs or applications that may be appropriate in IECSE services. Certainly, in the near future, there will be a number of personal organizational and reporting software available to address many of the reporting and preparation requirements of the contemporary IECSE teacher.

Another critical element of communication in the consultation process is ensuring that priority services and support activities are delivered as planned. This guarantee is related to the following:

- Providing professional development materials to the ECE teacher. This may include teaching resources developed by the IECSE teacher, journal articles, web links, video streaming links or videotapes, and learning materials for the child

- Making sure that similar materials promised by related services staff (when related services are provided in accord with IEP requirements) also are provided in a timely manner

- Making sure that joint communications to parents from the IECSE teacher and ECE partner teacher, such as periodic progress reports or notice of conferences, are sent and received in a timely manner

Working with School District Administrators and Community-Based ECE Program Administrators

The need for engagement of administrators in ensuring the success of the consultation model in IECSE services cannot be underestimated. Based on formal and informal conversations and communications, a number of IECSE teachers provide services to children in community-based programs without any formal agreements between the local school district and the host program. Furthermore, many IECSE teachers report that in their role as agents of a school district, their responsibilities in coordinating IEP-focused interventions in community-based settings and their professional qualifications and training have never been formally described to child care or preschool administrators, potential ECE partners, or the parents of the children on their caseloads. A number of sample communications/letters that address this problem are included in Appendix A. Although the problem is remedial, the problem is serious. There is no reason that IECSE teachers should continue to operate as if they were covert agents of the local school district. Continuing to provide IECSE services without explicit agreement about the objectives and form (consultation model) of IECSE service delivery will undermine the credibility of the IECSE teacher and grossly affect the prospects for successful adoption of the consultation model. Broader concerns related to communication between school district administrators and early childhood program administrators have been addressed in the previous discussion of affinity networks.

Working with ECE Partner Teachers Who Differ in Their Beliefs, Practices, Experiences, or Attitudes

Working with other adults who may not share the same interests, motivation, professional commitment, life experiences, or formal education is a reality in many occupations. The importance of these factors is magnified in the consultation relationship that is the focus of IECSE intervention. Negotiation of these differences is the science and art of consultation and is pivotal in shaping the outcome of the consultation process. The implications of these differences will be apparent in the strategies that the IECSE teacher selects to transfer knowledge and skills as well as in his or her adoption of selected interpersonal communication skills. This is the challenge of consultation and may be the primary reason why some IECSE teachers elect the default option of direct instruction of children in pull-out or small-group instruction.

There are at least four factors that come into play in working effectively with ECE partner teachers who may not share the same beliefs and attitudes or who may not engage in the same professional practices. One factor is the self-confidence of the IECSE teacher with respect to his or her role as "expert." This is a particularly delicate topic that often generates passionate discussion among IECSE teachers. The issue revolves around the perception of the role and responsibilities of the expert. Some IECSE teachers resist this role adamantly, whereas others express discomfort with this role. Other IECSE teachers acknowledge that although this may be a valid expectation on the part of parents, ECE partner teachers, and child care and preschool administrators, they have grave concerns about the potentially negative implications of acting as "expert." There are research findings (Dinnebeil et al., 2006b) that describe an expectation of expertise on the part of key stakeholders. ECE partner teachers reported that they expected IECSE teachers to know about disability conditions and special education instructional strategies. Given the promise of the IECSE service delivery model, this is a reasonable expectation. The target child has, in fact, qualified for special education or early intervention services and has an IFSP or IEP to guide the direction of his or her development. Also, the IECSE teacher may have been identified, publicly, as the primary agent of the local school district as the result of letters of introduction and formal agreements for services. The IECSE teacher has been designated as the key special education professional responsible for coordination of IEP-focused services for the target child.

To the extent that the IECSE teacher does not accept this role as "expert" or is not comfortable with his or her expertise in early childhood special education practices, his or her confidence and effectiveness are compromised. Discomfort in the role of expert may be an honest admission of inadequate preprofessional preparation or limited professional experience. It is not unusual for a novice IECSE teacher to be a graduate of an early childhood teacher education program and not a special education program. In this case, the teacher may have had limited formal education in special education content or skills. He or she also may be employed under a temporary ECSE license. Although recent graduates of K–12 special education teacher education programs may enjoy an advantage with respect to knowledge of disability conditions and special education teaching strategies, they would not be aware of ECE curriculum and methods or the progression of early development. Confidence or lack of confidence in special education expertise is not an insignificant problem for an IECSE professional. A reasonable recommendation that would contribute to the success of a consultation model would be to avoid hiring teachers in IECSE positions if they are not appropriately prepared and licensed. If this is not possible, a remedial professional development program focused on special education content and instruction is recommended for IECSE teachers who are less than fully qualified.

The second factor that affects interaction with individuals who share different perspectives and expectations are the skills of the IECSE teacher with respect to personal and professional organization and interpersonal communication. Unlike knowledge of special education practices, most IECSE teachers have had little or no formal training in developing organizational and/or interpersonal skills associated with effective consultation. It also is apparent that some IECSE teachers are more comfortable in interpersonal communication and may be more facile than some of their peers. The good news is that organizational and communication skills can be learned and will improve with practice. This is a positive and empowering realization for all IECSE teachers. Development of effective interpersonal communication skills is as necessary in the delivery of high-quality IECSE services as knowledge of special education content and practices. There is a recognized set of skills associated with effective interpersonal communication (see Chapter 5). These skills have traditionally been associated with the disciplines of counseling and clinical psychology (Brems, 2001). Emerging interest in these skills has been evident in early intervention Part C programs (Keyser, 2008; Park & Turnbull, 2003) as well as in coursework and field experiences related to parent and professional partnerships in special education. The link between effective communication and IECSE service delivery is apparent. The development of high-quality interpersonal communication skills and the intentional use of selected communication skills during site visits is the linchpin of effective and productive consultation.

The third factor that will influence interaction with ECE partner teachers is personal and professional experience. This is awareness that the interaction of personal maturity and professional experience can shape the motivation and expectations of ECE partner teachers. The IECSE teacher may be paired with an ECE partner teacher who is similar in age, may share similar life experiences and values, and may have similar aspirations in advancing his or her career. Other partner teachers may be significantly older and/or may have limited formal education. These older partner teachers also may have extensive personal and professional experience in community-based ECE programs. Although these partner teachers may have limited expectations for career growth, they may be very interested in gaining knowledge and skills that have immediate utility in their classrooms. It has been proposed that efforts to match IECSE teachers with compatible partners may be beneficial in accelerating IECSE services; however, this may not always be possible. Whatever the basis for assigning partners, it is recommended that in reviewing the progress of partnerships, differences in the characteristics of ECE partner teachers should be factored into assessment of the progress of the relationship. It would be inappropriate to expect that every IECSE partnership would progress quickly and effectively. Differences in ECE teacher response to the partnership opportunity; variations in the characteristics of children; differences in personal motivation, personal concerns, and challenges facing the family of the partner teacher; and professional expectations all factor into the dynamics of the relationship.

Part B 619 supervisors or K–12 special education supervisors could consider the use of a GAS model (previously described in Chapter 5) or a variation of this approach in an effort to balance caseloads. GAS is similar to the statistical principle of covariance. In covariance, there is an attempt to consider differences in characteristics of research participants—for example, with respect to their level of some variable of interest. As an example, if researchers were interested in evaluating the effects of a model reading program that focused on improved retention on the skills of a group of fourth graders, the researchers might wish to determine the level of comprehension of these students before they participated in the reading instruction. It is possible that there would be differences in this skill across all of the students selected for this study before instruction began. In recognizing differences in comprehension skills of these students, the researchers might be able to examine the effect of this reading instruction model on students with poor comprehension, average comprehension, and advanced comprehension skills. Although the reading program might result in improved skills for all of these students, the effect of the instruction might be more or less dramatic for students in each of the three achievement groups. Also, the researchers might find the reading program has much greater impact on one or two of the student subgroups but not all three subgroups.

This same model could be applied in assigning ECE partner teachers to the caseload of an IECSE teacher, though the sophistication or simplicity of the model could vary considerably. The benefit of the use of a system for analysis of IECSE teacher caseloads is that the IECSE teacher and his or her supervisor will be more aware of the nature of the IECSE and ECE partner teacher relationships. They also will be more aware of the potential allocation of supervisory resources that may be necessary to support different partnerships. Also, as children and ECE partner teachers enter and exit the caseload during the year, the Part B 619 or special education supervisor may be more thoughtful about assigning additional ECE partner teachers based on expected progress of ongoing partnerships and anticipated challenges in the development of new partnerships.

A relatively simple form of a GAS model could consist of analysis of a limited number of features of the IECSE teacher and his or her potential ECE partner teachers. For example, a 25-year-old pre-K teacher who holds a bachelor's degree in ECE, has 3 years of experience as head teacher in the ECE program, and is beginning master's degree study in Elementary Science Education might be considered a good match for a 28-year-old IECSE teacher. An ECE teacher with this profile might be considered to be a Category 3 teacher. A 37-year-old Head Start teacher with an associate's degree and a CDA credential who has 9 years experience in several different pre-K programs, including 4 years in Head Start, and is considering seeking a bachelor's degree might be considered a Category 2 teacher. A 40-year-old pre-K teacher with an associate's degree who has been working for 15 years in ECE and 10 years in a church-related pre-K program that has limited experience with children with special needs might be viewed as a Category 1 teacher.

The intent of this type of "profiling" is not to diminish the contributions or competence of ECE partners but to acknowledge differences in time, effort, and resources that may be necessary in supporting a partnership. Furthermore, this type of proactive categorization also allows for rational assignment of caseload based on expected responsiveness of ECE partner teachers, some awareness of their experience, an estimation of confidence and competence, and some assessment of the professional and personal motivation of the ECE partner teacher with respect to interest in acquisition of knowledge and skills. It is important to note that a GAS-type system is somewhat delicate. The intent and utility of a coding or categorization system is easily misunderstood. It is important that the intent of this system be clearly communicated as an attempt to allocate an appropriate level of support and resources of the local school district to ensure the success of this partnership versus an attempt to limit attention to some ECE partner teachers or to predict success or failure of some IECSE relationships.

The last, or fourth, factor that can influence the probability of success of a partnership is administrative support of the consultation model. Administrative personnel must recognize their responsibilities in supporting the consultation model. Formal agreements and public recognition of the roles and responsibilities of the IECSE teacher and his or her ECE partner certainly are evidence of proactive support of the model. Sensitivity in supporting placement of children with special needs within the child care or preschool program in an effort to "match" IECSE teachers with positive, energetic, and receptive ECE partner teachers also will improve the prospects for success of consultation. Supportive ECE program administrators also can provide logistical support such as arranging for a roving instructor or substitute teacher, designating private space for consultation, and engaging school district personnel in assisting in developing in-service training opportunities, thereby verifying their support for local school district presence in their program.

Effective partnerships do not usually happen naturally or by chance. Partnerships also may not develop despite the goodwill of one or both parties. Administrators, as well as IECSE teachers, should consider a range of factors in developing a proactive model for assignment of IECSE teacher and partner teacher dyads. The critical factors that influence partnerships should be consciously targeted and addressed. Consideration of these factors can serve as a tool for administrators and teachers as they make decisions regarding allocation of resources, assignment of caseloads, and allocation of resources for professional development.

Some form of proactive conjecture concerning anticipated successes and challenges in the creation and development of a partnership could become an important tool for planning caseload assignments and facilitating the progression of effective partnerships. It is more important to understand the conceptual underpinnings of such a model rather than to develop a precise formula to objectify these factors. Ultimately, improved outcomes for ECE partner teachers and students, as well as the improvement of IECSE services, can result from the intentional and proactive use of a tool that would consider factors such as those proposed in assessing specific IECSE–ECE teacher partnerships. Deliberate consideration of these factors that potentially shape or obstruct the progression of IECSE partnerships is recommended. This will allow the committed IECSE teacher and her supervisor to anticipate the unique nature of each IECSE partnership, as well as to address factors that might contribute to building more effective relationships.

Recharging the Battery: Lifelong Learning

Because there are usually few IECSE teachers within a single school district or region, opportunities for professional support and development must be planned. Although association with classroom-based ECSE teachers is helpful, it is not sufficient to support the professional development needs of IECSE teachers. IECSE teachers should create self-advocacy groups within geographic regions. These self-advocacy groups could be sponsored by a special education resource center or some other regional agency. The objectives of a self-advocacy group might include proactive inclusion of content and practice strands at state conferences that are specific to IECSE services, development of regional listserv or social network groups for IECSE teachers, and support for other professional activities that would improve the professional practice of IECSE teachers. Because there are a limited number of IECSE teachers within a region or school district and most states do not require specific training or certification for IECSE teachers, it is unlikely that many colleges and universities would offer professional development opportunities for IECSE teachers. It might be possible, however, within the platform of distance learning, for several major teacher-training institutions within a state to develop a consortium to address the professional development needs of IECSE teachers. As an example, a limited number of graduate seminar options that focus on the roles and responsibilities of IECSE teachers could be developed by several colleges and universities and offered on a rotating schedule across several semesters via distance learning. The use of a web-based instruction model could address minimum course enrollment requirements, whereas traditional on-campus course sections for IECSE teachers might never meet minimum enrollment requirements. Also, by creating a rolling professional development program for IECSE teachers, each of the cooperating institutions would be able to focus on a single course or seminar that would be offered once a year versus development of multiple course or seminar options. Some of these courses or seminars also could be offered in summer sessions. This might be an incentive for some university faculty members to commit to coordinating these practice-specific courses or seminars.

The PIECES professional development tool also could be used to poll IECSE teachers regarding their professional development interests. A group of IECSE teachers could meet in a caucus format at annual professional development conferences such as the statewide Association for the Education of Young Children (AEYC) conference or state department of education professional development conferences. Interested IECSE professionals also could seek to develop a limited number of presentations or poster sessions at these conferences that were specific to IECSE services. Although it is difficult for many teachers to attend national conferences, the DEC annual conference usually features several presentations and posters that address content and skills that are appropriate for IECSE teachers. Of course, the publications of the DEC often feature articles that are relevant to IECSE services. Membership in an organization such as the DEC is recommended for IECSE teachers, because this is the primary professional development organization that addresses IECSE services.

Finally, there is unlimited potential for self-advocacy in Internet-based social networking. A group of professionals with a limited number of practitioners in any region or state, such as IECSE teachers, can be well-served by active Internet communication. There always will be the challenge in management of content and communications within social network and professional development sites; however, with the advent of multiple messaging systems (e.g., Twitter) and the growing sophistication of personal communication devices, creation and management of dedicated resources sites will become less burdensome.

Summary

Although the quality of interaction and support of the IECSE teacher and her ECE partner teacher is the linchpin of an effective consultation and coaching relationship, the logistics associated with the IECSE service delivery model are critical elements in a successful partnership. LEA and child development program administrators must assume responsibility and initiative for defining and promulgating the nature of the consultation or coaching model for parents, ECE teachers, and the early childhood education community. IECSE teachers also must advocate for, and engage in, proactive planning focused on developing relationships with exemplary preschool programs and cultivating long-term partnerships with committed and engaged ECE personnel. Finally, the careful assignment of IECSE teacher caseloads must be tempered by an awareness of the scope of responsibilities that define the professional landscape of the IECSE professional.

References

Administration on Children, Youth and Families. (2009). *FY 2010: Office of Head Start monitoring protocol*. Washington, DC: Author.

Allen, K.E., & Schwartz, I.S. (1996). *The exceptional child: Inclusion in early childhood education*. Albany, NY: Delmar.

Bagnato, S.J. (2007). *Authentic assessment for early childhood intervention: Best practices*. New York: Guilford Press.

Bagnato, S.J., & Neisworth, J. (2005). Recommended practices in early intervention/early childhood special education assessment. In S. Sandall, M.L. Hemmeter, B.J. Smith, & M.E. McLean (Eds.), *DEC recommended practices in early intervention/early childhood special education* (pp. 17–28). Longmont, CO: Sopris West.

Bagnato, S.J., Neisworth, J., & Munson, S.M. (1997). *LINKing assessment and early intervention: An authentic assessment alternative*. Baltimore: Paul H. Brookes Publishing Co.

Barnard, K.E. (1997). Influencing parent–child interactions for children at risk. In M.J. Guralnick (Ed.), *The effectiveness of early intervention* (pp. 249–268). Baltimore: Paul H. Brookes Publishing Co.

Barretto, A., Wacker, D.P., Harding, J., Lee, J., & Berg, W.K. (2006). Using telemedicine to conduct behavioral assessments. *Journal of Applied Behavior Analysis, 39*(3), 333–340.

Baumgart, D., Brown, L., Pumpian, I., Nisbet, J., Ford, A., Sweet, M., & Schroeder, J. (1982). Principle of partial participation and individualized adaptations in educational programs for severely handicapped. *Journal of the Association for Persons with Severe Handicaps, 7*, 17–27.

Belsky, J. (2006). Early child care and early childhood development: Major findings of the NICHD study of early child care. *European Journal of Developmental Psychology, 3*, 95–110.

Bolton, R. (1979). *People skills*. New York: Touchstone, Simon & Schuster.

Bondy, A.S., & Frost, L.A. (1998). *Picture Exchange Communication System (PECS)*. Cherry Hill, NJ: Pyramid Education Consultants.

Brems, C. (2001). *Basic skills in psychotherapy and counseling*. Pacific Grove, CA: Brookes/Cole.

Bronfenbrenner, U. (1979). *The ecology of human development: Experiments by nature and design*. Cambridge, MA: Harvard University Press.

Buysse, V., & Peisner-Feinberg, E. (2010). Recognition & response: Response to intervention (RTI) for pre-k. *Young Exceptional Children, 13*(4), 2–13.

Buysse, V., & Wesley, P.W. (2004). A framework for understanding the consultation process: Stage-by-stage. *Young Exceptional Children, 7*, 2–9.

Buysse, V., & Wesley, P.W. (2005). *Consultation in early childhood settings*. Baltimore: Paul H. Brookes Publishing Co.

Buysse, V., & Wesley, P.W. (2006). Evidence-based practice: How did it emerge and what does it really mean for the early childhood field? In V. Buysse & P.W. Wesley (Eds.), *Evidence-based practice in the early childhood field* (pp. 1–34). Washington, DC: ZERO TO THREE Press.

Campbell, P.H. (1987). The integrated programming team: An approach for coordinating professionals of various disciplines in programs for students with severe and multiple handicaps. *Journal of The Association for Persons with Severe Handicaps, 12*(2), 107–116.

Campbell, P.H. (2004). Participation-based services: Promoting children's participation in natural settings. *Young Exceptional Children, 8*(1), 20–29.

Campbell, P.H., & Sawyer, L.B. (2004). *Natural Environments Rating Scale.* Philadelphia: Thomas Jefferson University, Child and Family Studies Research Programs.

Campbell, P.H., & Sawyer, L.B. (2007). Supporting learning opportunities in natural settings through participation-based services. *Journal of Early Intervention, 29*(4), 287–305.

Carta, J.J., Schwartz, I.S., Atwater, J.B., & McConnell, S.R. (1991). Developmentally appropriate practice: Appraising its usefulness for young children with disabilities. *Topics in Early Childhood Special Education, 11*(1), 1–20.

Case-Smith, J., & Cable, J. (1996). Perceptions of occupational therapists regarding service delivery models in school-based practice. *The Occupational Therapy Journal of Research, 16*(1), 23–44.

Case-Smith, J., & Rogers, J. (2005). School-based occupational therapy. In J. Case-Smith (Ed.), *Occupational therapy for children* (pp. 795–826). St. Louis, MO: Elsevier Mosby.

Cepeda, N.J., Pashler, H., Vul, E., Wixted, J.T., & Rohrer, D. (2006). Distributed practice in verbal recall tasks: A review and quantitative synthesis. *Psychological Bulletin, 132,* 354–380.

Chandler, L., & Maude, S. (2007). Teaching about inclusive settings and natural learning environments. In P. Winton, J. McCollum, & C. Catlett (Eds.), *Effective professionals: Evidence and application in early childhood and early intervention* (pp. 207–226). Washington, DC: ZERO TO THREE Press.

Chiara, L., Schuster, J.W., Bell, J., & Wolery, M. (1995). Small-group massed-trial and individually distributed trial instruction with preschoolers. *Journal of Early Intervention, 19,* 203–217.

Child Care and Early Education Research Connections. (2007). *Early childhood comprehensive systems: A key topic resource list.* New York: Author.

Childers, J.B., & Tomasello, M. (2002). Two-year-olds learn novel nouns, verbs and conventional actions from massed or distributed practice. *Developmental Psychology, 38*(6), 867–978.

Clinton, H.R. (1996). *It takes a village to raise a child and other lessons children teach us.* New York: Touchstone.

Collaborate. (n.d.). In *Merriam-Webster's Online Dictionary,* Retrieved June 22, 2008, from http://www.merriam-webster.com/

Corn, A., Hatlen, P., Huebner, K.M., Ryan, F., & Siller, M. (1995). *National agenda for children and youths with visual impairments, including those with multiple disabilities.* New York: AFB Press.

Council for Exceptional Children. (2009). *What every special educator should know: Ethics, standards, and guidelines for special educators* (6th ed., Rev.). Arlington, VA: Author.

Craig, S., Haggart, A., Gold, S., & Hull, K. (2000). Expanding the circle of inclusion: The childcare director's role. In S. Sandall & M. Ostrosky (Eds.), *Young Exceptional Children Monograph Series No. 2* (pp. 27–36). Denver, CO: Division for Early Childhood of the Council for Exceptional Children.

Cripe, J.W., & Venn, M.L. (1997). Family-guided routines for early intervention services. *Young Exceptional Children, 1*(1), 18–26.

Davis, G.A. (1966). The current status of research and theory in human problem solving, *Psychological Bulletin, 66*(1).

DeBoer, A. (1995). *Working together: The art of consulting & communicating.* Longmont, CO. Sopris West.

Dettmer, P., Thurston, L., & Dyck, N. (1993). *Consultation, collaboration, and teamwork for students with special needs.* Boston: Allyn & Bacon.

DeVore, S. (2007, November). *You're a consultant so what do you do.* Retrieved from http://www.preschooloptions.org/tools/so_you_are.pdf

DeVore, S., & Bowers, B. (2006). Childcare for children with disabilities: Families search for specialized care and cooperative childcare partnerships. *Infants and Young Children, 19*(3), 203–212.

DeVore, S., & Russell, K. (2007). Early childhood education and care for children with disabilities: Facilitating inclusive practice. *Early Childhood Education Journal, 35*(2), 189–198.

Dinnebeil, L.A., Buysse, V., Rush, D., & Eggbeer, L. (2007). Becoming effective collaborators and change agents. In P. Winton, J. McCollum, & C. Catlett (Eds.), *Effective professionals: Evidence and application in early childhood and early intervention* (pp. 227–245). Washington, DC: ZERO TO THREE Press.

Dinnebeil, L., Denov, A., Hicks, L., & McInerney, W. (2007, October). *Supporting itinerant early childhood special education teachers through effective supervision.* Paper presented at the 2007 International DEC Conference, Niagara Falls, Ontario, Canada.

Dinnebeil, L.A., Fox, C., & Rule, S. (1998). Influences on collaborative relationships: Exploring dimensions of effective communication and shared beliefs. *Infant Toddler Intervention: The Transdisciplinary Journal, 8*, 263–278.

Dinnebeil, L.A., Hale, L., & Rule, S. (1996). A qualitative analysis of parents' and service coordinators' descriptions of variables that influence collaborative relationships. *Topics in Early Childhood Special Education, 16*(3), 322–347.

Dinnebeil, L.A., & McInerney, W.F. (2001). An innovative practicum to support early childhood inclusion through collaborative consultation. *The Journal of the Teacher Education Division of the Council for Exceptional Children, 24*(3), 263–266.

Dinnebeil, L., McInerney, W., Denov, A., Garofalo, L., Hicks, L., Loehrer, A., et al. (2007). *Performance Indicators for Early Childhood Education Specialists.* Unpublished document.

Dinnebeil, L.A., McInerney, W., Fox, C., & Juchartz-Pendry, K. (1998). An analysis of the perceptions and characteristics of early childhood personnel regarding inclusion in community-based programs: Implications for training and preparation. *Topics in Early Childhood Special Education, 18*, 118–128.

Dinnebeil, L.A., McInerney, W.F., & Hale, L. (2006a). "Shadowing" itinerant ECSE teachers: A descriptive study of itinerant teacher activities. *Journal of Research in Childhood Education, 21*(1), 41–52.

Dinnebeil, L., McInerney, W., & Hale, L. (2006b). Understanding the roles and responsibilities of itinerant ECSE teachers through Delphi research. *Topics in Early Childhood Special Education, 26*(3), 153–166.

Dinnebeil, L., McInerney, W., Roth, J., & Ramaswamy, V. (2001). Itinerant early childhood special education services: Service delivery in one state. *Journal of Early Intervention, 24*, 36–45.

Dinnebeil, L.A., & Rule, S. (1994). Variables that influence collaboration between parents and service coordinators. *Journal of Early Intervention, 18*, 361–379.

Division for Early Childhood. (2007). *Promoting positive outcomes for children with disabilities: Recommendations for curriculum, assessment, and program evaluation.* Missoula, MT: Author.

Division for Early Childhood. (2008). *DEC position on inclusion.* Missoula, MT: Author.

Division for Early Childhood. (2009). *DEC code of ethical conduct.* Missoula, MT: Author.

Division for Early Childhood/National Association for the Education of Young Children. (2009). *Early childhood inclusion: A joint position statement of the Division for Early Childhood (DEC) and the National Association for the Education of Young Children (NAEYC).* Chapel Hill: The University of North Carolina, FPG Child Development Institute.

Donovan, J.J., & Radosevich, D.J. (1999). A meta-analytic review of the distribution of practice effect: Now you see it, now you don't. *Journal of Applied Psychology, 84*(5), 795–805.

Dunn, W. (1990). A comparison of service provision models in school-based occupational therapy services. A pilot study. *The Occupational Therapy Journal of Research, 10*, 300–320.

Dunst, C.J., & Bruder, M.B. (2002). Valued outcomes of service coordination, early intervention, and natural environments. *Exceptional Children, 68*, 361–375.

Dunst, C.J., & Bruder, M.B. (2006). Early intervention service coordination models and service coordination practices. *Journal of Early Intervention, 28*, 155–165.

Ebbinghaus, H. (1885/1964). *Memory: A contribution to experimental psychology* (H.A. Ruger & C.E. Bussenius, Trans.). New York: Dover.

Eligibility, recruitment, selection, enrollment and attendance in Head Start, 45 C.F.R. § 1305 (2008).

Erchul, W.P., & Martens, B.K. (2002). *School consultation: Conceptual and empirical bases of practice* (2nd ed.). New York: Kluwer Academic/Plenum.

Erchul, W.P., & Sheridan, S.M. (2008). *Handbook of research in school consultation.* Mahwah, NJ: Lawrence Erlbaum Associates.

Fialka, J. (2001). The dance of partnership: Why do my feet hurt? *Young Exceptional Children, 4*, 21–27.

Fixsen, D.L., Blasé, K.A., Horner, R., & Sugai. G. (2009, February). *Intensive technical assistance. Scaling Up Brief #2.* Chapel Hill: The University of North Carolina, FPG Child Development Institute, State Implementation and Scaling Up of Evidence Based Practices (SISEP).

Fixsen, D.L., Blasé, K.A., Timbers, G.D., & Wolf, M.M. (2007). In search of program implementation: 792 replications of the Teaching–Family model. *The Behavior Analyst Today, 8*, 96–110.

Fox, L., & Lentini, R.H. (November, 2006). You got it! Teaching social and emotional skills. *Young Children, 61*(6), 36–42.

Friend, M., & Cook, L. (2000). *Interactions: Collaboration skills for school professionals.* New York: Longman.

Fuchs, D., & Fuchs, L. (2006). Introduction to response to intervention: What, why and how valid is it? *Reading Research Quarterly, 41*, 93–99.

Gilbertson, D., Witt, J.C., Singletary, L.L., & VanDerHeyden, A. (2007). Supporting teacher use of interventions: Effects of response dependent performance feedback on teacher implementation of a math intervention. *Journal of Behavioral Education, 16*, 311–326.

Glaser, R. (1990). The reemergence of learning theory within instructional research. *American Psychologist, 45*, 29–39.

Godby, S., Gast, D.L., & Wolery, M.A. (1987). Comparison of time delay and system of least prompts in teaching object identification. *Research in Developmental Disability, 8*(2), 283–305.

Gray, C. (2010). *The new social story book: 10th anniversary edition*. Arlington, TX: Future Horizons.

Grisham-Brown, J., & Hemmeter, M.L. (1998). Writing IEP goals and objectives: Reflecting an activities-based approach to instruction for children with disabilities. *Young Exceptional Children, 1*, 2–10.

Grisham-Brown, J., Hemmeter, M.L., & Pretti-Frontczak, K. (2005). *Blended practices for teaching young children in inclusive settings*. Baltimore: Paul H. Brookes Publishing Co.

Grisham-Brown, J., Pretti-Frontczak, K., Hemmeter, M.L., & Ridgley, R. (2002). Teaching IEP goals and objectives in the context of classroom routines and activities. *Young Exceptional Children, 6*(1), 18–27.

Hall, G., George, A.A., Steigelbauer, S., & Dirksen, D. (2006). *Measuring implementation in schools: Using the tools of the concerns-based adoption model*. Austin, TX: Southwest Education Development Laboratory.

Hanft, B.E., & Place, P.A. (1996). *The consulting therapist*. San Antonio, TX: Therapy Skill Builders.

Hanft, B.E., Rush, D.D., & Shelden, M.L. (2004). *Coaching families and colleagues in early childhood*. Baltimore: Paul H. Brookes Publishing Co.

Haring, N.G., & Eaton, M.D. (1978). Systematic instructional procedures: An instructional hierarchy. In N.G. Haring, T.C. Lovitt, M.D. Eaton, & C.L. Hansen (Eds.), *The fourth R: Research in the classroom* (pp. 23–40). Columbus, OH: Charles E. Merrill Publishing Co.

Harms, T., Clifford, R.M., & Cryer, D. (2005). *Early Childhood Environment Rating Scale–Revised Edition*. New York: Teachers College Press.

Harms, T., Cryer, D., & Clifford, R.M. (2003). *Infant/Toddler Environment Rating Scale–Revised Edition*. New York: Teachers College Press.

Harms, T., Cryer, D., & Clifford, R.M. (2007). *Family Child Care Environment Rating Scale–Revised Edition*. New York: Teachers College Press.

Harris, K.C., & Klein, M.D. (2002). Itinerant consultation in early childhood special education: Issues and challenges. *Journal of Educational and Psychological Consultation, 13*(3), 237–247.

Harris, K.C., & Klein, M.D. (2004). An emergent discussion of itinerant consultation in early childhood special education. *Journal of Educational and Psychological Consultation, 15*(2), 123–126.

Hemmeter, M.L. (2000). Classroom-based interventions: Evaluating the past and looking toward the future. *Topics in Early Childhood Special Education, 20*(1), 56–56–61.

Hemmeter, M.L., & Rous, B. (1997). *Teachers' expectations of children's transition into kindergarten or ungraded primary programs: A national survey*. Unpublished manuscript.

Horn, E., Lieber, J., Li, S., Sandall, S., & Schwartz, I. (2000). Supporting young children's IEP goals in inclusive settings through embedded learning opportunities. *Topics in Early Childhood Special Education, 20*(4), 208–223.

Horton, G.E., & Brown, D. (1990). The importance of interpersonal skills in consultee-centered consultation: A review. *Journal of Counseling and Development, 68*(4), 423–426.

Hunt, P., Soto, G., Maier, J., & Doering, K. (2003). Collaborative teaming to support students at risk and students with severe disabilities in general education classrooms. *Exceptional Children, 69*, 315–332.

Hunt, P., Soto, G., Maier, J., Liboiron, N., & Bae, S. (2004). Collaborative teaming to support preschoolers with severe disabilities who are placed in general education early childhood programs. *Topics in Early Childhood Special Education, 24*, 123–142.

Hunt, P., Soto, G., Maier, J., Muller, E., & Goetz, L. (2002). Collaborative teaming to support students with augmentative and alternative communication needs in general education classrooms. *AAC Alternative and Augmentative Communication, 18*, 20–35.

Hynes, K., & Habasevich-Brooks, T. (2008). The ups and downs of child care: Variations of child care quality and exposure across the early years. *Early Childhood Research Quarterly, 23*, 559–574.

Individuals with Disabilities Education Act (IDEA) of 1990, PL 101-476, 20 U.S.C. §§ 1400 *et seq.*

Individuals with Disabilities Education Improvement Act of 2004, PL 108-446, 20 U.S.C. §§ 1400 *et seq.*

Interactive Collaborative Autism Network. (2009). *Direct instruction: Introduction.* Retrieved September 1, 2010, from http://www.autismnetwork.org/modules/academic/direct/index.html

Johnson, J.E., & Johnson, K.M. (1992). Clarifying the developmental perspective in response to Carta, Schwartz, Atwater, and McConnell. *Topics in Early Childhood Special Education, 12*(4), 439–457.

Johnson, L.J., & LaMontagne, M.J. (1993). Using content analysis to examine the verbal or written communication of stakeholders within early intervention. *Journal of Early Intervention, 17,* 73–79.

Jordan, J.B., Gallagher, J.J., Hutinger, P.L., & Karnes, M.B. (1988). *Early childhood special education: Birth to three.* Reston, VA: Council for Exceptional Children.

Jost, G. (1987). Die Associationsfestigkeit in iher Abhängigkeit von der Verteilung der Wiederholungen. *Zeitschriftfür Psychologie, 14,* 436–472.

Jung, L.A. (2003). More is better: Maximizing natural learning opportunities. *Young Exceptional Children, 6,* 21–26.

Jung, L.A. (2007). Writing SMART objectives and strategies that fit the routine. *Young Exceptional Children, 39,* 54–58.

Jung, L.A., Gomez, C., Baird, S.M., & Galyon Keramidas, C.L. (2008). Designing intervention plans: Bridging the gap between individualized education programs and implementation. *Young Exceptional Children, 41,* 26–33.

Kalis, T.M., Vannest, K.J., & Parker, R. (2007). Praise counts: Using self-monitoring to increase effective teaching practices. *Preventing School Failure, 51,* 20–27.

Karlan, G.R. (1991). *Environmental communication teaching.* Lafayette, IN: Purdue University: Office of Special Education, U.S. Department of Education.

Kavale, K.A., & Forness, S.R. (2000). History, rhetoric, and reality: Analysis of the inclusion debate. *Remedial & Special Education, 21*(5), 279–296.

Kemmis, B.L., & Dunn, W. (1996). Collaborative consultation: The efficacy of remedial and compensatory interventions in school contexts. *American Journal of Occupational Therapy, 50*(9), 709–717.

Keyser, J. (2008). *From parents to partners.* St. Paul, MN: Redleaf Press.

King-Sears, M. (2008). Using teacher and researcher data to evaluate the effects of self-management in an inclusive classroom. *Preventing School Failure, 52,* 25–34.

Kinlaw, D.C. (1999). *Coaching for commitment* (2nd ed.). San Francisco, CA: Jossey-Bass/Pfeiffer.

Kiresuk, T.J., Smith, A., & Cardillo, J.E. (Eds.). (1994). *Goal attainment scaling: Applications, theory and measurement.* Mahwah, NJ: Lawrence Erlbaum Associates.

Klein, M.D., & Harris, K.C. (2004). Considerations in the personnel preparation of itinerant early childhood special education consultants. *Journal of Educational and Psychological Consultation, 15*(2), 151–165.

Kohler, F.W., Crilley, K.M., Shearer, D.D., & Good, G. (1997). Effects of peer coaching on teacher and student outcomes. *Journal of Educational Research, 90,* 240–251.

Kohler, F.W., McCullough, K.M., & Buchan, K.A. (1995). Using peer coaching to enhance preschool teachers' development and refinement of classroom activities. *Early Education and Development, 6,* 215–239.

Linder, T. (1993). *Transdisciplinary play-based assessment: A functional approach to working with young children.* Baltimore: Paul H. Brookes Publishing Co.

Linstone, H.A., & Turoff, M. (2002). *The Delphi method: Techniques and applications.* Retrieved June 1, 2010, from http://www.is.njit.edu.pubs/delphibook/ch1.html

Losardo, A., & Notari-Syverson, A. (2001). *Alternative approaches to assessing young children.* Baltimore: Paul H. Brookes Publishing Co.

Mautone, J.A., Luiselli, J.K., & Handler, M.W. (2006). Improving implementation of classroom instruction through teacher-directed behavioral consultation: A single case demonstration. *International Journal of Behavioral and Consultation Therapy, 2,* 432–438.

McClelland, M.M., Acock, A.C., & Morrison, F.J. (2006). The impact of kindergarten learning-related skills on academic trajectories at the end of elementary school. *Early Childhood Research Quarterly, 26,* 471–490.

McCollum, J., Gooler, F., Appl, D.J., & Yates, T. (2001). PIWI: Enhancing parent–child interaction as a foundation for early intervention. *Infants and Young Children, 14,* 34–46.

McCollum, J.A., & Yates, T. (1994). Dyad as focus, triad as means: A family-centered approach to supporting parent–child interactions. *Infants and Young Children, 6*(4), 54–66.

McEwen, I. (2000). *Providing physical therapy services under Parts B & C of the Individuals with Disabilities Education Act (IDEA).* Alexandria, VA: Section on Pediatrics, American Physical Therapy Association.

McGinnis, E., & Goldstein, A.P. (1990). *Skillstreaming in early childhood. Teaching prosocial skills to the preschool and kindergarten child.* Champaign, IL: Research Press.

McInerney, W., Dinnebeil, L.A., & Hale, L. (2005). *A model to prioritize IEP objectives for instruction: The MEPI model.* Unpublished document.

McLaughlin, M.J., & Jordan, G.B. (1999). Logic models: A tool for telling your program's story. *Evaluation and Program Planning, 22,* 65–72.

McLean, M.E., Bailey, D.B., & Wolery, M. (1996). *Assessing infants and preschoolers with special needs* (2nd ed.). Columbus, OH: Merrill.

McWilliam, R.A. (1996a). How to provide integrated therapy. In R. McWilliam (Ed.), *Rethinking pull-out services in early intervention: A professional resource* (pp. 147–184). Baltimore: Paul H. Brookes Publishing Co.

McWilliam, R.A. (1996b). *Rethinking pull-out services in early intervention: A professional resource.* Baltimore: Paul H. Brookes Publishing Co.

McWilliam, R.A. (2005). Interdisciplinary models practices. In S. Sandall, M.L. Hemmeter, B.J. Smith & M. McLean (Eds.), *DEC recommended practices: A comprehensive guide* (pp. 127–146). Longmont, CO: Sopris West.

McWilliam, R.A., & Casey, A.M. (2007). *Engagement of every child in the preschool classroom.* Baltimore: Paul H. Brookes Publishing Co.

McWilliam, R.A., Casey, A.M., & Sims, J. (2009). The routines-based interview: A method for gathering information and assessing needs. *Infants and Young Children, 23,* 224–233.

McWilliam, R.A., Ferguson, A., Harbin, G., Porter, D.M., & Vandiviere, P. (1998). The family-centeredness of individualized family services plans. *Topics in Early Childhood Special Education, 18,* 69–82.

Meisels, S.J., & Atkins-Burnett, S. (2000). The elements of early childhood assessment. In J.A. Shonkoff & S.J. Meisels (Eds.), *Handbook of early childhood intervention* (2nd ed.; pp. 231–257). New York: Cambridge University Press.

Milbourne, S., & Campbell, P.H. (2007). *CARA's kit—Consultant version: Creating adaptations for routines and activities.* Philadelphia: Thomas Jefferson University, Child and Family Studies Research Programs.

Miranda-Linne, F., & Melin, L. (1992). Acquisition, generalization, and spontaneous use of color adjectives: A comparison of incidental teaching and traditional discrete trial procedures for children with autism. *Research in Developmental Disabilities, 13,* 191–210.

Mitchell, A. (2009). *Quality rating improvement systems as the framework for early care and education system reform.* Retrieved December 1, 2009, from http://www.buildinitiative.org/files/QRIS-Framework.pdf

Mooney, P., Ryan, J.B., Uhing, B.M., Reid, R., & Epstein, M.H. (2005). A review of self-management strategies targeting outcomes for students with emotional and behavioral disorders. *Journal of Behavioral Education, 14,* 203–221.

National Child Care Information Center. (2009). *QRS Quality Standards.* Retrieved June 22, 2009, from http://nccic.acf.hhs.gov/poptopics/qrs-criteria-websites.html

National Institute of Child Health and Human Development Early Child Care Research Network. (2006). Child care effect sizes for the NICHD study of early child care and youth development. *American Psychologist, 61,* 99–116.

National Research Council. (2008). *Early childhood assessment: Why, what, and how.* Washington, DC: The National Academies Press.

Neitzel, J., & Wolery, M. (2009). *Implementation checklist for time delay.* Chapel Hill, NC: the National Professional Development Center on Autism Spectrum Disorders, FPG Child Development Institute, The University of North Carolina.

Neuman, S.B., Dwyer, J., & Koh, S. (2007). *Child/Home Early Language and Literacy Observation (CHELLO).* Baltimore: Paul H. Brookes Publishing Co.

No Child Left Behind Act of 2001, PL 107-110, 115 Stat. 1425, 20 U.S.C. §§ 6301 *et seq.*

Noell, G.H., Witt, J.C., Slider, N.J., Connell, J.E., Gatti, S.L., Williams, K.L., et al. (2005). Treatment implementation following behavior consultation in the schools: A comparison of three follow-up strategies. *School Psychology Review, 34,* 87–106.

Nolet, V., & McLaughlin, M.J. (2000). *Accessing the general curriculum: Including students with disabilities in standards-based reform.* Thousand Oaks, CA: Corwin Press.

Noonan, M.J. (2006). Procedures for challenging behavior. In M.J. Noonan & L. McCormick (Eds.), *Young children with disabilities in natural environments: Methods and procedures* (pp. 219–249). Baltimore: Paul H. Brookes Publishing Co.

Noonan, M.J., & McCormick, L. (2006). *Young children with disabilities in natural environments: Methods and procedures.* Baltimore: Paul H. Brookes Publishing Co.

Notari-Syverson, A., & Losardo, A. (2008). Assessment for learning: Teaching about alternative assessment approaches. In P.J. Winton, J.A. McCollum, & C. Catlett (Eds.), *Practical approaches to early childhood professional development* (pp. 161–186). Washington, DC: ZERO TO THREE Press.

Odom, S.L., & Cox, A. (2009, December). *Promoting the use of evidence-based practice for preschool children with autism spectrum disorders.* Paper presented at the 2009 OSEP National Early Childhood Conference, Arlington, VA.

Odom, S.L., & Diamond, K.E. (1998). Inclusion of young children with special needs in early childhood education: The research base. *Early Childhood Research Quarterly, 13,* 3–26.

Odom, S.L., Horn, E., Marquart, J.M., Hanson, M.J., Wolfberg, P., Bechman, P., et al. (1999). On the forms of inclusion: Organizational context and individualized service models. *Journal of Early Intervention, 22,* 185–199.

Odom, S.L., & Munson, L. (1996). Assessing social performance. In M. McLean, D.B. Bailey, & M. Wolery (Eds.), *Assessing infants and preschoolers with special needs* (pp. 398–434). Columbus, OH: Merrill.

Office of Special Education Programs. (2009). *Table 3-RE5, Part B, Individuals with Disabilities Education Act implementation of FAPE requirements.* Washington, DC: U.S. Department of Education.

Ohio Department of Education. (2008). *Operating standards for Ohio educational agencies serving children with disabilities.* Columbus, OH: Author.

Ostrosky, M.M., & Kaiser, A.P. (1991). Preschool classroom environments that promote communication. *Teaching Exceptional Children, 23,* 6–10.

Park, J., & Turnbull, A.P. (2003). Service integration in early intervention: Determining interpersonal and structural factors for its success. *Infants and Young Children, 16,* 48–58.

Peisner-Feinberg, E., Buysse, V., Ayers, L., & Soukakou, E. (in press). Recognition & response: Response to intervention (RTI) for pre-k. To appear in C. Groark, S.M. Eidelman, L. Kaczmarek, & S. Maude (Eds.), *Early childhood intervention: Programs and policies for special needs children.* Santa Barbara, CA: ABC-CLIO.

Pence, K.L., Justice, L.M., & Wiggins, A.K. (2008). Preschool teachers' fidelity in implementing a comprehensive language-rich curriculum. *Language, Speech, & Hearing Services in Schools, 39,* 329–341.

Pianta, R.C. (2004). Transitioning to school: Policy, practice, and reality. *The Evaluation Exchange, 10,* 5–6.

Pianta, R.C., & Kraft-Sayre, M. (2003). *Successful kindergarten transition: Your guide to connecting children, families, and schools.* Baltimore: Paul H. Brookes Publishing Co.

Pianta, R.C., La Paro, K.M., & Hamre, B.K. (2008). *Classroom Assessment Scoring System™ (CLASS™).* Baltimore: Paul H. Brookes Publishing Co.

Pretti-Frontczak, K., & Bricker, D. (2000). Enhancing the quality of individual education plan (IEP) goals and objectives. *Journal of Early Intervention, 23,* 92–105.

Pretti-Frontczak, K.L., & Bricker, D. (2004). *An activity-based approach to early intervention* (3rd ed.). Baltimore: Paul H. Brookes Publishing Co.

Rainforth, B. (1997). Analysis of physical therapy practice acts: Implications for role release in educational settings. *Pediatric Physical Therapy, 9*(2), 54–61.

Rainforth, B., & York-Barr, J. (1997). *Collaborative teams for students with severe disabilities: Integrating therapy and educational services.* Baltimore: Paul H. Brookes Publishing Co.

Rathel, J.M., Drasgow, E., & Christle, C.C. (2008). Effects of supervisor performance feedback on increasing preservice teachers' positive communication behaviors with students with emotional and behavioral disorders. *Journal of Emotional and Behavioral Disorders, 16*(2), 67–77.

Raven, B.H. (1992). *The bases of power: Origins and recent developments.* New York: Wiley.

Raver, S.A. (2004). Monitoring child progress in early childhood special education settings. *Teaching Exceptional Children, 36*(6), 52–57.

Rea, C.P., & Modigliani, V. (1985). The effect of expanded versus massed practice on the retention of multiplication facts and spelling lists. *Human Learning, 4,* 11–18.

Rhymer, K.N., Evans-Hampton, T.N., McCurdy, M., & Watson, T.S. (2002). Effects of varying levels of treatment integrity on toddler aggressive behavior. *Special Services in the School, 18*, 75–82.

Riley-Tillman, T.C., & Chafouleas, S.M. (2003). Using interventions that exist in the natural environment to increase treatment integrity and social influence in consultation. *Journal of Educational and Psychological Consultation, 14*, 139–156.

Rosenkoetter, S., Schroeder, C., Rous, B., Hains, A., Shaw, J., & McCormick, K. (2009). *A review of research in early childhood transition: Child and family studies. Technical Report #5.* Lexington: University of Kentucky, Human Development Institute, National Early Childhood Transition Center.

Rous, B.S., & Hallam, R. (2006). *Tools for transition in early childhood.* Baltimore: Paul H. Brookes Publishing Co.

Rous, B.R., Hallam, R., Harbin, G., McCormick, K., & Jung, L.A. (2007). The transition process for young children with disabilities: A conceptual framework. *Infants and Young Children, 20*, 135–148.

Rous, B., Myers, C.T., & Stricklin, S.B. (2007). Strategies for supporting transitions for young children with special needs and their families. *Journal of Early Intervention, 30*, 1–18.

Rovee-Collier, C. (1995). Time windows in cognitive development. *Developmental Psychology, 31*(2), 147–169.

Rule, S., Losardo, A., Dinnebeil, L.A., Kaiser, A., & Rowland, C. (1998). Research challenges in naturalistic intervention. *Journal of Early Intervention, 21*, 283–293.

Rule, S., Utley, G., Qian, A., & Eastmond, N. (1999). *Strategies for preschool intervention in everyday settings (SPIES) video series.* Logan: Utah State University.

Rush, D.D., Shelden, M.L.L., & Hanft, B.E. (2003). Coaching families and colleagues: A process for collaboration in natural settings. *Infants and Young Children, 16*(1), 33–47.

Sandall, S., Hemmeter, M.L., Smith, B.J., & McLean, M.E. (Eds.). (2005). *DEC recommended practices: A comprehensive guide for practical application in early intervention/early childhood special education.* Missoula, MT: Division for Early Childhood.

Sandall, S.R., & Schwartz, I.S. (2002). *Building blocks for teaching preschoolers with special needs.* Baltimore: Paul H. Brookes Publishing Co.

Seabrook, R., Brown, G.D.A., & Solity, J. (2005). Distributed and massed practice: From laboratory to classroom. *Applied Cognitive Psychology, 19*(1), 107–122.

Sheridan, S.M., Kratochwill, T.R., & Bergan, J.R. (1996). *Conjoint behavioral consultation: A procedural manual.* New York, NY: Plenum Publishing Corporation.

Shonkoff, J.P., & Phillips, D.A. (2000). *From neurons to neighborhoods: The science of early childhood development.* Washington, DC: National Academies Press.

Showers, B., & Joyce, B. (1996). The evolution of peer coaching. *Educational Leadership, 53*, 12–17.

Sigafoos, J., O'Reilly, M., Ma, C.H., Edrisinha, C., Cannella, H., & Lancioni, G.E. (2006). Effects of embedded instruction versus discrete-trial training on self-injury, correct responding, and mood in a child with autism. *Journal of Intellectual & Developmental Disability, 3*(4), 196–203.

Sladeczek, I.E., Elliott, S.N., Kratochwill, T.R., Robertson-Mjaanes, S., & Stoiber, K.C. (2001). Application of goal attainment scaling to a conjoint behavioral consultation case. *Journal of Educational and Psychological Consultation, 12*, 45–58.

Smith, M.W., Brady, J.P., & Anastasopoulos, L. (2008). *Early Language & Literacy Classroom Observation (ELLCO) Pre-K.* Baltimore: Paul H. Brookes Publishing Co.

Smith, S., & Collett-Klingenberg, L. (2009). *Implementation checklist for visual boundaries.* Madison: The National Professional Development Center on Autism Spectrum Disorders, Waisman Center, University of Wisconsin.

Snyder, P.A., Wixson, C.S., Talapatra, D., & Roach, A.T. (2008). Assessment in early childhood: Instruction-focused strategies to support response-to-intervention frameworks. *Assessment for Effective Intervention, 34*, 25–34.

Stokes, T.F., & Baer, D.M. (1977). An implicit technology of generalization. *Journal of Applied Behavior Analysis, 10*(2), 349–367.

Striffler, N., & Fire, N. (1999). Embedding personnel development into early intervention service delivery: Elements in the process. *Infants and Young Children, 11*, 50–61.

Stroh, L.K., & Johnson, H.H. (2006). *The basic principles of effective consulting.* Mahwah, NJ: Lawrence Erlbaum Associates.

Sugai, G., Horner, R.H., Dunlap, G., Hieneman, M., Lewis, T.J., Nelson, C.M., et al. (2000). Applying positive behavior support and functional behavioral assessments in schools. *Journal of Positive Behavior Interventions, 2*, 131–143.

Suk-Hyang, L., Palmer, S.B., & Wehmeyer, M.L. (2009). Goal-setting and self-monitoring for students with disabilities: Practical tips and ideas for teachers. *Intervention in School and Clinic, 44*, 139–145.

Terrace, H.S. (1963). Discrimination learning with and without "errors." *Journal of the Experimental Analysis of Behavior, 6*, 1–27.

Terrace, H.S. (1972). By-products of discrimination learning. In G.H. Bower (Ed.), *The psychology of learning and motivation* (Vol. 5, pp. 195–265). New York: Academic Press.

Thorndike, E.L. (1912). *Education: A first book*. New York: Macmillan.

Turnbull, A., Turnbull, R., Erwin, E.J., & Skodak, L.C. (2006). *Families, professionals. and exceptionality: Positive outcomes through partnerships and trust* (Fifth ed.). Columbus, OH: Pearson-Merill Prentice Hall.

Vail, C.O., Tschantz, J.M., & Bevill, A. (1997). Dyads and data in peer coaching: *Early childhood teaching in action. Teaching Exceptional Children, 30*, 11–13.

Vander Linde, E., Morrongiello, B.A., & Rovee-Collier, C. (1985). Determinants of retention in 8-week-old infants. *Developmental Psychology, 21*, 601–613.

Venn, M.L., Wolery, M., & Greco, M. (1996). Effects of every-day and every-other-day instruction. *Journal of Autism and Other Developmental Disabilities, 11*, 15–28.

Walsh, S., Rous, B., & Lutzer, C. (2000). The federal IDEA natural environments provisions. In S. Sandall & M. Ostrosky (Eds.), *Young Exceptional Children Monograph Series No. 2* (pp. 3–15). Denver, CO: Division for Early Childhood of the Council for Exceptional Children.

Webster-Stratton, C. (1992). *The incredible years*. Seattle, WA: Umbrella Press.

Wesley, P.A., & Buysse, V. (2006). Ethics and evidence in consultation. *Topics in Early Childhood Special Education, 26*, 131–141.

Wilkinson, L.A. (2006). Monitoring treatment integrity: An alternative to the 'consult and hope' strategy in school-based behavioural consultation. *School Psychology International, 27*, 426–438.

Wilkinson, L.A. (2008). Self-management for children with high-functioning autism spectrum disorders. *Intervention in School and Clinic, 43*, 150–157.

Wilson, K.E., Erchul, W.P., & Raven, B.H. (2008). The likelihood of use of social power strategies by school psychologists when consulting with teachers. *Journal of Educational and Psychological Consultation, 18*, 101–123.

Wilson, L.L., Mott, D.W., & Bateman, D. (2004). The asset-based context matrix: A tool for assessing children's learning opportunities and participation in natural environments. *Topics in Early Childhood Special Education, 24*(2), 110–120.

Winton, P. (2006). The inclusion of young children with disabilities: Professional development challenges. *TASH Connections, 32*(3), 12–16.

Wolery, M. (1994). Instructional strategies for teaching young children with special needs. In M. Wolery & J. Wilbers (Eds.), *Including children with special needs in early childhood programs* (pp. 119–150). Washington, DC: National Association for the Education of Young Children.

Wolery, M. (1996). Monitoring child progress. In M. McLean, D.B. Bailey, & M. Wolery (Eds.), *Assessing infants and preschoolers with special needs* (2nd ed., pp. 519–560), Columbus, OH: Merrill.

Wolery, M. (1997). Encounters with general early education: Lessons being learned. *Journal of Behavioral Education, 7*(1), 91–98.

Wolery, M. (2004). Monitoring child progress. In M. McLean, M. Wolery & D.B. Bailey (Eds.), *Assessing infants and preschoolers with special needs* (3rd ed., pp. 545–584). Englewood Cliffs, NJ: Prentice-Hall.

Wolery, M. (2005). DEC Recommended practices: Child-focused practices. In S. Sandall, M.L. Hemmeter, B.J. Smith, & M.E. McLean (Eds.), *DEC recommended practices: A comprehensive guide for practical application* (pp. 71–106). Longmont, CO: Sopris.

Wolery, M., Anthony, L., Caldwell, N.K., Snyder, E.D., & Morgante, J.D. (2002). Embedding and distributing constant time delay in circle time and transitions. *Topics in Early Childhood Special Education, 22*, 14–25.

Wolery, M., Ault, M.A., & Doyle, P. (1992). *Teaching students with moderate to severe disabilities: Use of response prompting strategies*. New York: Longman.

Wolery, M., Brashers, M.S., & Neitzel, J.C. (2002). Ecological congruence assessment for classroom activities and routines: Identifying goals and intervention practices in childcare. *Topics in Early Childhood Special Education, 22*, 131–142.

Wood, J.T. (2004). *Interpersonal communication: Everyday encounters* (4th ed.). Belmont, CA: Wadsworth.

Wortham, S.C. (2005). *Assessment in early childhood (4th ed.)*. Upper Saddle River, NJ: Prentice Hall.

Sample Letters of Introduction and Administrative Agreements

GOLDEN LOCAL SCHOOL DISTRICT

4521 Oak Lane
Aspen Ridge, OH 41234
Telephone: 330-541-6789 Fax: 330-541-6780
Carol Mitchell, Ed.D., SUPERINTENDENT

Ms. Michelle Quintera
Director, Jack & Jill Child Care Center
Oak Glen, OH 41235

Dear Ms. Quintera,

Let me introduce Sarah Albright, Itinerant Preschool Special Needs Teacher with Golden Local School District. Sarah will be working with Jacob Hill, who is enrolled in your center. As you are aware from being involved in the team discussion, Sarah will be working with Jacob's teachers at Jack & Jill Child Care Center to incorporate into their program the goals that are identified on Jacob's individualized education program (IEP).

Sarah's job is to provide educational services for preschool-age children with special needs who are enrolled in community-based early childhood programs like yours. Itinerant early childhood services may be provided in homes, child care centers, home-based child care programs, preschools, kindergarten classrooms, Head Start classrooms, or any other early childhood setting. Sarah travels to a number of different programs to work with the children on her caseload and their teachers. Her visiting schedule varies depending on the needs of the children, but it is usually once a week for about an hour.

In her role, Sarah wears many hats—she is a consultant, a resource person, and a teacher. Her main role is to collaborate with the classroom teacher and/or child care provider, staff members, and families so that children with special needs can receive the most appropriate learning experiences. She also may spend time with children in their classrooms or homes as needed. She is available to provide suggestions, strategies, resources, and ideas to support the classroom teacher and/or child care provider. She and the teacher will work out a system so they can best work together. It will be important that they can find some uninterrupted time each week when they can meet to discuss and share information.

I appreciate the opportunity to work with your center. If you have any questions about our itinerant preschool program, please do not hesitate to call me at any time. Together, we will make this a great educational experience for the children, teachers, and families!

Sincerely,

Jennifer Reynolds

Jennifer Reynolds, Ed.S.
Supervisor, Preschool Special Needs Program
Telephone: 330-538-2222

GOLDEN LOCAL SCHOOL DISTRICT
4521 Oak Lane
Aspen Ridge, OH 41234
Telephone: 330-541-6789 Fax: 330-541-6780
Carol Mitchell, Ed.D., SUPERINTENDENT

Hello!

My name is Sarah Albright, Itinerant Preschool Special Needs Teacher with Golden Local School District. My job is to provide learning services for preschool-age children with special needs who attend community-based early childhood programs such as yours [*or insert name of program*]. Itinerant early childhood services may be provided in homes, day care centers, family day cares, preschools, kindergarten classrooms, Head Start classrooms, or any other early childhood setting. I travel to a number of different programs to work with children with special needs and their teachers. My visiting schedule varies depending on the needs of the children with whom I work, but it is usually once a week for about an hour.

In my role, I wear many hats—I am a consultant, a resource person, and a teacher. My main role is to work with the classroom teacher, staff members, and families so that the children with special needs with whom I work can have the most appropriate learning experiences. In this case, my job will be to work with you to help you understand how the learning goals that are identified in Jacob's individualized education program (IEP) can be met in your program. I am available to help provide you with suggestions for teaching strategies, learning resources, and any other ideas that might be helpful.

I look forward to working with you and Jacob this school year. I will be visiting your program [*insert visiting schedule*]. We will discuss the best ways for us to work together to help Jacob meet his learning goals. Please do not hesitate to call me with questions or concerns. Together, we will make this a great year for Jacob, his peers, and Jacob's family!

Sincerely,

Sarah Albright

Sarah Albright
Golden Local School District
Preschool Itinerant Services
4521 Oak Lane
Aspen Ridge, OH 41234
Telephone: 330-538-7642 Fax: 330-538-7677
Carol Mitchell, Ed.D., Superintendent
e-mail: salbright@goldenlocal.edu

GOLDEN LOCAL SCHOOL DISTRICT

4521 Oak Lane
Aspen Ridge, OH 41234
Telephone: 330-541-6789 Fax: 330-541-6780
Carol Mitchell, Ed.D., SUPERINTENDENT

August 29, 2011

Hello. My name is Sarah Albright. I have been assigned by the Golden Local School District to provide support to Jacob Hill and his teacher during the 2010–2011 school year. As you know, Jacob has an individualized education program (IEP) that specifies learning objectives that he could achieve this year at Jack & Jill Child Care Center. As the local school district representative, it is my responsibility to work with you and Jacob's teacher(s) in addressing these learning objectives. In providing support services, I plan to visit your school once a week for approximately 1 hour. During this time, I will be observing Jacob, familiarizing myself with the classroom schedule and routines, and developing a relationship with Jacob's teacher. Occasionally, I may ask to meet with Jacob's teacher outside of the classroom to discuss her progress with Jacob. My visitation schedule may change somewhat in response to Jacob's progress as well as the schedule of my "partner" teacher. I am excited about working with Jacob and the staff of Jack & Jill Child Care Center. I have heard great things about the center from Jacob's mother.

I thought you might like to know about my background and previous experiences. I have been an itinerant (traveling) preschool special education teacher for the last 3 years. Two of these years were with the Cincinnati Public Schools. Prior to my teaching as an itinerant teacher, for 4 years I was a primary school teacher (Grades 3–5) of students with mild intellectual impairment, also in Cincinnati. I graduated from Kent State University with certification in special education (Grades K–12—Mental Retardation and Learning Disability). I expect to complete my master's degree at the University of Toledo in early childhood special education in May 2012. I hold a supplemental license from the Ohio Department of Education in early childhood special education. Last year, I worked with children and their teachers at Children's World and St. Paul Lutheran Preschool. Please feel free to contact the directors of these programs for a reference.

I am looking forward to working with you and Jacob's teacher(s). If you have any questions about my responsibilities, please contact my supervisor, Jennifer Reynolds (330-538-2222), at the Golden Local Schools. If you wish to contact me, you may reach me at 330-538-7642 or by e-mail at salbright@goldenlocal.edu. Thank you, and best wishes for the school year.

Sincerely,

Sarah Albright

Sarah Albright
Itinerant Preschool Special Education Teacher
Golden Local Schools

GOLDEN LOCAL SCHOOL DISTRICT

4521 Oak Lane
Aspen Ridge, OH 41234
Telephone: 330-541-6789 Fax: 330-541-6780
Carol Mitchell, Ed.D., SUPERINTENDENT

Hello!

My name is Sarah Albright. I am an itinerant preschool special needs teacher with Golden Local School District. We met at Jacob Hill's individualized education program (IEP) meeting last year. I will be the teacher who comes to your home child care program to work with you and Jacob, and to help you understand how to work with him on his IEP-focused learning objectives when I am not there. I will be visiting Jacob once a week for about an hour, as agreed upon at the IEP meeting and as stated in Jacob's IEP.

In my role as an itinerant (or "traveling") teacher, I wear several hats. I am a consultant, a provider of resources, and a teacher. My main responsibility is to work with you so that Jacob will enjoy appropriate learning experiences that are focused on the learning outcomes in his IEP. My job will be to help you better understand how the learning goals that are identified in Jacob's IEP can be met. I will provide suggestions for teaching strategies as well as resources and ideas that might be helpful. At times, I may work with Jacob myself, but more often my job will be to make sure that you are confident that you can work on Jacob's learning objectives when I am not there.

I look forward to working with you and Jacob. Please do not hesitate to call me at my office at Jefferson School (telephone number below). Please leave a message if I am not in. You may also send me e-mail (address below). Together, we will create a positive experience for Jacob.

Sincerely,

Sarah Albright

Sarah Albright
Golden Local School District
4521 Oak Lane
Aspen Ridge, OH 41234
Telephone: 330-538-7642
Fax: 330-538-7677
e-mail: salbright@goldenlocal.edu

GOLDEN LOCAL SCHOOL DISTRICT

4521 Oak Lane
Aspen Ridge, OH 41234
Telephone: 330-541-6789 Fax: 330-541-6780
Carol Mitchell, Ed.D., SUPERINTENDENT

Hello!

My name is Sarah Albright. I am an itinerant preschool special needs teacher with Golden Local School District. We met at Jacob Hill's individualized education program (IEP) meeting last year. I will be the teacher who comes to Jack & Jill Child Care Center to work with Jacob and to help Jacob's teachers understand how to work with him when I am not at the center. I will be visiting Jacob once a week for about an hour, as agreed on at the IEP meeting and as stated in Jacob's IEP.

In my role as an itinerant (or "traveling") teacher, I wear several hats. I am a consultant, a provider of resources, and a teacher. My main responsibility is to work with Jacob's teacher and other staff members at Jack & Jill so that Jacob will enjoy appropriate learning experiences that are focused on the learning outcomes in his IEP. My job will be to work with Jacob's teachers and the staff at Jack & Jill to help them better understand how the learning goals that are identified in Jacob's IEP can be met in their program. I will provide suggestions for teaching strategies as well as resources and ideas that might be helpful. At times, I may work with Jacob myself, but more often my job will be to make sure that his teachers are confident that they can work on Jacob's learning objectives when I am not at Jack & Jill. Of course, 'we' (myself and my 'partner' teacher at Jack & Jill) will also be working with you to be sure that we are all working on the same goals.

I look forward to working with you and the staff of the Jack & Jill Child Care Center this school year. Please do not hesitate to call me at my office at Jefferson School (telephone # below). Please leave a message if I am not in. You may also send me e-mail (address below). Together, we will create a positive experience for you and Jacob.

Sincerely,

Sarah Albright

Sarah Albright
Itinerant Preschool Special Needs Teacher
Golden Local School District
4521 Oak Lane
Aspen Ridge, OH 41234
Telephone: 330-538-7642
Fax: 330-538-7677
e-mail: salbright@goldenlocal.edu

Letter of Agreement
Itinerant Early Childhood Special Education Services

The purpose of this agreement is to specify the nature of itinerant early childhood special education services (ECSE) to be provided by _____ [school district)] for _____ [child's name], a child with an individualized education program (IEP) who is enrolled in _____ [community child care program].

During the 2010–2011 school year, these IECSE services will be provided by _____ _____ [IECSE teacher], who will be working with the teacher(s) and staff of the classroom in which _____ [child's name] is enrolled. Ms./Mr. _____ holds a degree in early childhood special education and has been working as an IECSE teacher for _____ years. She also holds a teaching license from the [enter name of state department of education] in the area(s) of _____.

As the local school district representative, it is the responsibility of the itinerant teacher to work with the teacher(s) at your site to address _____'s [child's name] IEP objectives. Rather than focusing his or her work solely on the child, the itinerant teacher will work with your teachers so that they are able to address the child's IEP goals within the regular classroom environment and during typical preschool activities. This will require the itinerant teacher to develop a collaborative partnership with your teachers. The itinerant teacher will be available to share teaching resources as well as knowledge and teaching strategies with your teachers.

As stated in _____'s IEP, the itinerant teacher is scheduled to visit _____ [community child care program] for no less than 1 hour per week during the school year; however, this schedule may be modified upon agreement of the teaching partners and with your approval. The itinerant teacher also will inform his or her supervisor of any planned changes in the visiting and/or consultation schedule. On occasion, the itinerant teacher may need to meet with his or her partner teacher(s) outside of the classroom environment to discuss issues related to child progress, teaching strategies, and related issues.

The itinerant teacher and the early childhood education teachers will discuss the child's progress with his or her parents at least monthly. Update communications will be formal (e.g., file copy) and informal (e.g., phone, e-mail).

The itinerant teacher may be contacted at the following telephone number or e-mail address: _____ [telephone] or _____ [e-mail]. The supervisor of this teacher, _____, also may be contacted at _____ [telephone] or _____ [e-mail].

Signatures:

_____   _____
Preschool Program Director (or Representative)   Date

_____   _____
School District Representative   Date

_____   _____
Parent/Caregiver   Date

Sample Forms

Consultation Planning forms

Planning for Consultation Session: Sample A

Date of visit: <u>9/23/10</u>   Location: <u>Lutheran EC Learning Center</u>

IECSE teacher: <u>L. Winkler</u>   ECE partner teacher: <u>M. Conner</u>

Session #: <u>3</u>   Duration of session: <u>60 mins.</u>

Child: <u>E.M.</u>

Focus of session:

☒ Prioritization of IEP objectives   ☐ Monitoring of child progress
☐ MATRIX planning to embed instruction   ☐ Discussion of transition to kindergarten
☐ Discussion of peer pairing   ☐ Discussion of transition to another program
☐ Monitoring of partner progress   ☐ Assessment of child
☐ Development of task analysis of teaching skill

☐ Modification of materials: _____

☐ Provision of information and/or media on disability conditions: _____

☐ Demonstration of incidental teaching skill: _____

☐ Demonstration of direct instruction teaching skill: Use of DRO/DRA procedure _____

☐ Review of Internet resources: _____

Supplies and materials:

☐ Materials: _____

☐ Toy(s): _____

☐ Microswitch: _____

☐ CD or video: _____

☐ Child monitoring form: _____

☐ ECE partner teacher monitoring form: _____

☐ Journal article: _____

☒ Other: <u>MEPI Summary</u>

Reflection on coaching session (narrative/rating system)

☒ Objective(s) met   ☐ Objective(s) partially met
☐ Objective(s) NOT met

Comments:

We discussed E's IEP and how to determine which IEP objectives needed to be addressed by M during the week via direct and/or embedded instruction. We discussed rationale for why some objectives might need more teacher attention than others via use of the MEPI model. M was able to identify some activities and opportunities in the curriculum where instruction could be embedded.

Left overview of MEPI model, which includes examples of how IEP objectives can be prioritized.

Date of next coaching session: 10/1/10

Focus of next session: Matching priority IEP objectives with state prekindergarten learning standards and opportunities for instruction via development of curriculum matrix.

Planning for Consultation Session: Sample B

Date of visit: <u>10/7/11</u>   Location: <u>Lincoln Center - Head Start</u>

IECSE teacher: <u>V. McNamara</u>   ECE partner teacher: <u>S. Sykes</u>

Session #: <u>5</u>   Duration of session: <u>90 mins.</u>

Child: <u>T.P.</u>

Focus of session:

☐ Prioritization of IEP objectives   ☐ Monitoring of child progress
☒ MATRIX planning to embed instruction   ☐ Discussion of transition to kindergarten
☐ Discussion of peer pairing   ☐ Discussion of transition to another program
☐ Monitoring of partner progress   ☐ Assessment of child
☐ Development of task analysis of teaching skill

☐ Modification of materials: _____

☐ Provision of information and/or media on disability conditions: _____

☐ Demonstration of incidental teaching skill: _____

☐ Demonstration of direct instruction teaching skill: Use of DRO/DRA procedure _____

☐ Review of internet resources: _____

Supplies and materials:

☐ Materials: _____

☐ Toy(s): _____

☐ Microswitch: _____

☒ CD or video: <u>SPIES—Examples of Embedded Instruction</u>

☐ Child monitoring form: _____

☐ ECE partner teacher monitoring form: _____

☐ Journal article: _____

☒ Other: <u>MATRIX form</u>

Reflection on coaching session (narrative / rating system)

☐ Objective(s) met   ☒ Objective(s) partially met
☐ Objective(s) NOT met

Comments:

We reviewed the relationship between priority IEP objectives and the classroom curriculum with use of a MATRIX planning model. Opportunities to link IEP objectives with state standards and opportunities for direct and embedded instruction were discussed. We agreed on when and where two of T's IEP objectives could be addressed during the week and completed a MATRIX planning form.

Date of next coaching session: 10/14/11

Focus of next session: Addressing additional IEP objectives in MATRIX
Discussing teaching strategies that match priority IEP objectives already in the curriculum matrix

Planning for Consultation Session

Date of visit: _____   Location: _____

IECSE teacher: _____   ECE partner teacher: _____

Session #: _____   Duration of session: _____

Child: _____

Focus of session:

☐ Prioritization of IEP objectives   ☐ Monitoring of child progress
☐ MATRIX planning to embed instruction   ☐ Discussion of transition to kindergarten
☐ Discussion of peer pairing   ☐ Discussion of transition to another program
☐ Monitoring of partner progress   ☐ Assessment of child
☐ Development of task analysis of teaching skill

☐ Modification of materials: _____

☐ Provision of information and/or media on disability conditions: _____

☐ Demonstration of incidental teaching skill: _____

☐ Demonstration of direct instruction teaching skill: Use of DRO/DRA procedure _____

☐ Review of internet resources: _____

Supplies and materials:

☐ Materials: _____

☐ Toy(s): _____

☐ Microswitch: _____

☐ CD or video: _____

☐ Child monitoring form: _____

☐ ECE partner teacher monitoring form: _____

☐ Journal article: _____

☐ Other: _____

Reflection on coaching session (narrative / rating system)

☐ Objective(s) met   ☐ Objective(s) partially met
☐ Objective(s) NOT met

Comments:

_____

_____

_____

_____

_____

_____

_____

_____

_____

_____

_____

_____

_____

_____

_____

_____

Date of next coaching session: _____

Focus of next session: _____

_____

_____

_____

_____

_____

_____

_____

Professional Development

PIECES: *Performance Indicators for Early Childhood Education Specialists*

◻ Introduction

The roles and responsibilities of an itinerant early childhood special education (IECSE) teacher vary greatly from those of an ECSE teacher who manages his or her own classroom. Whereas the classroom-based ECSE teacher "stays put" and manages the learning environment for a group of children, the IECSE teacher travels from site to site, visiting for a minimum of 4 hours per month, providing assistance and support to other teachers who work with children with disabilities throughout the week who are on the itinerant teacher's caseload. Although the itinerant ECSE model is used in Ohio and across the country, there is little support for itinerant ECSE teachers who assume these unique roles. The purpose of this document is to describe roles and responsibilities of itinerant ECSE teachers and outline indicators of high-quality performance.

Odom and his colleagues (1999) defined two primary models of itinerant ECSE service delivery—direct and consultative. The Ohio Department of Education has adopted a policy stressing the importance of a consultative model of itinerant ECSE service delivery, one that supports the successful inclusion of young children who have individualized education programs (IEPs) in community-based early childhood programs. This policy can be found at http://www.ode.state .oh.us/ece/superintendent/programs/Itinerant%20ECSE%20Policy%20Brief%20web%20 version3.pdf

Knowledge and Skills for Itinerant Early Childhood Special Educators

To be effective, an ECSE teacher must have prerequisite knowledge and skills related to the following:
a. Principles of early childhood special education and specialized instruction
b. Typical and atypical child development
c. Early childhood and early childhood special education curriculum and assessment practices
d. Operational and program standards for a range of community-based early childhood programs (e.g., Head Start, child care, Title I, kindergarten)

In addition to the knowledge and skills described here, the itinerant ECSE teacher also must have skills and knowledge related to the following:
e. Consultation and coaching strategies
f. Collaboration and problem-solving techniques
g. Leadership and team building

Since the launch of this work, the Office of Early Learning and School Readiness/ODE realized that consultative skills are applicable to any team relationship to ensure all team members can support child progress. This can be applicable to center-based teachers who are team teaching with general preschool teachers or related service personnel integrating services within an early childhood setting. As we move towards team sharing to ensure child progress performance measure established by federal Office of Special Education Programs (OSEP), consultation to ensure continued support for children is necessary.

(continued)

Characteristics critical to the itinerant ECSE service delivery, which cannot be measured directly but are important to note, include the following:
- Cultural sensitivity in interacting with families and staff
- Flexibility in service delivery
- Diplomacy in problem solving
- Creativity in developing the design of intervention plans
- Leadership in working with the team

In addition, readers should note that the knowledge and skills described in this document are not the only competencies needed by early childhood special educators. The Council for Exceptional Children's Common Core and Early Childhood Specialty Standards provide a comprehensive overview of the knowledge and skills needed by beginning early childhood special educators. These standards can be found at http://www.cec.sped.org/Content/NavigationMenu/ProfessionalDevelopment/ProfessionalStandards/default.htm

Finally, the field of early childhood special education has identified a code of ethics that guides the practice of early childhood special educators, including itinerant ECSE teachers. This code of ethical conduct is available at http://www.dec-sped.org/pdf/positionpapers/Code%20of%20Ethics.pdf

◼ PURPOSE OF THIS DOCUMENT

The purpose of this document is to provide a method of self-assessment for itinerant ECSE teachers. Supervisors might also be interested in using this document to support the performance of itinerant ECSE teachers they supervise. In addition, this document provides performance-based examples at three levels: *basic, proficient,* and *distinguished.* Itinerant ECSE teachers who are new to their positions can be expected to operate at the "basic" level of performance, whereas those with more experience and expertise can be expected to operate at either the "proficient" or "distinguished" levels. We hope this document is useful to those wishing to improve their performance as itinerant ECSE teachers as well as to those who supervise the work of itinerant ECSE teachers.

This document was supported in whole or in part by the U.S. Department of Education through the Ohio Department of Education. It was made possible through a grant from the Ohio Department of Education in SFY 2007, Project Number 063099-SAC 86E5-L849. The opinions expressed herein do not necessarily reflect the position or policy of the U.S. Department of Education or the Ohio Department of Education, and no official endorsement by the U.S. Department of Education or the Ohio Department of Education is implied. The authors would like to thank Project DIRECT (Defining Itinerant Roles for Early Childhood Teachers): Angie Denov, Lisa Garofalo, and Linda Hicks, of the Cincinnati Public Schools; Ann Loehrer, of the Dublin City Schools; and Amanda Mueller, of the Bellevue City Schools, all in Ohio, for their contributions.

(continued)

◼ ORGANIZATION OF THIS DOCUMENT

The performance indicators outlined in this document are divided into three parts. Embedded within each part are a series of rubrics designed to help itinerant ECSE teachers and/or their supervisors identify their current or desired skill level. These are described previously.

Part A focuses on requisite knowledge and skills related to ECSE service delivery and includes the following:
1. Knowledge of the organizational context of the child's environment
2. The ability to design and implement child-focused interventions, which assumes
   a. Knowledge of typical and atypical child development
   b. The ability to appropriately use special education intervention strategies
   c. An understanding of how aspects of the environment affects children's development and learning
   d. The ability to embed interventions into routines and daily activities
   e. The ability to monitor the effect of the intervention on children's progress towards meeting IEP goals
   f. The ability to assess the effectiveness of interventions

Part B focuses on communication skills and specialized knowledge related to coaching and information sharing in order to develop family, professional, and community relationships that support learning in the LRE, including the following:
1. The ability to build a collaborative team
   a. The ability to identify and actively include key members of the child's IEP team
   b. The ability to guide the team to use conflict resolution and problem-solving strategies
2. The ability to establish and implement a plan for regular communication among team members
   a. The use of systematic procedures to communicate with team members
   b. The ability to document communication events
3. The ability to demonstrate appropriate use of specific interpersonal communication skills to establish ongoing relationships with families and providers
   a. The ability to adhere to schedules and follow through on requests
   b. The use of appropriate communication strategies
4. The ability to help others develop skills and use strategies via a coaching model that includes the following components:
   a. Jointly identifying opportunities for coaching and intended outcomes
   b. Observing of the partner teacher's skills
   c. Demonstrating or modeling the targeted skill
   d. Observing the partner teacher using the skill or strategy
   e. Providing feedback about the partner teacher's performance
   f. Continuing through the cycle of observation, demonstration, and feedback until the intended outcome is achieved
   g. Providing information to support the child's success in the community-based program

(continued)

Part C focuses on how the IECSE teacher uses specialized knowledge to coordinate and facilitate integrated service delivery to support learning in the LRE in the following ways:

1. Coordinates and monitors service delivery
    a. Coordinates and monitors delivery of services specified on the child's IEP
    b. Effectively plans for visits
    c. Coordinates and completes paperwork as required by federal, state, and local guidelines
    d. Meets mandated timelines for procedural compliance
    e. Designs and implements professional development (PD) activities

Each skill area is described using a continuum of rubrics ranging from basic to proficient. This design allows the reader to use this document for both planning and self-evaluation purposes in program improvement.

(continued)

Directions for completion: Review each of the numbered components under each part of the PIECES and use the descriptors to rate the IECSE teacher's level of competence. Provide comments that identify specific components of the rated item that were considered in rating the IECSE teacher. If a certain competency is not one that is expected of the IECSE teacher, leave it blank.

■ Part A

The IECSE teacher uses specialized knowledge and skills to collaborate and consult with parents, educators, related services professionals, administrators, and children to support learning in the LRE.

1. **Demonstrates knowledge of the organizational context of the child's environment:**
   When helping others to embed interventions, it is essential that the IECSE teacher understand the context of the early childhood environment. For example, skilled IECSE teachers understand what routines and activities best lend themselves to embedded interventions. They are aware of the reality of their partner teacher's day and make suggestions that are practical and realistic. They can also identify the relevant characteristics of a routine or activity and describe its learning potential for children. They are familiar with the operational and program standards of community-based programs.

☐ **Basic**	☐ **Proficient**	☐ **Distinguished**
Demonstrates an understanding of the basic activities, routines, and procedures during the time of the IECSE's scheduled visit	Demonstrates an understanding of the activities, routines, and procedures of the child's daily/weekly learning environment	Demonstrates an understanding of the activities, routines, procedures, and policies across all of the child's daily/weekly environments
Comments:		

2. **Designs and implements child-focused interventions:**
   The IECSE teacher demonstrates the ability to design and implement intervention strategies that will successfully help children with disabilities reach developmental goals. It is essential that the IECSE teacher have knowledge and skills related to curriculum development and implementation for both children who are typically developing and children with disabilities.

(continued)

The IECSE teacher demonstrates the ability to appropriately use child-focused intervention strategies. For example, the IECSE teacher uses response-prompting strategies, peer-mediated strategies, and basic reinforcement techniques appropriate to address children's IEP goals.

☐ **Basic**	☐ **Proficient**	☐ **Distinguished**
Uses a limited number of intervention strategies that are directly aligned to the skills identified as goals and objectives on the child's IEP	Uses a variety of intervention strategies that are directly aligned to the skills identified as goals and objectives on the child's IEP	Uses a broad range of multiple intervention strategies that result in progress and mastery of the skills identified as goals and objectives on the child's IEP
Comments:		

a. **Demonstrates knowledge of typical and atypical child development:**
Knowledge of typical and atypical development is central to designing and implementing interventions that help children learn. The IECSE teacher is familiar with developmental milestones as well as the effects of disabling conditions on children's development (across all developmental domains). The IECSE teacher demonstrates a realistic understanding of children's capabilities across the preschool period as well as across developmental domains and uses this knowledge to prepare and implement developmentally appropriate activities within which interventions are embedded. The IECSE teacher applies knowledge of child development to make appropriate modifications or adaptations to activities.

☐ **Basic**	☐ **Proficient**	☐ **Distinguished**
Prepares and implements a limited number of developmentally appropriate activities that can be modified or adapted for the child with atypical development	Consistently prepares and implements a variety of developmentally appropriate activities that can be modified or adapted for the child with atypical development	Prepares and implements a broad range of developmentally appropriate activities that can easily be modified or adapted for the child with atypical development
Comments:		

(continued)

b. **Demonstrates the ability to appropriately use special education intervention strategies**

c. **Demonstrates an understanding of how aspects of the environment affect children's development and learning:**
   The IECSE teacher assesses the learning environment (e.g., the physical surroundings, the daily schedule, interactions between adults and children and between child and his or her peers) to ensure that the environment can and will support the child's development (e.g., use of the ECERS). Assessing the environment includes observing the child's participation in routines and activities that occur throughout the day as well as the responsibilities of the partner teacher or parent during those routines or activities (to determine feasibility of adult implementation of intervention strategies).

☐ **Basic**	☐ **Proficient**	☐ **Distinguished**
Is aware that dimensions of the environment have an impact on learning and development and can make basic suggestions for adaptations or modifications	Can analyze and describe how the environment affects learning and development and works with others to modify the environment to meet the needs of the child (and his or her peers)	Can conduct an environmental analysis using an instrument such as the ECERS and make suggestions to others regarding modifications that would support children's learning and development
Comments:		

d. **Embeds interventions into routines and daily activities:**
   The IECSE teacher is able to implement embedded interventions into routines and activities across the day. The interventions are educationally sound and are designed around the principles of naturalistic instruction (e.g., follows the child lead, addresses functional skills, incorporates systematic interventions, and logical/natural consequences).

(continued)

☐ **Basic**	☐ **Proficient**	☐ **Distinguished**
Designs and implements embedded basic interventions during routines and activities that occur during the scheduled time of the itinerant visit	Designs and implements complex interventions during routines and times that occur during the scheduled time of the itinerant visit	Designs and helps the partner teacher implement complex interventions in routines across the day
Comments:		

e. **Monitors the effect of the interventions on children's progress towards meeting IEP goals:**
The IECSE teacher is able to implement sound data monitoring strategies sensitive to children's progress. The IECSE teacher is knowledgeable about a broad range of data monitoring strategies (e.g., time sampling, anecdotal records, frequency counts) and can apply these appropriately to children's IEP goals. The IECSE teacher enlists the help of others in data monitoring efforts and provides appropriate support to them in order to ensure success.

☐ **Basic**	☐ **Proficient**	☐ **Distinguished**
Uses simple data collection strategies to monitor children's progress Can explain the strategies to others but does not share responsibility for data collection during the scheduled time of the itinerant visit	Uses a range of data collection strategies that are sensitive to children's progress and helps others use those strategies as well	Employs a broad range of data collection strategies that are specific to the nature of the desired skill or behavior Helps others become the primary data collectors through collaboratively designing systems that are easy to use and maintain
Comments:		

(continued)

f. **Assesses effectiveness of implemented interventions:**
    The IECSE teacher is able to use data collected to make sound decisions about the
    success of the intervention and children's progress in collaboration with others on the
    team. For example, the IECSE teacher analyzes the data for patterns and trends and
    makes decisions based on it.

☐ **Basic**	☐ **Proficient**	☐ **Distinguished**
Assesses the effectiveness of the planned interventions and may make some adjustments	Regularly assesses the effectiveness of the planned interventions and makes adjustments as needed	Regularly reflects on and assesses the effectiveness of planned interventions in collaboration with the IEP team, and makes adjustments as needed
Comments:		

Part B

The IECSE teacher uses communication skills and specialized knowledge to develop family,
professional, and community relationships, which support learning in the LRE.

1. **Builds a collaborative team:**
    The IECSE teacher is a team leader because his or her associations cut across the home,
    community-based program, and LEA. He or she has leadership skills that enable him or her
    to build a team that works collaboratively in order to best meet the needs of the child. He
    or she identifies and actively includes key members of the child's IEP team:
    a. As team leader, it is essential that the IECSE teacher **involves and actively includes
        all of the key stakeholders in the IEP team.** Skilled IECSE teachers actively include
        all stakeholders by working to ensure that team meetings are held when people can
        attend. Skilled IECSE teachers also help prepare less-knowledgeable team members by
        providing background information and explaining what is going to happen in the meet-
        ing before the meeting. Skilled IECSE teachers make sure that all team members have
        opportunities to contribute to the discussion by inviting less talkative members to speak
        and make sure that everyone understands what is being discussed.

(continued)

☐ **Basic**	☐ **Proficient**	☐ **Distinguished**
Identifies and involves services such as related service providers listed on the IEP as the only key members of the team	Designs and implements complex interventions during routines and times that occur during the scheduled time of the itinerant visit	Contacts and makes sure to actively include all of the child's stakeholders as well as service providers listed on the IEP, the partner teacher, and parent(s)
Comments:		

b. **Guides the team to use conflict resolution and problem-solving strategies:** Conflict resolution strategies include skills such as active listening, effective questioning, summarizing another's comments to clarify intent and meaning, and monitoring discussions so everyone has a chance to voice her or his opinion. The problem-solving process broadly reflects the following stages: a) identification of the problem, b) determining possible causes of the problem, c) brainstorming possible strategies to address the problem, d) choosing and implementing a strategy, and e) evaluating the effectiveness of the chosen strategy.

☐ **Basic**	☐ **Proficient**	☐ **Distinguished**
Participates in the team's group process but does not take an active role in resolving conflicts or problem solving among team members	Facilitates the team's group process including taking an active role in resolving conflicts and problem solving among team members	Leads the team's group process including taking a proactive role in resolving conflicts and problem solving among team members
Comments:		

2. **Establishes and implements a plan for regular communication among team members:**
   a. The IECSE teacher **uses systematic procedures to communicate with members of the collaborative team:** He or she recognizes the importance of communication in order to ensure that all team members are receiving important information in a coordinated manner.

(continued)

☐ **Basic**	☐ **Proficient**	☐ **Distinguished**
Communicates with members of the collaborative team through a limited number of methods and participates in meetings	Communicates with members of the collaborative team through a variety of methods and participates in goal-directed meetings	Communicates with members of the collaborative team through a system of communication of various methods and facilitates goal-directed meetings
Comments:		

b. **Documents communication:**
   In addition to fostering effective communication across all team members, the IECSE teacher keeps appropriate records of communications in order to document decisions concerning the child's program.

☐ **Basic**	☐ **Proficient**	☐ **Distinguished**
Maintains records of required communication among team members	Maintains records of ongoing communication among all team members	Maintains thorough records of ongoing communication among all team members in and out of the child's learning environment
Comments:		

3. **Demonstrates appropriate use of specific interpersonal communication skills to establish ongoing relationships with families and providers:**
   a. **Adheres to schedule and follows through on requests for materials and assistance:** The IECSE teacher is dependable and adheres to the set schedule for visits and provides appropriate notification to all concerned parties if he or she cannot adhere to the schedule. The IECSE teacher follows through with requests by others in a timely manner.

(continued)

☐ **Basic**	☐ **Proficient**	☐ **Distinguished**
Is sensitive to the attitudes and needs of staff and parents towards inclusion when developing a schedule and procedure for making requests	Is sensitive to the attitudes and needs of staff and parents toward inclusion; adheres to an agreed upon schedule and establishes trust by following through on requests for materials and assistance	Is sensitive to the attitudes and needs of staff and parents towards inclusion, adheres to an agreed upon schedule, and establishes trust by following through on requests for materials and assistance in a timely manner
Comments:		

b. **Uses appropriate communication strategies:**
   The IECSE teacher uses appropriate communication strategies to facilitate open and effective lines of communication with others. He or she creates a comfortable atmosphere for discussions. Body language demonstrates interest in a partner. He or she provides his or her partner with undivided attention by displaying appropriate eye contact and positive body language. He or she encourages his or her partner to talk and lets the partner steer or direct conversation.

☐ **Basic**	☐ **Proficient**	☐ **Distinguished**
Establishes two-way communication with families and community-based ECE providers by responding to staff and parent concerns in a timely manner	Establishes open and respectful communication with families and community-based ECE providers when opportunities arise and uses some open communication strategies	Establishes open and respectful communication with families and community-based ECE providers through the intentional use of a variety of communication strategies, which include questioning, summarizing, problem solving, and active listening
Comments:		

(continued)

4. **Helps others develop skills and use strategies via a coaching model that includes the following components:**
   a. Joint identification of opportunities for coaching and intended outcomes
   b. Observing the partner teacher's baseline skill development
   c. Demonstrating or modeling the targeted skill
   d. Observing the partner teacher use the skill or strategy
   e. Providing feedback about the partner teacher's performance
   f. Continuing through the cycle of observation, demonstration, and feedback until the intended outcome is achieved
   g. Providing information to support the child's success in the community-based program

The IECSE teacher jointly identifies skills that the partner teacher will acquire, refine, or enhance. The IECSE teacher collaborates with the partner teacher to identify skills or teaching behaviors that can be used to address children's developmental goals. The IECSE teacher is able to identify skills or behaviors that the partner teacher must acquire as opposed to those that are already in the partner teacher's repertoire and should be enhanced or refined.

☐ **Basic**	☐ **Proficient**	☐ **Distinguished**
Identifies skills or strategies the partner teacher could use to address children's developmental goals based on information already known about the partner teacher	Works in partnership with the partner teacher to identify skills or strategies the partner teacher could learn or refine that could be used to address children's developmental goals	Works in partnership with the partner teacher to identify and operationally define skills (e.g., use of an intervention strategy) that the partner teacher could use to address developmental goals for children
Comments:		

   a. **Identifies opportunities for the partner teacher to acquire, refine, or enhance those skills:**
   In partnership with the partner teacher, the IECSE teacher identifies times and situations during the day in which to help the partner teacher acquire or practice skills. The IECSE teacher is realistic and pragmatic about implementation of a coaching model and respects the demands on the partner teacher's time and other responsibilities.

(continued)

☐ **Basic**	☐ **Proficient**	☐ **Distinguished**
Identifies a learning opportunity during the day in which the partner teacher could learn to use or refine use of a new skill or strategy	Along with the partner teacher, identifies a few learning opportunities during which the partner teacher could learn to use or refine use of a new skill or strategy	Along with the partner teacher, identifies multiple learning opportunities that vary in terms of context yet are realistic to implement in a written intervention plan in conjunction with the partner teacher
Comments:		

b. **Uses observation to gather information about the partner teacher's skill level:**
The IECSE teacher employs systematic observation strategies to gather information about the partner teacher's use of a skill and documents those observations to share with the partner teacher.

☐ **Basic**	☐ **Proficient**	☐ **Distinguished**
Observes partner teacher's use of a skill or strategy	Observes across multiple instances and takes notes on observations to share with the partner teacher	Observes across multiple instances and systematically records observations in a way that will assist the partner teacher in acquiring or improving his or her skill
Comments:		

c. **Demonstrates or models a skill to the partner teacher:**
The IECSE teacher uses the information gained through observation to develop strategies for modeling or demonstrating a skill to the partner teacher. The IECSE teacher ensures that the partner teacher is an active participant in the modeling/demonstrating process by explicitly inviting the partner teacher to observe and then demonstrate correct use of a skill or strategy.

(continued)

☐ **Basic**	☐ **Proficient**	☐ **Distinguished**
Invites the partner teacher to observe the IECSE teacher correctly use the skill	Invites the partner teacher to observe the IECSE teacher correctly using the skill and discusses the demonstration afterwards	Invites the partner teacher to observe the IECSE teacher correctly using the skill, discusses the demonstration afterward, and provides for additional opportunities to demonstrate the skill
Comments:		

d. **Observes the partner teacher using the skill or strategy:**
e. **Provides feedback about the partner teacher's performance:** The IECSE teacher provides feedback (verbal and/or written) that enables the partner teacher to improve his or her use of a skill or strategy. This feedback is specific and constructive and is provided in a timely manner to promote acquisition or refinement of the targeted skill or strategy.

☐ **Basic**	☐ **Proficient**	☐ **Distinguished**
After observing the partner teacher use a skill, provides verbal feedback that is specific and constructive, thus enabling the partner teacher to learn from the coaching process	After observing the partner teacher use a skill, provides verbal and written feedback that is specific and constructive, thus enabling the partner teacher to learn from the coaching process	After observing the partner teacher use a skill, provides verbal and written feedback that is specific and constructive and invites the partner teacher to self-evaluate his or her use of a skill
Comments:		

(continued)

f. **Continuing through the cycle of observation, demonstration, and feedback until the intended outcome is achieved**

g. **Provides information to support the child's success in the community-based program:**
The IECSE teacher provides information in multiple forms (e.g., print, media, digital) that is relevant to the child's success in the program. This information is relevant and useful to team members (i.e., written at an appropriate reading level or in a useful format). It can include information about the child's condition, intervention strategies to address developmental goals, or community resources.

☐ **Basic**	☐ **Proficient**	☐ **Distinguished**
Shares helpful ideas with team members based on personal knowledge and experience when asked	Provides partners with helpful information in a variety of useful formats from outside sources when asked to do so as well as independent of a request	Uses a broad network of resources found within the school district, community, state, and/or beyond that provides support, advocacy, and information to meet the team's needs
Comments:		

■ Part C

The IECSE teacher uses specialized knowledge to coordinate and facilitate integrated service delivery to support learning in the LRE.

1. **Coordinates and monitors delivery of services specified on the child's IEP:**
   a. **Through effective monitoring practices, the IECSE teacher ensures that all services outlined on the child's IEP are being delivered as intended.** The IECSE teacher also works with the team to ensure that services are coordinated and integrated within the child's program.

(continued)

☐ **Basic**	☐ **Proficient**	☐ **Distinguished**
Reviews IEP with partner teacher and related service providers and coordinates scheduling of services at convenient times	Collaboratively integrates services within child's daily routines, reviews child's progress with team periodically, and makes appropriate adjustments to ensure effective service delivery	Facilitates regular team communication (e.g., meetings, telephone conferences) to monitor child's progress and service effectiveness, share expert information, and problem solve
Comments:		

b. **Effectively plans for visits:**
   The IECSE teacher develops plans for visits that reflect an efficient use of time and effort for both him- or herself and the partner teacher. Plans are developed in collaboration with partner teachers and the IECSE teacher works to ensure that the plans can be implemented effectively. For example, if the plan for the visit includes time for the IECSE and partner teacher to work on skill development via a coaching method, the IECSE teacher works with the partner teacher to ensure that the partner teacher has uninterrupted time to participate in a coaching session.

☐ **Basic**	☐ **Proficient**	☐ **Distinguished**
Meets with partner teacher periodically to discuss child's progress, plan learning activities, provide information, and make suggestions for interventions	Organizes consultation visits by identifying visit goals for child/partner/self, preparing for appropriate consultation/coaching activities and arrangements, documenting visit data, and determining interim activities for partner/self	Meets with partner on a regular basis to engage in a collaborative, systematic process for planning, reflecting, and problem solving. Partners make refinements to the process as the consultation relationship develops.
Comments:		

(continued)

c. **Coordinates and completes paperwork as required by federal, state, and local guidelines:**
   The IECSE teacher has the responsibility of maintaining a record-keeping system that ensures compliance with all relevant guidelines concerning paperwork and documentation.

☐ **Basic**	☐ **Proficient**	☐ **Distinguished**
Completes and distributes required paperwork related to child's educational services and develops appropriate IEPs	Uses an organized system to maintain documentation of communication, services, and child progress and develops well-designed IEPs	Ensures that all team members complete required paperwork related to child's educational services and provides technical support to colleagues with less experience
Comments:		

d. **Meets mandated timelines for procedural compliance:**
   The IECSE teacher provides leadership to the team to ensure that all mandated timelines for procedural compliance are being met.

☐ **Basic**	☐ **Proficient**	☐ **Distinguished**
Individually meets federal and state-mandated timelines for educational procedures	Collaborates with team members to meet federal and state-mandated timelines for educational procedures	Organizes and facilitates a team plan to meet federal and state-mandated timelines for educational procedures
Comments:		

(continued)

e. **Designs and implements professional development (PD) activities:** The IECSE teacher provides individual and group professional development activities designed to support successful inclusion in community-based programs. In addition to meeting the individualized learning needs of team members, the IECSE teacher works with center-based programs to design and conduct professional development activities including workshops or discussion groups.

☐ **Basic**	☐ **Proficient**	☐ **Distinguished**
Provides basic educational information requested by parents and partners	Determines partners' preferred learning style(s), provides relevant information from a variety of sources, and links partners to support systems	Identifies needs of community program staff related to inclusion and arranges for or provides pertinent professional development activities
Comments:		

Components of an Effective IECSE Consultation/Coaching Services Model

Active monitoring of child progress	Analysis of EC learning environment	Continuous feedback regarding EC partner teacher progress
Prioritizing child individual-ized education program (IEP) objectives to be addressed in the early childhood (EC) learning environment	Transfer of knowledge, skills, attitudes, and values to EC partner teacher	Administrative support— proactive and reactive
Development of effective interpersonal communication skills	Communication with families who have children receiving early childhood special education (IECSE) services	Self-advocacy and professional development

CODE OF ETHICS

The Code of Ethics of the Division for Early Childhood (DEC) of the Council for Exceptional Children is a public statement of principles and practice guidelines supported by the mission of DEC.

The foundation of this Code is based on sound ethical reasoning related to professional practice with young children with disabilities and their families and with interdisciplinary colleagues. Foremost, is our value of respecting the autonomy of families as they make decisions for their young children with disabilities while also practicing a mutual respect for our colleagues in the field. We, as early childhood professionals, practice within the principles and guidelines outlined below as well as uphold the laws and regulations of our professional licensure standards.

The Code's purpose is to: (1) identify the key principles guiding our professional conduct; and (2) provide guidance for practice and personal dilemmas in our conduct of research and practice. The Code is intended to assist professionals in resolving conflicts as they arise in practice with children and families and with other colleagues.

The following principles and guidelines for practice include:

   I.   Professional Practice;
   II.   Professional Development and Preparation;
   III.   Responsive Family Practices; and
   IV.   Ethical and Evidence Based Practices.

I.   **PROFESSIONAL PRACTICE** encompasses the practice principles to promote and maintain high standards of conduct for the early childhood special education professional. The early childhood special education professional should base his or her behaviors on ethical reasoning surrounding practice and professional issues as well as an empathic reflection regarding interactions with others. We are committed to beneficence acts for improving the quality of lives of young children with disabilities and their families. The guidelines for practice outlined below provide a framework for everyday practice when working with children and families and with other professionals in the field of early childhood special education.

     Professional and Interpersonal Behavior

       1. We shall demonstrate in our behavior and language respect and appreciation for the unique value and human potential of each child.

       2. We shall demonstrate the highest standards of personal integrity, truthfulness, and honesty in all our professional activities in order to inspire the trust and confidence of the children and families and of those with whom we work.

       3. We shall strive for the highest level of personal and professional competence by seeking and using new evidence based information to improve our practices while also responding openly to the suggestions of others.

       4. We shall serve as advocates for children with disabilities and their families and for the professionals who serve them by supporting both policy and programmatic decisions that enhance the quality of their lives.

(continued)

CODE OF ETHICS

5. We shall use individually appropriate assessment strategies including multiple sources of information such as observations, interviews with significant caregivers, formal and informal assessments to determine children's learning styles, strengths, and challenges.

6. We shall build relationships with individual children and families while individualizing the curricula and learning environments to facilitate young children's development and learning.

Professional Collaboration

1. We shall honor and respect our responsibilities to colleagues while upholding the dignity and autonomy of colleagues and maintaining collegial interprofessional and intraprofessional relationships.

2. We shall honor and respect the rights, knowledge, and skills of the multidisciplinary colleagues with whom we work recognizing their unique contributions to children, families, and the field of early childhood special education.

3. We shall honor and respect the diverse backgrounds of our colleagues including such diverse characteristics as sexual orientation, race, national origin, religious beliefs, or other affiliations.

4. We shall identify and disclose to the appropriate persons using proper communication channels errors or acts of incompetence that compromise children's and families' safety and well being when individual attempts to address concerns are unsuccessful.

II. **PROFESSIONAL DEVELOPMENT AND PREPARATION** is critical to providing the most effective services for young children with disabilities and their families. Professional development is viewed and valued as an ongoing process guided by high standards and competencies for professional performance and practice. Professionals acquire the knowledge, skills, and dispositions to work with a variety of young children with disabilities and their families within natural and inclusive environments promoting children's overall growth, development and learning, and enhancing family quality of life. Finally, professionals continually should seek and interpret evidence based information for planning and implementing individually appropriate learning environments linked to ongoing assessment and collaboration with parents and professional team members.

1. We shall engage in ongoing and systematic reflective inquiry and self-assessment for the purpose of continuous improvement of professional performance and services to young children with disabilities and their families.

2. We shall continually be aware of issues challenging the field of early childhood special education and advocate for changes in laws, regulations, and policies leading to improved outcomes and services for young children with disabilities and their families.

3. We shall be responsible for maintaining the appropriate national, state, or other credential or licensure requirements for the services we provide while maintaining our competence in practice and research by ongoing participation in professional development and education activities.

4. We shall support professionals new to the field by mentoring them in the practice of evidence and ethically based services.

III. **RESPONSIVE FAMILY CENTERED PRACTICES** ensure that families receive individualized, meaningful, and relevant services responsive to their beliefs, values, customs, languages, and culture. We are committed to enhancing the quality of children's and families' lives by promoting family well-being and participation in typical life activities. The early childhood special education professional will demonstrate respect for all families, taking into consideration and acknowledging diverse family structures, culture, language, values, and customs. Finally, families will be given equal voice in all decision making relative to their children. The following practice guidelines provide a framework for enhancing children's and families' quality of lives.

CODE OF ETHICS

Enhancement of Children's and Families' Quality of Lives

1. We shall demonstrate our respect and concern for children, families, colleagues, and others with whom we work, honoring their beliefs, values, customs, languages, and culture.

2. We shall recognize our responsibility to improve the developmental outcomes of children and to provide services and supports in a fair and equitable manner to all families and children.

3. We shall recognize and respect the dignity, diversity, and autonomy of the families and children we serve.

4. We shall advocate for equal access to high quality services and supports for all children and families to enhance their quality of lives.

Responsive Family Centered Practices

1. We shall demonstrate our respect and appreciation for all families' beliefs, values, customs, languages, and culture relative to their nurturance and support of their children toward achieving meaningful and relevant priorities and outcomes families' desire for themselves and their children.

2. We shall provide services and supports to children and families in a fair and equitable manner while respecting families' culture, race, language, socioeconomic status, marital status, and sexual orientation.

3. We shall respect, value, promote, and encourage the active participation of ALL families by engaging families in meaningful ways in the assessment and intervention processes.

4. We shall empower families with information and resources so that they are informed consumers of services for their children.

5. We shall collaborate with families and colleagues in setting meaningful and relevant goals and priorities throughout the intervention process including the full disclosure of the nature, risk, and potential outcomes of any interventions.

6. We shall respect families' rights to choose or refuse early childhood special education or related services.

7. We shall be responsible for protecting the confidentiality of the children and families we serve by protecting all forms of verbal, written, and electronic communication.

IV. **ETHICAL AND EVIDENCE BASED PRACTICES** in the field of early childhood special education relies upon sound research methodologies and research based practices to ensure high quality services for children and families. As professionals researching and practicing within the field, it is our responsibility to maintain ethical conduct in building a cadre of practices based on evidence. Establishing an evidence base not only involves critically examining available research evidence relative to our professional practices, it also involves continually engaging in research to further refine our research-based or recommended practices.

Sound and ethical research strategies always should be used including adherence to institutional review board procedures and guidelines prior to the conduct of research and use of peer-reviewed venues for published dissemination of findings. Honoring and respecting the diversity of children and families should guide all research activities.

Evidence Based Practices

1. We shall rely upon evidence based research and interventions to inform our practice with children and families in our care.

(continued)

CODE OF ETHICS

2. We shall use every resource, including referral when appropriate, to ensure high quality services are accessible and are provided to children and families.

3. We shall include the diverse perspectives and experiences of children and families in the conduct of research and intervention.

Ethical Practice in Research

1. We shall use research designs and analyses in an appropriate manner by providing a clear rationale for each. We shall provide enough information about the methodologies we use so that others can replicate the work.

2. We shall maintain records of research securely; no personal information about research participants should be revealed unless required by law.

3. We shall conduct on-going research and field work that is consistent with and builds upon the available cadre of evidence based practices.

4. We shall utilize collaborative and interdisciplinary research for strengthening linkages between the research and practice communities, as well as for improving the quality of life of children with disabilities and their families.

ACKNOWLEDGEMENTS

DEC appreciates the work of DEC members who participated in the revision of the Code of Ethics: Harriet Boone (chair), Cynthia Core, Sharon Darling, Terri Patterson, Cheryl Rhodes, & Dianna Valle-Riestra.

APPROVED BY THE DEC EXECUTIVE BOARD: SEPTEMBER 1996
REAFFIRMED: APRIL 16, 1999
REAFFIRMED: DECEMBER 5, 2002
APPROVED FOR FIELD REVIEW: OCTOBER 27, 2008
APPROVED BY THE DEC EXECUTIVE BOARD: AUGUST 11, 2009

Division for Early Childhood
27 Fort Missoula Road • Missoula, MT • 59804 • Phone: 406-543-0872 • Fax: 406-543-0887
E-mail: dec@dec-sped.org • www.dec-sped.org

Early Childhood Inclusion

A Joint Position Statement of the Division for Early Childhood (DEC) and the National Association for the Education of Young Children (NAEYC)

Today an ever-increasing number of infants and young children with and without disabilities play, develop, and learn together in a variety of places – homes, early childhood programs, neighborhoods, and other community-based settings. The notion that young children with disabilities[1] and their families are full members of the community reflects societal values about promoting opportunities for development and learning, and a sense of belonging for every child. It also reflects a reaction against previous educational practices of separating and isolating children with disabilities. Over time, in combination with certain regulations and protections under the law, these values and societal views regarding children birth to 8 with disabilities and their families have come to be known as early childhood inclusion.[2] The most far-reaching effect of federal legislation on inclusion enacted over the past three decades has been to fundamentally change the way in which early childhood services ideally can be organized and delivered.[3] However, because inclusion takes many different forms and implementation is influenced by a wide variety of factors, questions persist about the precise meaning of inclusion and its implications for policy, practice, and potential outcomes for children and families.

The lack of a shared national definition has contributed to misunderstandings about inclusion. DEC and NAEYC recognize that having a common understanding of what inclusion means is fundamentally important for determining what types of practices and supports are necessary to achieve high quality inclusion. This DEC/NAEYC joint position statement offers a definition of early childhood inclusion. The definition was designed not as a litmus test for determining whether a program can be considered inclusive, but rather, as a blueprint for identifying the key components of high quality inclusive programs. In addition, this document offers recommendations for how the position statement should be used by families, practitioners, administrators, policy makers, and others to improve early childhood services.

Definition of Early Childhood Inclusion

Early childhood inclusion embodies the values, policies, and practices that support the right of every infant and young child and his or her family, regardless of ability, to participate in a broad range of activities and contexts as full members of families, communities, and society. The desired results of inclusive experiences for children with and without disabilities and their families include a sense of belonging and membership, positive social relationships and friendships, and development and learning to reach their full potential. The defining features of inclusion that can be used to identify high quality early childhood programs and services are access, participation, and supports.

What is meant by Access, Participation, and Supports?

Access. Providing access to a wide range of learning opportunities, activities, settings, and environments is a defining feature of high quality early childhood inclusion. Inclusion can take many different forms and can occur in various organizational and community contexts, such as homes, Head Start, child care, faith-based programs, recreational programs, preschool, public and private pre-kindergarten through early elementary education, and blended early childhood education/early childhood special education programs. In many cases, simple modifications can facilitate access for individual children. Universal design is a concept that can be used to support access to environments in many different types of settings through the removal of physical and structural barriers. Universal Design for Learning (UDL) reflects practices that provide multiple and varied formats for instruction and learning. UDL principles and practices help to ensure that *every* young child has access to learning environments, to typical home or educational routines and activities, and to the general education curriculum. Technology can enable children with a range of functional abilities to participate in activities and experiences in inclusive settings.

Participation. Even if environments and programs are designed to facilitate access, some children will need additional individualized accommodations and supports to participate fully in play and learning activities with peers and adults. Adults promote belonging, participation, and engagement of children with and without disabilities in inclusive settings in a variety of intentional ways. Tiered models in early childhood hold promise for helping adults organize assessments and interventions by level of intensity. Depending on the individual needs and priorities of young children and families, implementing inclusion involves a range of approaches—from embedded, routines-based teaching to more explicit interventions—to scaffold learning and participation for all children. Social-emotional development and behaviors that facilitate participation are critical goals of high quality early childhood inclusion, along with learning and development in all other domains.

Supports. In addition to provisions addressing access and participation, an infrastructure of systems-level supports must be in place to undergird the efforts of individuals and organizations providing inclusive services to children and families. For example, family members, practitioners, specialists, and administrators should have access to ongoing professional development and support to acquire the knowledge, skills, and dispositions required to implement effective inclusive practices. Because collaboration among key stakeholders (e.g., families, practitioners, specialists, and administrators) is a cornerstone for implementing high quality early childhood inclusion, resources and program policies are needed to promote multiple opportunities for communication and collaboration among these groups. Specialized services and therapies must be implemented in a coordinated fashion and integrated with general early care and education services. Blended early childhood education/early childhood special education programs offer one example of how this might be achieved.[4] Funding policies should promote the

Division for Early Childhood of the
Council for Exceptional Children
27 Fort Missoula Road | Missoula, MT 59804
Phone 406.543.0872 | Fax 406.543.0887
Email dec@dec-sped.org | Web www.dec-sped.org

naeyc

National Association for the Education of Young Children
1509 16th Street NW | Washington, DC 20036-1426
Phone 202.232.8777 Toll-Free 800.424.2460 | Fax 202.328.1846
Email naeyc@naeyc.org | Web www.naeyc.org

pooling of resources and the use of incentives to increase access to high quality inclusive opportunities. Quality frameworks (e.g., program quality standards, early learning standards and guidelines, and professional competencies and standards) should reflect and guide inclusive practices to ensure that all early childhood practitioners and programs are prepared to address the needs and priorities of infants and young children with disabilities and their families.

Recommendations for Using this Position Statement to Improve Early Childhood Services

Reaching consensus on the meaning of early childhood inclusion is a necessary first step in articulating the field's collective wisdom and values on this critically important issue. In addition, an agreed-upon definition of inclusion should be used to create high expectations for infants and young children with disabilities and to shape educational policies and practices that support high quality inclusion in a wide range of early childhood programs and settings. Recommendations for using this position statement to accomplish these goals include:

1. *Create high expectations for every child to reach his or her full potential.* A definition of early childhood inclusion should help create high expectations for every child, regardless of ability, to reach his or her full potential. Shared expectations can, in turn, lead to the selection of appropriate goals and support the efforts of families, practitioners, individuals, and organizations to advocate for high quality inclusion.

2. *Develop a program philosophy on inclusion.* An agreed-upon definition of inclusion should be used by a wide variety of early childhood programs to develop their own philosophy on inclusion. Programs need a philosophy on inclusion as a part of their broader program mission statement to ensure that practitioners and staff operate under a similar set of assumptions, values, and beliefs about the most effective ways to support infants and young children with disabilities and their families. A program philosophy on inclusion should be used to shape practices aimed at ensuring that infants and young children with disabilities and their families are full members of the early childhood community and that children have multiple opportunities to learn, develop, and form positive relationships.

3. *Establish a system of services and supports.* Shared understandings about the meaning of inclusion should be the starting point for creating a system of services and supports for children with disabilities and their families. Such a system must reflect a continuum of services and supports that respond to the needs and characteristics of children with varying types of disabilities and levels of severity, including children who are at risk for disabilities. However, the designers of these systems should not lose sight of inclusion as a driving principle and the foundation for the range of services and supports they provide to young children and families. Throughout the service and support system, the goal should be to ensure access, participation, and the infrastructure of supports needed to achieve the desired results related to inclusion. Ideally, the principle of natural proportions should guide the design of inclusive early childhood programs. The principle of natural proportions means the inclusion of children with disabilities in proportion to their presence in the general population.

   A system of supports and services should include incentives for inclusion, such as child care subsidies, and adjustments to staff-child ratios to ensure that program staff can adequately address the needs of every child.

4. *Revise program and professional standards.* A definition of inclusion could be used as the basis for revising program and professional standards to incorporate high quality inclusive practices. Because existing early childhood program standards primarily reflect the needs of the general population of young children, improving the overall quality of an early childhood classroom is necessary, but might not be sufficient, to address the individual needs of every child. A shared definition of inclusion could be used as the foundation for identifying dimensions of high quality inclusive programs and the professional standards and competencies of practitioners who work in these settings.

5. *Achieve an integrated professional development system.* An agreed-upon definition of inclusion should be used by states to promote an integrated system of high quality professional development to support the inclusion of young children with and without disabilities and their families. The development of such a system would require strategic planning and commitment on the part of families and other key stakeholders across various early childhood sectors (e.g., higher education, child care, Head Start, public pre-kindergarten, preschool, early intervention, health care, mental health). Shared assumptions about the meaning of inclusion are critical for determining who would benefit from professional development, what practitioners need to know and be able to do, and how learning opportunities are organized and facilitated as part of an integrated professional development system.

6. *Influence federal and state accountability systems.* Consensus on the meaning of inclusion could influence federal and state accountability standards related to increasing the number of children with disabilities enrolled in inclusive programs. Currently, states are required to report annually to the U.S. Department of Education the number of children with disabilities who are participating in inclusive early childhood programs. But the emphasis on the prevalence of children who receive inclusive services ignores the quality and the anticipated outcomes of the services that children experience. Furthermore, the emphasis on prevalence data raises questions about which types of programs and experiences can be considered inclusive in terms of the intensity of inclusion and the proportion of children with and without disabilities within these settings and activities. A shared definition of inclusion could be used to revise accountability systems to address both the need to increase the number of children with disabilities who receive inclusive services and the goal of improving the quality and outcomes associated with inclusion.

Endnotes

1   Phrases such as "children with special needs" and "children with exception-alities" are sometimes used in place of "children with disabilities."

2   The term "inclusion" can be used in a broader context relative to opportunities and access for children from culturally and linguistically diverse groups, a critically important topic in early childhood requiring further discussion and inquiry. It is now widely acknowledged, for example, that culture has a profound influence on early development and learning, and that early care and education practices must reflect this influence. Although this position statement is more narrowly focused on inclusion as it relates to disability, it is understood that children with disabilities and their families vary widely with respect to their racial/ethnic, cultural, economic, and linguistic backgrounds.

3   children ages 3–21 are entitled to a free, appropriate public education (FAPE) in the least restrictive environment (LRE). LRE requires that, to the extent possible, children with disabilities should have access to the general education curriculum, along with learning activities and settings that are available to their peers without disabilities. Corresponding federal legislation applied to infants and toddlers (children birth to 3) and their families specifies that early intervention services and supports must be provided in "natural environments," generally interpreted to mean a broad range of contexts and activities that generally occur for typically developing infants and toddlers in homes and communities. Although this document focuses on the broader meaning and implications of early childhood inclusion for children birth to eight, it is recognized that the basic ideas and values reflected in the term "inclusion" are congruent with those reflected in the term "natural environments." Furthermore, it is acknowledged that fundamental concepts related to both inclusion and natural environments extend well beyond the early childhood period to include older elementary school students and beyond.

4   Blended programs integrate key components (e.g., funding, eligibility criteria, curricula) of two or more different types of early childhood programs (e.g., the federally funded program for preschoolers with disabilities [Part B-619] in combination with Head Start, public pre-k, and/or child care) with the goal of serving a broader group of children and families within a single program.

APPROVED BY DEC EXECUTIVE BOARD: April 2009

APPROVED BY NAEYC GOVERNING BOARD: April 2009

Suggested citation

DEC/NAEYC. (2009). *Early childhood inclusion: A joint position statement of the Division for Early Childhood (DEC) and the National Association for the Education of Young Children (NAEYC).* Chapel Hill: The University of North Carolina, FPG Child Development Institute.

Permission to copy not required — distribution encouraged.

http://community.fpg.unc.edu/resources/articles/Early_Childhood_Inclusion

Acknowledgments

Coordination of the development and validation of this joint position statement was provided by the National Professional Development Center on Inclusion (NPDCI), a project of the FPG Child Development Institute funded by a grant from the U.S. Department of Education, Office of Special Education Programs. NPDCI work group members included Camille Catlett, who directed the validation process, Virginia Buysse, who served as the lead writer, and Heidi Hollingsworth, who supervised the analysis of respondent comments and the editorial process.

DEC and NAEYC appreciate the work of Joint DEC-NAEYC Work Group members who participated in the development of the initial definition and position statement: Terry Harrison, NJ Department of Health and Senior Services; Helen Keith, University of Vermont; Louise Kaczmarek, University of Pittsburgh; Robin McWilliam, Siskin Children's Institute and the University of Tennessee at Chattanooga; Judy Niemeyer, University of North Carolina at Greensboro; Cheryl Rhodes, Georgia State University; Bea Vargas, El Papalote Inclusive Child Development Center; and Mary Wonderlick, consultant. Input from the members of the DEC Executive Board and the NAEYC Governing Board, as well as key staff members in both organizations, also is acknowledged.

Index

Page numbers followed by *f* indicate figures, by *t* indicate tables, and by *n* indicate notes.